Raewyn Connell

Research
Politics
Social Change

MELBOURNE UNIVERSITY PRESS
An imprint of Melbourne University Publishing Limited
Level 1, 715 Swanston Street, Carlton, Victoria 3053, Australia
mup-contact@unimelb.edu.au
www.mup.com.au

First published 2023
Text © Raewyn Connell, 2023
Design and typography © Melbourne University Publishing Limited, 2023

This book is copyright. Apart from any use permitted under the *Copyright Act 1968* and subsequent amendments, no part may be reproduced, stored in a retrieval system or transmitted by any means or process whatsoever without the prior written permission of the publishers.

Every attempt has been made to locate the copyright holders for material quoted in this book. Any person or organisation that may have been overlooked or misattributed may contact the publisher.

Cover design by Peter Long Design
Typeset in 12/15.5pt Adobe Garamond Pro by Cannon Typesetting
Printed in Australia by McPherson's Printing Group

 A catalogue record for this book is available from the National Library of Australia

9780522879629 (paperback)
9780522879636 (ebook)

Contents

Introduction ... 1

Masculinities
1. Toward a new sociology of masculinity (1985) ... 11
2. Masculinities in global perspective (2016) ... 28

Gender
3. Theorising gender (1985) ... 53
4. Rethinking gender from the South (2014) ... 72

Class
5. The Australian ruling class (1975) ... 93
6. Moloch mutates (2002) ... 109

Education
7. Poverty and education (1994) ... 131
8. The neoliberal cascade and education (2013) ... 152

Fieldwork
9. Fieldwork (2006, 2010) ... 175

Social science and Southern theory
10. Why is classical theory classical? (1997) ... 197
11. Social science on a world scale (2015) ... 220

Acknowledgements ... 236
References ... 241
Index ... 262

Introduction

1

Singers have their Greatest Hits, painters their Retrospectives, chess masters their collections of Best Games. But a researcher? A *social* researcher? It seems vainglorious to try to collect the best. So much of social science is collaborative, so much depends on organisations, networks and movements, shared ideas and engagements. Anyway, how do we know what's the greatest or the best?

But it may be worth looking at a social researcher's trajectory, way of working, situation in the world—and the knowledge those conditions allow. Much of my writing is based on life-history interviews, which ask for that kind of information from other people. This book is not a life history, but perhaps it can be a case study: a collection of the changing work of one researcher over nearly fifty years.

2

Why do social research? I had a clear purpose when I began. It was the mid-1960s and the war in Vietnam was building towards its horrifying peak. Australia, a minor player in that war, was ruled by a corrupt, reactionary gang of politicians and businessmen. It was a deeply unjust society: the rich lived in mansions, the poor struggled for basic living conditions, Indigenous people were treated with particular viciousness. I was finishing a degree in history, a subject I loved, in a university department that emphasised close-focus documentary work. I was being taught to concentrate on small and remote problems, while the world went up in flames. I asked myself what kind of knowledge really mattered in this world, and social science came top of the list. So I enrolled for graduate study in social science, and by the 1970s was a full-time researcher and teacher.

Of course, many others were concerned with these issues; there was a movement. I had some busy years as a student activist, campaigning, writing manifestos, marching in demonstrations and trying to start collectives. When I began an academic job, a longer-term effort became possible: building research and teaching programs, and connecting with groups able to use research findings. That was a crucial point: if knowledge mattered, part of my job was to make it available.

Therefore, as well as writing articles for academic journals and papers for conferences, I wrote and spoke in other forums: for unions, social movements, the Labor Party, teacher organisations, literary magazines and mass media. Later, I wrote some reports for governments and for the United Nations, not to mention a pamphlet on socialist strategy for a left union group. When the internet arrived, I set up, with a colleague's help, a website called *www.raewynconnell.net*. I have given video and audio talks, some of which became podcasts or YouTube videos.

So, if this book tells a story, it's about what happens when the ambition to produce knowledge relevant to social justice and change meets the practical conditions of work in universities, located—most of them—far from the centre of the global economy of knowledge.

3

I have been sharply critical of universities, and have fought, not very successfully, to make them more democratic. *The Good University* spells out that idea. Despite my criticism, I have relied on what universities gave me: a salary and office, co-workers and students, research funds, the possibility of travel, and many friendships. Academic researchers depend absolutely on the skills of administrative, professional, technical and maintenance workers, and on other organisations, including libraries, publishers and professional associations, to provide the practical environment for our work.

From the start, much of my research has been done through teamwork. Collaborative projects are under-represented in this book, so I'll emphasise the fact here. Some projects were designed jointly, then carried out and written up together. For the projects that I designed myself, I usually had research associates who soon became colleagues and co-authors. Collaborations are not magic: some led to conflict, some stalled. But most did generate energy, and in some there was a wonderful interplay of intellectual excitement and personal support. I'm very grateful to all the groups I have worked with.

4

About the author: I was born during World War II and grew up in the shadow of the atom bomb—literally, as eastern Australia was downwind from British bomb tests in the 1950s. I'm descended from settler-colonial families who joined the British invasion of Australia in the nineteenth century. I've had class privilege, race privilege and language privilege. I went to public-sector schools and universities in Australia and was given, for the time, an excellent education. I gained a love of history and literature, an interest in psychology, a curiosity about natural science, and a grounding in several European languages, only one of them dead.

I have held teaching jobs in three Australian universities and one in the United States, and have taught for shorter stints in other countries. I have been a union member all my working life; I'm now a life member of the National Tertiary Education Union. I joined the Australian Labor Party in the 1960s and stayed a member until the 1990s, when the party lurched so far to the right that I got seasick. I belong to several professional associations for social science, and have been to more conferences than I could shake a stick at. Being a professor in rich countries meant money and visa privilege for international travel. I have visited about thirty countries for lectures, seminars, conferences, interviews and discussions.

5

Social research on a substantial scale is not cheap. I decided early that to get funding I would sell my soul to the state, but not to the corporate world. I have had grants for basic research from the national agency, the Australian Research Council, and its predecessor, and for applied projects from federal and state government agencies such as departments of Health and Education.

I don't make a sharp distinction between applied and basic research, but I'm conscious of different ways that research agendas develop. Sometimes they start from an expressed need for new knowledge. In the early years of the HIV/AIDS pandemic, activists from the gay community in Sydney, hard hit by illness and deaths, proposed to social scientists at Macquarie University a joint effort to produce knowledge about sexual practices that was urgently needed by community educators. We were able to get government funding, and a long-term research program followed. In other cases, a critique of current knowledge is the starting point; finding that information is missing, or a certain field is stuck or intellectually cramped, or otherwise in need of a new departure. That was the position with knowledge about masculinity in the 1980s (Chapter 1), and about the Australian ruling class in the 1970s (Chapter 5).

There are times when the work goes on without much drama, each study adding some detail to what was known before. There are times when things stagnate, or an apparently promising approach gets nowhere. Research projects do fail, though we hate to say so. There are times, too, when things move unexpectedly fast, when one move leads to another at a rising pace. I learned to bodysurf as a child, on Sydney's lovely beaches. There's a great pleasure in catching a wave just as it breaks, and feeling the surge of ocean all around as you plane through the water. Sometimes research has felt like that.

6

An important part of research is communicating about it. I think of writing as a craft, and I've searched for good models. I write a little poetry and read a great deal more, and I've paid attention to poets' technique. (I once recited passages from Allen Ginsberg's 'Howl', backed by a band playing 12-bar blues, to an amazed inner-city audience in Sydney. Yes, it was the sixties!) In prose, I've learned from writers such as Patrick White and Alice Munro. In the research world, I've learned style mainly from the historians I admire. Whatever the models, I've aimed to write in a clear and unpretentious way that would still convey complex ideas and sustained arguments.

That demands thinking about the readers—what they bring to the encounter, and what my writing can and cannot do for them. I have tried to teach that approach, too. I have held writing workshops, and a few years ago wrote a booklet, *Writing for Research*, which is available to download for free from my website. So far it has been accessed 55 000 times: please go there, it should be a lot more!

7

What kind of knowledge has this effort produced? That sounds like a question from a very fierce and final examination paper: Define your working life in 200 words, and don't write on both sides of the paper. I'll try to answer within the word limit.

I have tried to produce a realistic social science, grounded empirically and flexible about method. I emphasise practice, things actually done in specific situations; and social agency, the capacities of people and groups to transform their situations. I try to recognise the here-and-now-ness of practice, its embodiment and its place, in local or in global terms.

The main aim has been knowledge relevant to struggles for social justice. That requires analyses of social structure, and much of my work has been to map existing patterns of power, privilege and oppression and to understand their dynamics. There are multiple structures in social life, and I have tried to clarify their entanglements in education, in organisations, in intimate relations and in the economy of knowledge.

A concern with agency has a strong consequence: we must be concerned with the effects of action, the downstream. The historicity of social life is fundamental; social science must concern time, transformation and possibility. To grapple with questions of social justice—which now include survival in the face of environmental catastrophe—is to be concerned with pathways towards structural transformations. That, I think, has been the basic direction of my work.

8

So, how to compose a collection? I have written in a variety of genres. I decided to focus on articles written for journals—more self-contained than chapters from books, reporting empirical and theoretical work directly. Rather than assemble favourite pieces, making a random assortment of topics, I decided to concentrate on specific pathways that I have followed over a span of years: concerning the making of masculinities, theories of gender, class structure, social issues in education, and the global economy of knowledge.

By choosing an early and late article from each, I hope to illustrate the transformation of knowledge itself, as well as its environment. Two broad changes will be very plain. One is the advent of neoliberal ideas and corporate-friendly policies, which became powerful in Australian life from the 1980s (chapters 6 and 8 particularly). The other is the development of postcolonial or Southern perspectives in the social sciences, a shift that has gained momentum more recently (chapters 2, 4 and 11).

My criteria unexpectedly produced a tilt towards theoretical writing. I mostly do theory in close connection with empirical work. Some rebalancing was needed. I used the old social scientist's fallback: take a sample. I have taken extracts from three fieldwork projects and offer them in Chapter 9.

I have used an author's privilege to make small edits here and there to improve readability. To keep the book to a reasonable length, in various chapters I have cut passages that seemed less relevant or interesting today, while keeping the most significant parts of the argument in full. These cuts are indicated in the text.

So, here it is. It may or may not have my Best Games and Greatest Hits, but it is the best *collection* of my work that I can put together. I'd like to think it could be an inspiration to new researchers, though I realise it's just as likely to be an Awful Warning. Whatever it is, be welcome to my house!

Masculinities

1
Toward a new sociology of masculinity (1985)

THE WOMEN'S LIBERATION movement of the 1960s–70s promised a revolutionary change in knowledge. By the end of the 1970s not only had a new field called 'women's studies' been created, but women's concerns were being brought into the social sciences and humanities, and even the natural sciences. Yet, more was needed. To understand inequality also required 'studying up': that is, studying the groups that held resources and power. In gender relations, that mainly meant studying men and masculinity. At the time, the leading concept for gender analysis in the human sciences was 'sex roles'. That included the idea of a 'male role'. But role theory was a profoundly inadequate way of understanding power and inequality. Something more was needed, and this article was an attempt to say what it was.

The article was co-authored with Tim Carrigan and John Lee. They were my research assistants on a grant from the national government's Australian Research Grants Committee for a project called 'Theory of Class and Patriarchy'—possibly the first grant the ARGC ever gave for social theory. Both Tim and John were activists in the gay liberation movement, and Tim was finishing a PhD about theory. We decided to start with issues about masculinity, which were under-researched. Our first attempt to write up our work, in 1983, produced an 89-page duplicated booklet with the ironic title 'Hard and Heavy Phenomena', a phrase from a popular book that attempted to define what masculinity was about. We recast the text as a journal article and gave it a sober title: 'Toward a New Sociology of Masculinity'. We sent this to an Australian journal, which had difficulties with its length, then sent it to a US journal that welcomed longer articles. It was published in *Theory and Society* in 1985.

The paper offered a very detailed review and critique of the 'male role' literature; an account of the impact of women's liberation on the situation of men; a sardonic commentary on the newly popular genre of Books About Men; an account of gay liberation thinking about masculinity, from which came key ideas about hegemony and new masculinities; and an outline of the new approach we proposed. It was an outrageously long paper, of over 23000 words. That is too long to reprint in full here, and most of the early sections focus on now-forgotten authors and ideas. So I have chosen the final section, 'Outline of a Social Analysis of Masculinity', which presents the positive ideas that turned out to be influential: the plurality of masculinities, the complex way masculinities are made, the idea of hegemonic masculinity, historical shifts in the gender order, and political struggles over masculinity.

We were lucky to have published this in the United States. There was much more controversy about masculinity in the global North than in Australia at the time. Our discussion caught a wave. The paper was soon anthologised and translated. It came at the right time and helped to shape the field.

Looking back, it is easy to see its limitations. The empirical basis was quite limited. We gathered studies from psychology, sociology and anthropology, but there wasn't much depth in masculinities research at the time. A good deal of that was soon to come; but another weakness was not so easily fixed. Almost all the research we gathered, and all the ideas we debated, came from the global North. In the same year that we circulated 'Hard and Heavy Phenomena', Ashis Nandy published his brilliant book about the making of masculinities under colonialism, *The Intimate Enemy*. It was published in Delhi, and I didn't hear about it for another fifteen years.

Outline of a social analysis of masculinity

Men in the framework of gender relations

The starting point for any understanding of masculinity that is not simply biologistic or subjective must be men's involvement in the social relations that constitute the gender order. In a classic article Gayle Rubin (1975) has defined the domain of the argument as 'the sex/gender system', a patterning of social relations connected with reproduction and gender division that is found in all societies, though in varying shapes. This system is historical, in the fullest sense; its elements and relationships are constructed in history and are all subject to historical change (Connell 1985). It is also internally differentiated, as Juliet Mitchell (1971) argued more than a decade ago. Two aspects of its organization have been the foci of research in the past decade: the division of labor and the structure of power. (The latter is what Kate Millett (1970) originally called 'sexual politics', and is the more precise referent of the concept 'patriarchy'.) To these we must add the structure of cathexis, the social organization of sexuality and attraction—which as the history of homosexuality demonstrates is fully as social as the structures of work and power.

The central fact about this structure in the contemporary capitalist world (like most other social orders, though not all) is the subordination of women. This fact is massively documented, and has enormous ramifications—physical, mental, interpersonal, cultural—whose effects on the lives of women have been the major concerns of feminism. One of the central facts about masculinity, then, is that men in general are advantaged through the subordination of women.

To say 'men in general' is already to point to an important complication in power relations. The global subordination of women is consistent with many particular situations in which women hold power over men, or are at least equal. Close-up research on families shows a good many households where wives hold authority in practice (Kessler et al. 1985). The fact of mothers' authority over young sons has been noted in most discussions of the psychodynamics of masculinity. The intersections of gender relations with class and race relations yield many other situations where rich white heterosexual women, for instance, are employers of working-class men, patrons of homosexual men, or politically dominant over black men.

To cite such examples and claim that women are therefore not subordinated in general would be crass. The point is, rather, that contradictions between local situations and the global relationships are endemic. They are likely to be a fruitful source of turmoil and change in the structure as a whole.

The overall relation between men and women, further, is not a confrontation between homogeneous, undifferentiated blocs. Our argument has perhaps established this sufficiently by now; even some role theorists, notably Helen Hacker (1957), recognized a range of masculinities. We would suggest, in fact, that the fissuring of the categories of 'men' and 'women' is one of the central facts about patriarchal power and the way it works. In the case of men, the crucial division is between hegemonic masculinity and various subordinated masculinities.

Even this, however, is too simple a phrasing, as it suggests a masculinity differentiated only by power relations. If the general remarks about the gender system made above are correct, it follows that masculinities are constructed not just by power relations but by their interplay with a division of labor and with patterns of emotional attachment. For example, as Alan Bray (1982) has clearly shown, the character of men's homosexuality, and of its regulation by the state, is very different in the mercantile city from what it was in the pre-capitalist countryside.

The differentiation of masculinities is psychological—it bears on the kind of people that men are and become—but it is not only psychological. In an equally important sense it is institutional, an aspect of collective practice. In a notable recent study of British printing workers, Cynthia Cockburn (1983) has shown how a definition of compositors' work as hypermasculine has been sustained despite enormous changes in technology. The key was a highly organized practice that drove women out of the trade, marginalized related labor processes in which they remained, and sustained a strongly-marked masculine 'culture' in the workplace. What was going on here, as many details of her study show, was the collective definition of a hegemonic masculinity that not only manned the barricades against women but at the same time marginalized or subordinated other men in the industry (e.g. young men, unskilled workers, and those unable or unwilling to join the rituals). Though the details vary, there is every reason to think such processes are very general. Accordingly we see social definitions of masculinity as being embedded in the dynamics of institutions—the working of the state, of corporations, of unions, of families—quite as much as in the personality of individuals.

Forms of masculinity and their interrelationships

In some historical circumstances, a subordinated masculinity can be produced collectively as a well-defined social group and a stable social identity, with some well-recognized traits at the personal level. A now familiar case in point is the 'making of the modern homosexual' (Plummer 1981) in the late nineteenth and early twentieth centuries. One aspect of the collective process here was a change in forms of policing that criminalized homosexuality as such, creating a criminal sexual 'type'. And one aspect of the psychological process was the creation of 'camp' personal style, both internalizing and sardonically transforming the new medical and clinical definition of the homosexual as a type of person.

In other circumstances, a subordinated masculinity may be a transient identity. The printing apprentices in Cockburn's study provide one example of this. Another is provided by the New Guinea culture studied by Gilbert Herdt (1981), where younger men gain their masculinity through ritualized homosexuality under the guardianship of older men. In other cases again, the collective and individual processes do not correspond. There may be stable enough personalities and configurations of motive produced, which for various reasons do not receive a clear social definition. A historic case of this is the vague social identity of English homosexuality before the advent of 'Molly' at the end of the seventeenth century. Closer to home, another example would seem to be the various forms of effeminate heterosexual masculinity being produced today. There are attempts to give such masculinities an identity: for instance by commercial exploitation of hippie styles of dress; and by conservative transvestite organizations such as the Beaumont Society (UK) or the Seahorse Club (Australia). But for the most part there is no very clear social definition of heterosexual effeminacy. It is popularly assimilated to a gay identity when it is noticed at all—an equation its publicists furiously but unavailingly protest.

The ability to impose a particular definition on other kinds of masculinity is part of what we mean by 'hegemony'. Hegemonic masculinity is far more complex than the accounts of essences in the masculinity books would suggest. It is not a 'syndrome' of the kind produced when sexologists like John Money (1970) reify human behavior into a 'condition', or when clinicians reify homosexuality into a pathology. It is, rather, a question of how particular groups of men inhabit positions of power and wealth, and how they legitimate and reproduce the social relationships that generate their dominance.

An immediate consequence of this is that the culturally exalted form of masculinity, the hegemonic model so to speak, may only correspond to the actual characters of a small number of men. On this point at least the 'men's liberation' literature had a sound insight. There is a distance, and a tension, between collective ideal and actual lives. Most men do not really act like the screen image of John Wayne or Humphrey Bogart; and when they try to, it is likely to be thought comic (as in the Woody Allen movie *Play It Again, Sam*) or horrific (as in shoot-outs and 'sieges'). Yet very large numbers of men are complicit in sustaining the hegemonic model. There are various reasons: gratification through fantasy, compensation through displaced aggression (e.g. poofter-bashing by police and working-class youths), etc. But the overwhelmingly important reason is that most men benefit from the subordination of women, and hegemonic masculinity is centrally connected with the institutionalization of men's dominance over women. It would hardly be an exaggeration to say that hegemonic masculinity is hegemonic so far as it embodies a successful strategy in relation to women.

This strategy is necessarily modified in different class situations, a point that can be documented in the research already mentioned on relationships inside families. A contemporary ruling-class family is organized around the corporate or professional career of the husband. In a typical case the well-groomed wife is subordinated not by being under the husband's thumb—he isn't in the house most of the time—but by her task of making sure his home life runs on wheels to support his self-confidence, his career advancement, and their collective income. In working-class homes, to start with, there is no 'career'; the self-esteem of men is eroded rather than inflated in the workplace. For a husband to be dominant in the home is likely to require an assertion of authority without a technical basis; hence a reliance on traditional ideology (religion or ethnic culture) or on force. The working man who gets drunk and belts his wife when she doesn't hold her tongue, and belts his son to make a man of him, is by no means a figure of fiction (Kessler et al. 1985; Johnson 1981).

To think of this as 'working-class authoritarianism' and see the ruling-class family as more liberal would be to mistake the nature of power. Both are forms of patriarchy, and the husbands in both cases are enacting a hegemonic masculinity. But the situations in which they do so are very different, their responses are not exactly the same, and their impact on wives and children is likely to vary a good deal.

The most important feature of this masculinity, alongside its connection with dominance, is that it is heterosexual. Though most literature on the family and masculinity takes this entirely for granted, it should not be. Psychoanalytic evidence goes far to show that conventional adult heterosexuality is constructed, in the individual life, as one among a number of possible paths through the emotional forest of childhood and adolescence. It is now clear that this is also true at the collective level, that the pattern of exclusive adult heterosexuality is a historically-constructed one. Its dominance is by no means universal. For this to become the hegemonic form of masculine sexuality required a historic redefinition of sexuality itself, in which undifferentiated 'lust' was turned into specific types of 'perversion'—the process that is documented, from the under side, by the historians of homosexuality already mentioned. A passion for beautiful boys was compatible with hegemonic masculinity in renaissance Europe, emphatically not so at the end of the nineteenth century. In this historical shift, men's sexual desire was to be focused more closely on women—a fact with complex consequences for them—while groups of men who were visibly not following the hegemonic pattern were more specifically labelled and attacked. So powerful was this shift that even men of the ruling classes found wealth and reputation no protection. It is interesting to contrast the experiences of the Chevalier d'Éon, who managed an active career in diplomacy while dressed as a woman (in a later era he would have been labelled a 'transvestite'), with that of Oscar Wilde a hundred years later.

'Hegemony', then, always refers to a historical situation, a set of circumstances in which power is won and held. The construction of hegemony is not a matter of pushing and pulling between ready-formed groupings, but is partly a matter of the *formation* of those groupings. To understand the different kinds of masculinity demands, above all, an examination of the practices in which hegemony is constituted and contested—in short, the political techniques of the patriarchal social order.

This is a large enterprise, and we can only note a few points about it here. First, hegemony means persuasion, and one of its important sites is likely to be the commercial mass media. An examination of advertising, for instance, shows a number of ways in which images of masculinity are constructed and put to work: amplifying the sense of virility, creating anxiety and giving reassurance about being a father, playing games with stereotypes (men washing dishes), and so on (Atwan et al. 1979). Studying versions of masculinity in Australian mass media, Glen Lewis (1983) points to an important qualification to the usual conception of media influence. Commercial television in fact gives a lot of airplay to 'soft' men, in particular slots such as hosts of daytime quiz shows. What comes across is by no means unrelieved machismo; the inference is that television companies think their audiences would not like that.

Second, hegemony closely involves the division of labor, the social definition of tasks as either 'men's work' or 'women's work', and the definition of some kinds of work as more masculine than others. Here is an important source of tension between the gender order and the class order, as heavy manual labor is generally felt to be more masculine than white-collar and professional work—though perhaps not management (Tolson 1977). Third, the negotiation and enforcement of hegemony involves the state. The criminalization of male homosexuality as such was a key move in the construction of the modern form of hegemonic masculinity. Attempts to reassert it after the struggles of the last twenty years, for instance by fundamentalist right-wing groups in the United States, are very much addressed to the state—attempting to get homosexual people dismissed as public school teachers, for instance, or erode court protection for civil liberties. Much more subtly, the existence of a skein of welfare rules, tax concessions, and so on which advantage people living in conventional conjugal households and disadvantage others (Baldock & Cass 1983) creates economic incentives to conform to the hegemonic pattern.

Psychodynamics

To argue that masculinity and femininity are produced historically is entirely at odds with the view that sees them as settled by biology, and thus as being pre-social categories. It is also at odds with the now most common view of gender, which sees it as a social elaboration, amplification, or perhaps exaggeration of the biological fact of sex—where biology says 'what' and society says 'how'. Certainly, the biological facts of maleness and femaleness are central to the matter; human reproduction is a major part of what defines the 'sex/gender system'. But all kinds of questions can be raised about the nature of the *relation* between biology and the social. The facts of anatomical and physiological variation should caution us against assuming that biology presents society with clear-cut categories of people. More generally, it should not be assumed that the relation is one of *continuity*.

We would suggest that the evidence about masculinity, and gender relations at large, makes more sense if we recognize that the social practice of gender arises—to borrow some terminology from Sartre—in *contradiction* to the biological statute (Connell 1982). It is precisely the property of human sociality that it transcends biological determination. To transcend is not to ignore: the bodily dimension remains a presence within the social practice. Not as a 'base', but as an *object of practice*. Masculinity invests the body. Reproduction is a question of strategies. Social relations continuously take account of the body and biological process and interact with them. 'Interact' should be given its full weight. For our knowledge of the biological dimension of sexual difference is itself predicated on the social categories, as the startling research of Kessler and McKenna (1978) makes clear.

In the field of this interaction, sexuality and desire are constituted, being both bodily pain and pleasure, and social injunction and prohibition. Where Freud (1930) saw the history of this interaction only as a strengthening prohibition by an undifferentiated 'society', and Marcuse (1955) as the by-product of class exploitation, we must now see the construction of the unconscious as the field of play of a number of historically developing power relations and gender practices. Their interactions constitute masculinities and femininities as particular patterns of cathexis.

Freud's work with his male patients produced the first systematic evidence of one key feature of this patterning. The repressions and attachments are not necessarily homogeneous. The psychoanalytic exploration of masculinity means diving through layers of emotion that may be flagrantly contradictory. For instance in the 'Wolf Man' case history, the classic of the genre, Freud (1918) found a promiscuous heterosexuality, a homosexual and passive attachment to the father, and an identification with women, all psychologically present though subject to different levels of repression. Without case study evidence, many recent authors have speculated about the degree of repression that goes into the construction of dominant forms of masculinity: the sublimated homosexuality in the cult of sport, repressed identification with the mother, and so on. Homosexual masculinity as a pattern of cathexis is no less complex, as we see for instance in Genet. If texts like *Our Lady of the Flowers* are, as Sartre (1964) claims, masturbatory fantasies, they are an extraordinary guide to a range and pattern of cathexes—from the hard young criminal to Divine herself—that show, among other things, Genet's homosexuality is far from a mere 'inversion' of heterosexual object-choice.

In this perspective the unconscious emerges as a field of politics. Not just in the sense that a conscious political practice can address it, or that practices that do address it must have a politics, as argued (against Freud) by the Red Collective in Britain (1978). More generally, the organization of desire is the domain of relations of power. When writers of the Books About Men ejaculate about 'the wisdom of the penis' (Goldberg (1976), who thinks the masculine ideal is a rock-hard erection), or when they dilate on its existential significance ('a firm erection on a delicate fellow was the adventurous juncture of ego and courage'—Mailer 1971), they have grasped an important point, though they have not quite got to the root of it. What is at issue here is power over women. This is seen by authors such as Lippert (1977), in an excellent paper exploring the connections of the male-supremacist sexuality of American automobile workers with the conditions of factory work. Bednarik's (1970) suggestion about the origins of popular sadism in the commercialization of sex and the degradation of working life is a more complex case of how the lines of force might work.

The psychodynamics of masculinity, then, are not to be seen as a separate issue from the social relations that invest and construct masculinity. An effective analysis will work at both levels; and an effective political practice must attempt to do so too.

Transformations

An 'effective political practice' implies something that can be worked on and transformed. The question of transformation, its possibilities, sources, and strategies, should be central to the analysis of masculinity.

It has had a very ambiguous status in the literature so far. The 'male role' literature has spoken a lot about changes in the role, but has had no very clear account of how they come about. Indeed this literature generally implies, without arguing the point very explicitly, that once a man has been socialized to his role that is more or less the end of it. On the other side, the gay movement, in its contest with psychiatrists who wished to 'cure' homosexuality, has had its own reasons for claiming that homosexual masculinity, once formed, is settled.

The strength of sexual desire as a motive is one reason why a pattern of cathexis may remain stable for most of a lifetime. Such stability can be found even in the most implausible patterns of cathexis, as the literature of sexual fetishism has abundantly shown, ever since Krafft-Ebing (1886) introduced his middle-European hair, handkerchief, corset and shoe enthusiasts. Yet the strength of desire can also be a mighty engine of change, when caught up in contradiction. And as the last two sections have suggested, contradiction is in fact endemic in the processes that construct masculinity.

The psychodynamics of change in masculinity is a question that so far has attracted little attention. There is one exception: the highly publicized, indeed sensationalized, case of male-to-female 'transsexuals'. Even this case has not brought the question quite into focus, because the transsexuals are mostly saying they are really women and their bodies should be adjusted to match, while their opponents say their bodies show they are really men and their psyches should be adjusted to match. Both look on masculinity and femininity as pure essences, though of different kinds. Roberta Perkins's (1983) fascinating study shows the true situation is much more complex and fraught. The conviction of being really a woman may grow, rather than being present from the start. It may not be complete; ambiguity and uncertainty are common. Those who push on must negotiate their way out of the social position of being a man and into that of being a woman, a process liable to corrode family relationships, lose jobs, and attract police attention. (The social supports of conventional masculine identities are very much in evidence.) Sexual ambiguity is exciting to many people, and one way of surviving—if one's physique allows it—is to become a transsexual prostitute or show girl. But this tends to create a new gender category—one becomes known as 'a transsexual'—rather than making a smooth transition into femininity. There is, in short, a complex interplay between motive and social circumstance; masculinity cannot be abandoned all at once, nor without pain.

Although very few are involved in a process as dramatic and traumatic as that, a good many men feel themselves to be involved in some kind of change having to do with gender, with sexual identity, with what it is to be a man. The 'androgyny' literature of the

1970s spoke to this in one way (Bem 1974), the literature about the importance of fathering spoke in another (Russell 1983). We have already seen some reasons to doubt that the changes discussed were as decisive as the 'men's movement' proclaimed. But it seems clear enough that there have been recent changes in the constitution of masculinity in advanced capitalist countries, of at least two kinds: a deepening of tensions around relationships with women, and the crisis of a form of heterosexual masculinity that is increasingly felt to be obsolete.

The psychodynamics of these processes remain obscure; we still lack the close-up research that would illuminate them. What is happening on the larger scale is somewhat clearer. Masculinities are constituted, we argued above, within a structure of gender relations that has a historical dynamic as a whole. This is not to say it is a neatly-defined and closely-integrated system—the false assumption made by Parsons (Parsons & Bales 1953), Chodorow (1978), and a good many others. This would take for granted what is currently being fought for. The dominion of men over women, and the supremacy of particular groups of men over others, is sought by constantly re-constituting gender relations as a system within which that dominance is generated. Hegemonic masculinity might be seen as what would function automatically if the strategy were entirely successful. But it never does function automatically. The project is contradictory, the conditions for its realization are constantly changing, and, most importantly, there is resistance from the groups being subordinated. The violence in gender relations is not part of the essence of masculinity—as Fasteau (1974), Nichols (1975), and Reynaud (1983), as well as many radical feminists (e.g. Dworkin 1981), present it—so much as a measure of the bitterness of this struggle.

The emergence of Women's Liberation at the end of the 1960s was, as feminists are now inclined to see it, the heightening of a resistance that is much older and has taken many other forms in the past. It did nevertheless represent two new and important things.

TOWARD A NEW SOCIOLOGY OF MASCULINITY (1985)

First, the transformation of resistance into a liberation project addressed to the whole gender order. Second, a breakdown of masculine authority; if not in the society as a whole, at least in a substantial group, the younger professional intelligentsia of western cities. Though it has not widened its base as fast as activists expected, the new feminism has also not gone under to the reaction that gained momentum in the late 1970s. Like Gay Liberation it is here to stay; and at least in limited milieux the two movements have achieved some changes in power relations that are unlikely to be reversed.

This dynamic of sexual politics has met up with a change in class relations that also has implications for masculinity. In a very interesting paper, Winter and Robert (1980) suggest that some of the familiar economic and cultural changes in contemporary capitalism—the growth of large bureaucratized corporations, the integration of business and government, the shift to technocratic modes of decision making and control—have implications for the character of 'male dominance'. We think they over-generalize, but at least they have pointed to an important conflict within and about hegemonic masculinity. Forms of masculinity well adapted to face-to-face class conflict and the management of personal capital are not so well suited to the politics of organizations, to professionalism, to the management of strategic compromises and consensus.

One dimension of the recent politics of capitalism, then, is a struggle about the modernization of hegemonic masculinity. This has by no means gone all one way. The recent ascendancy of the hard-liners in the American ruling class has involved the systematic reassertion of old-fashioned models of masculinity (not to mention femininity—*vide* Nancy Reagan).

The politics of 'men's liberation' and the search for androgyny have to be understood in this field of forces. They are, explicitly, a response to the new feminism—accepting feminism in a watered-down version, hoping that men could gain something from its advent. This required an evasion of the issue of power, and the limits were clearly marked by the refusal of any engagement with gay liberation. Yet there was an urgency about what the 'men's movement' publicists were saying in the early 1970s, which drew its force partly from the drive for the modernization of hegemonic masculinity already going on in other forms (Ehrenreich 1983).

The goal (to simplify a little) was to produce forms of masculinity able to adapt to new conditions, but sufficiently similar to the old ones to maintain the family, heterosexuality, capitalist work relations, and American national power (most of which are taken for granted in the Books About Men). The shift in the later 1970s that produced 'Free Men' campaigning for fathers' rights, and the ponderings of conservative ideologues on how to revive intelligent paternalism (e.g. Stearns 1979), is clearly connected with the anti-modernist movement in the American ruling class. This offered strategies for repairing men's authority in the face of the damage done by feminism, much as the Reagan foreign policy proposed to restore American hegemony internationally, and monetarism proposed a drastic disciplining of the working class. The political appeal of the whole package—mainly to men, given the 'gender gap' in politics—is notable.

The triumph of these ideas is not inevitable. They are strategies, responding to dilemmas of practice, and they have their problems too. Other responses, other strategies, are also possible; among them much more radical ones. The ferment that was started by the new left, and that produced the counterculture, the new feminism, gay liberation, and many attempts at communal households and collective childcare, has also produced a good deal of quiet experimentation with masculinity and attempts to work out in practice un-oppressive forms of heterosexuality. This is confined at present to a limited milieu, and has not had anything like the shape or public impact of the politics of liberation among gay men.

The moment of opportunity, as it appeared in the early 1970s, is past. There is no easy path to a major reconstruction of masculinity. Yet the initiative in sexual politics is not entirely in the hands of reaction, and the underlying tensions that produced the initiatives of ten years ago have not vanished. There are potentials for a more liberating politics, here and now. Not in the form of grand schemes of change, but at least in the form of coalitions among feminists, gay men, and progressive heterosexual men that have real chances of making gains on specific issues.

2

Masculinities in global perspective (2016)

IN THE TWENTY years after our new sociology of masculinity hit the streets, a great deal happened in this field. Descriptive studies in many localities multiplied, in what I call the ethnographic moment in masculinity research. The idea of multiple masculinities was widely adopted and the term 'hegemonic masculinity' became amazingly popular. I started a life-history project, interviewing four groups of Australian men who were facing pressures for change in constructing masculinity. A little later, I put the results of this study, together with the theoretical work and some historical and political reflection, in the book *Masculinities* (1995). Though rejected by the first publisher I sent it to, when it was accepted by other firms it circulated briskly in English, and has now been translated into twelve other languages.

Applications of this research soon appeared: in schools, health work, counselling, violence prevention, literary criticism and other fields. Invitations came to give public lectures and media interviews, and speak to conferences, workshops and seminars. I accepted as many as I could—not thinking then of the carbon cost. Travelling from Australia to other continents was expensive and exhausting, but I became acquainted with much more of the world, the researchers and the potential audience.

The idea of globalisation was suddenly popular in the 1990s, and I published a paper called 'Masculinities and Globalization' in the first issue of the new journal *Men and Masculinities*. This, too, was translated and anthologised. A few years later, I helped draft the documents, and gave the opening speech, for the UN Commission on the Status of Women, when that body became concerned with the role of men and boys in achieving gender equality. The background paper that I wrote, surveying worldwide research and debates, was published in the US journal *Signs* in 2005.

This sounds like the forward march of science in all its glory. We had created a new research field and were seeing it grow, develop practical applications and spread around the world. But it wasn't so simple. As the term 'hegemonic masculinity' became popular, its meaning often shifted. Either it lost the connection with inequalities, or became a synonym for domination or toxicity. My friend and colleague James Messerschmidt suggested trying to clarify and update this concept. Our paper was published in 2005 and has circulated very widely. But I fear some misunderstandings of the concept continue.

To complicate matters, the idea of globalisation was flawed. Claims that the world was now homogenised, or at least decoratively mixed together, were hard to reconcile with massive inequalities of wealth, deep imbalances of power, rapacious transnational corporations, and violent antagonisms about race, nation, gender, sexuality and religion. I was working on the global economy of knowledge (see chapters 10 and 11). After publishing *Southern Theory* in 2007, I worked on applying postcolonial ideas to gender issues.

This is the main statement about masculinities, published in *Theory and Society* in 2016. The paper argues for a world perspective, a more strongly historical concept of masculinities, and a close examination of the conditions for hegemony in the colonial and postcolonial world.

Introduction

Thirty years ago in this journal, three Australian authors proposed 'a new sociology of masculinity' (Carrigan, Connell & Lee 1985). They criticized the popular concept of a 'male sex role', offering instead a combination of feminist, gay liberation and psychoanalytic ideas. Their most influential idea was that multiple masculinities existed, that there was hierarchy among them, and that a hegemonic version, at the top of the hierarchy, connected the subordination of women to the subordination of marginalized groups of men. The term 'hegemonic masculinity' named a key mechanism sustaining an oppressive society, and implied that contesting this mechanism was an important strategy of change.

In the following decades, as research grew alongside public debates about men and masculinity, the concept of hegemonic masculinity was widely used. The concept has played a role in reform agendas, and has guided empirical investigations. It has also been vigorously criticized and re-formulated (Connell & Messerschmidt 2005). Questions have been raised about the idea of masculinity, the use of Gramscian ideas in understanding gender relations, the location of the concept in modern or postmodern thought, and the relation of hegemonic masculinity to identity, power and violence (Howson 2006; Meuser 2010; Zhan 2015; Pascoe & Bridges 2016).

Most of this research and debate has occurred within the global North. It is increasingly recognized that the resulting geopolitics of knowledge is a problem. For a deeper understanding of the issues raised in the debates about hegemonic masculinity, we need to learn not only from western Europe and north America but also from the majority world. We need, in short, to decolonize the study of masculinities.

In this paper I outline an approach to this task in three steps. I first examine conceptual difficulties about social reproduction and argue for a more consistently historical understanding of hegemony.

I then make the approach concrete by analyzing key processes in the formation of masculinities over the last 500 years of coloniality and global power. Finally I discuss how a postcolonial approach leads to an understanding of masculinity and hegemony on a world scale today.

This paper makes considerable use of documentation and research from the global South. The crucial feature of its method, however, is posing questions from Southern *perspectives*: about the character and impact of colonization, the postcolonial experience of neoliberal globalization, above all the dynamic that the Peruvian sociologist Aníbal Quijano (2000) has famously called 'the coloniality of power'. This requires looking at research in the metropole too, in new perspectives.

Decolonizing the discussion

Modern knowledge production has a global structure (Hountondji 1997). A worldwide division of labour, with its origins in colonial conquest, locates the production of theory in the global metropole and treats the periphery essentially as a data source. Intellectual workers in the periphery normally follow the intellectual authority of the North and seek recognition there. (Our 1985 article 'Toward a New Sociology of Masculinity' was a good example of this pattern.) Over the last two decades, however, there has been a sustained critique of Northern dominance in the social sciences, proposing globally inclusive agendas of theory (Connell 2007; Go 2013; Bhambra 2014; Rosa 2014). The same kind of discussion has developed in gender studies (Bulbeck 1998; Lugones 2007; Connell 2015).

These concerns have recently emerged in research on masculinity. Robert Morrell and Sandra Swart in South Africa (2005) pose the situation of the poorest part of the world's population as a key issue for masculinity studies. Margaret Jolly (2008: 1), introducing research on masculinities in the postcolonial Pacific, emphasises 'the crucial importance of colonialism in the construction of indigenous masculinities in both past and present'. Paul Amar (2011), in a critical review of Middle East masculinity studies, vigorously argues for a decolonial perspective. Michele Ford and Lenore Lyons (2012), introducing research on masculinities from south-east Asia, question universalized concepts and emphasise the need for local knowledge.

Kopano Ratele (2013), on the basis of experience in southern Africa, questions the assumption that 'traditional' masculinity automatically means patriarchal dominance. The Brasilian scholar Diego Santos Vieira de Jesus (2011) shows how a postcolonial approach to masculinities yields a broad historical framework that throws light on the colonizers and the imperial centre as well as the colonized. In a recent paper I have pointed to the global archive on masculinities and argued for the importance of ideas, as well as data, from the global South (Connell 2014).

The idea of hegemonic masculinity has to be considered in the light of these changes; and the question arises whether the idea of hegemony applies in the colonial world at all. The Indian historian Ranajit Guha, founder of *Subaltern Studies*, questioned this in an article called 'Dominance Without Hegemony and its Historiography' (1989). The imperial power, he argued, never achieved hegemony in colonial India. The British persuaded themselves that they operated by the rule of law; but this was self-deception, in a colony actually controlled by autocratic decrees and military force. The truth was revealed by the widespread acts of resistance that British rule continually encountered.

Guha did not concern himself much with gender, and his overall view has been contested. Ashis Nandy had already, in his brilliant book *The Intimate Enemy* (1983), traced a close interplay between the making of masculinities among the Indian colonized and the British colonizers. Nevertheless the problem Guha posed has grown in importance. The basic project of *Subaltern Studies* was to valorize the historical role of the poor and illiterate, the peasants and the nameless rebels, refusing to read history through the eyes of the powerful.

The problem with the Eurocentrism of global gender discourse is that it projects into gender analysis everywhere the image that the society of the global North holds of itself.

Specifically, it presumes coherence and a self-sustaining logic for any gender order. This is implicit in the concepts of 'patriarchy', 'sex/gender system', 'gender norms', 'gender regime' and 'heteronormativity'. Eurocentric gender research and policy-making assume that gender has a system-like character, a logical homogeneity, and, though it may change, it does so with continuity in time.

With these assumptions in the background, the concept of hegemony tends to become ahistorical, concerned with the *social reproduction* of a system. Hence the prevalence, in research on hegemonic masculinity, of ideas of identity formation, socialization, habitus and the internalization of social norms—which are actually black-box concepts produced by assuming a mechanism of social reproduction (Connell 1983). Hence the familiar slippage between notions of hegemony and notions of domination (Connell & Messerschmidt 2005), which are easily blurred when the reproduction of a hierarchical system is assumed.

Research in postcolonial contexts, however, calls exactly these assumptions into question. Historical *dis*continuity is the core of colonial conquest. Margrethe Silberschmidt (2004), researching HIV transmission in East Africa, rejects the idea that men's dangerous assertion of sexual privilege reflected the continuity of 'traditional' masculinity. She argues that gender violence resulted from the *breakdown* of traditional gender orders, under the pressures of colonialism and postcolonial economic change.

In a similar vein, when talking about feminist sexuality research in Africa, Jane Bennett (2008: 7) observes that mainstream methods textbooks tacitly assume a stable social environment. But a stable environment cannot be assumed for research in postcolonial conditions where 'relative chaos, gross economic disparities, displacement, uncertainty and surprise' are the norm not the exception. Discussing the 'water wars' in Cochabamba (Bolivia), Nina Laurie (2005) traces the clash of masculinities in this defeated neoliberal privatisation attempt. She too makes a strong argument that research in the global South cannot presume a consolidated gender order.

To discard global-North assumptions about social reproduction does not imply that gender concepts such as hegemonic masculinity must be abandoned. Rather, it requires that gender concepts should always be understood historically, as concepts that concern the making and transformation of gender orders through time. Hegemony is a historical possibility, a state of gender relations being struggled for, and struggled against, by different social forces. Since the accomplishment of hegemony is never guaranteed, the most useful way to conceptualize hegemonic masculinity is to treat it as a collective project for realizing gender hierarchy. And that, in the light of the postcolonial critique outlined above, is a process we now have to understand on a world scale.

Hegemony and empire in the history of masculinities

Constitutive violence and the making of colonial societies

Colonialism, as Guha said, involved massive violence. Some conquests destroyed a pre-colonial regime and so established rule over a subject population. The classic case was the invasion led by Cortés in México, smashing the Aztec empire and reducing indigenous men and women to a new kind of serfdom. In other cases, from Hispaniola to Australia, colonizing violence swept over a whole population and directly or indirectly destroyed most of it.

In a powerful argument Amina Mama (1997: 48) shows that to understand violence against women in postcolonial Africa we must understand the violence of colonialism. And to understand that, we must start with 'gender relations and gender violence at the imperial source'. The Christian societies of Europe that launched the global conquests of the last five hundred years were already patriarchal and organized for war. Until the machine gun and the aeroplane appeared, the only overwhelming weapon they had was the broadside-firing warship. It was their military organization and ruthlessness that enabled conquest on land.

This social technology involved constructions of masculinity. The masculinities of empire were *necessarily* bound up with the enabling of violence—violence sufficient to overcome the considerable military capabilities of colonized societies. When the colonizers sorted men into categories of 'manly' and 'effeminate', as they often did (Sinha 1995), it was groups perceived as warriors—Sikh, Pathan, Zulu, Cheyenne—who were admired, though not trusted.

In Northern research on 'gender-based violence', violence is usually understood as a consequence of gender arrangements, i.e. as a dependent variable. In postcolonial analyses like Mama's, violence is *constitutive* for gender relations. In an essay in the journal *Feminist Africa*, Jane Bennett (2010: 35) considers homophobic violence. She muses that, seen in the light of Southern experience, the connection between gender and violence changes shape: 'gender, as practiced conventionally despite diversity of contexts, *is* violence'.

The double movement of disrupting indigenous gender orders and creating new ones was a fundamental and persisting feature of colonialism. Memory of the disruption is the driving force in one of the most famous postcolonial documents, Chinua Achebe's (1958) great novel about masculinity in West Africa at the time of conquest, *Things Fall Apart*.

The dis-ordering of gender relations occurred in multiple ways, including rape, which was endemic in conquest and disrupted indigenous kinship and communal relations with the land; forced migrations, up to the huge scale of the Atlantic slave trade; the loss of women's land rights, a feature of colonialism in the Pacific (Stauffer 2004); and the suppression of gender groupings such as the two-souled people of indigenous North America (Williams 1986). Imperial expansion also disrupted gender relations among the colonizers. The early history of the British settlements in Australia is full of debate about sexual anarchy and gender imbalance (Reid 2007).

In the 1840s and 1850s there was a celebrated attempt to import a supply of women from England—a distance of 20 thousand kilometres—to become respectable servants and wives (Kiddle 1992).

The making of colonial societies deeply concerned gender. It required the management of reproductive bodies through relationships that organized sexuality, birth and childrearing, domestic work and the broad division of labour. Colonial economies required continuing workforces, and colonizing elites required family and inheritance structures.

In trying to stabilize the turbulent situations created by colonizing violence and the resistance of the colonized, the colonizing power brought into play mechanisms that can be seen as the initial hegemonic projects of colonialism. Establishing hegemony was a principal task of missionary religion, as Valentine Mudimbe (1994: 140) notes in his powerful analysis of Belgian colonization in the Congo. All over the colonized world, missionary religion concerned itself with imposing a new order on gender relations and especially sexuality.

Hegemony is a matter of institutions as well as beliefs. Where schools were introduced by colonial governments or churches, they were typically gender-segregated. Systems of law regulated indigenous marriage, women's rights and inheritance. Gender relations were a significant concern in colonial legal codes such as those written by the French for Cambodia (Haque 2012). Colonized men were recruited in considerable numbers into imperial armed forces, especially the British and French. Patriarchal households organized labour forces and allowed white men sexual access to slave and indigenous women (Saffioti 1969).

A spectrum of hegemonic mechanisms also developed among the colonizers. They were sketched in J. O. C. Phillips' (1987) pioneering study of settler-colonial masculinities in New Zealand, and can be seen very clearly in Robert Morrell's (2001) classic study of colonial Natal. Morrell traces the institutionalization of a hegemonic form of masculinity in the schools, military forces and civil society of the

British settlers. It was specifically a harsh and insistent masculinity adapted to the need to dominate a colonized population.

Nothing guaranteed that colonial strategies for hegemony would succeed. Indeed, the project was inherently contradictory. The dynamics of colonialism both created the need, and continually disrupted the results achieved. Colonialism disrupted gender order by continuing violence and dispossession; by the turbulence of the global capitalist economy; by continuing resistance, from Tupac Amaru to Abd el-Krim. There is every reason to think gender hegemony in colonial contexts was patchy, contested, and varied greatly from one part of the colonial world to another.

Out of colonialism: Hegemonic projects in resistance and development

Raymond Suttner (2005), in an illuminating study of the armed struggle against apartheid in South Africa, notes that colonial and apartheid authorities typically denied the manhood of African men. Indigenous men were treated as children in need of control—'boy' was an everyday term. Resistance by men, not surprisingly, took the shape of an assertion of manhood. The ANC mobilized stories of heroic resistance from the past, and young men often interpreted joining the struggle as a form of initiation into manhood.

Such collective masculinity projects are widespread among resistance movements, giving prestige to young men on the front line, such as Palestinian youth in the *intifada* (Peteet 1994). Post-conflict, this can lead to severe problems, with continuing community violence in South Africa (Xaba 2001), Timor Leste (Myrttinen 2012), and other cases.

It is important to note, therefore, the other dimensions of gender in resistance movements. Suttner (2005) carefully documents emotionality, confronting of pain, and desire for the presence of children, dimensions given legitimacy by leaders such as Chris Hani. Very similar conclusions are reached by Luisa Maria Dietrich Ortega

(2012) in an impressive study of militants in Latin American guerrilla movements. These movements had multiple forms of masculinity, a significant place for emotion, and an ideology of social equality which often gave women a prominent role. An oral-history study of gender issues in the Vietnamese wars for independence against the French and Americans is called *Even the Women Must Fight* (Turner & Phan 1998). Marnia Lazreg (1990: 768) says of the Algerian independence struggle that 'the very fact that women entered the war willingly was in and of itself a radical break in gender relations'.

Yet Lazreg and Maria Mies (1986) have remarked how often national liberation movements mobilized women for struggle, but on gaining independence installed patriarchal regimes. A striking example is the anticolonial rising in Ireland commemorated in W. B. Yeats' famous poem 'Easter 1916':

> All changed, changed utterly:
> A terrible beauty is born.

Across Dublin, women were in combat in all the insurgent battalions except one. That one was commanded by Eamon de Valera, who sent the women home (Townshend 2005). After independence, with a conservative Catholicism ascendant, women were thoroughly marginalized in Irish public life. After de Valera himself became head of government, he brought in a Constitution that *defined* woman's place as 'within the home' (1937 Constitution, Article 41).

Postcolonial societies have often shown a 'shifting terrain of gender relations', as Linden Lewis (2004) puts it in his study of Caribbean masculinity. Fatima Mernissi's pioneering fieldwork on masculinity (1975) found evidence of 'sexual anomie' among young men in Morocco, and great uncertainty in the transition between generations. In Egypt a couple of decades later, Mai Ghoussoub (2000) found evidence of a great cultural disturbance in gender relations, and 'a chaotic quest for a definition of modern masculinity'. Discussing Iran under the neocolonial regime before the

Islamic revolution, Al-e Ahmad (1962) described a thin and rootless masculinity among the middle class, 'a donkey in a lion's skin'.

Not all changes in gender relations, however, were chaotic. Some were driven by the policies of developmental states. In the Turkish successor state to the Ottoman empire, a military regime under the war hero Mustafa Kemal created a paradigm of secular development in which modernizing the position of women was a central, almost iconic, feature. But military masculinities remained hegemonic, with conscription as a rite of passage into manhood for generations of Turkish men (Sinclair-Webb 2000).

Economic development was another important arena of gender formation. Where steelmaking, machine manufacturing and large-scale extractive industry were launched, industrial labour provided a central definition of working-class masculinity. Mike Donaldson (1991) showed this for Wollongong in settler-colonial Australia, noting how the gradual destruction of working bodies became part of the enactment of masculinity, demonstrating toughness and endurance. Dunbar Moodie's (1994) study of gold mining in South Africa presents another striking case, with industrial militancy growing while older constructions of masculinity were displaced and family connections with pastoral homelands weakened.

Elite masculinities could change too, as they did in Japan. Starting in the Meiji era, a strong developmental state and a small group of powerful conglomerates, the *zaibatsu*, launched heavy industry and constructed finance, education and weapon systems. For a time Japan became an imperial power. It is not surprising that a strongly-marked hegemonic model of masculinity on a national scale was produced, the corporate *sarariiman* (Ito 1993; Dasgupta 2003). The model was based on stable long-term employment as a manager, a sharp gender division of labour in the home, and a steep hierarchy of authority in the workplace. These conditions eroded in the late twentieth century, accompanied by public debates about salaryman masculinity and greater recognition of diversity (Roberson & Suzuki 2003).

The social transformations of development, then, involved new waves of gender disordering, and new hegemonic projects. In Turkey and Japan this produced historically original constructions of masculinity that achieved hegemony at the national level. In other situations it seems that a sustainable hegemony was not achieved in the era of decolonization and development, though social dominance for groups of powerful men usually was. Achille Mbembe's famous *On the Postcolony* (2001) gives a scorching picture of power without hegemony in a postcolonial authoritarian state.

Masculinities in neoliberal development

Since the 1970s, development strategies in the periphery have diverged. Many countries under neoliberal regimes abandoned import replacement industrialization and turned to mining and agriculture to find 'comparative advantage' in world markets. Others used low wages as their comparative advantage in manufacturing for export (Connell & Dados 2014).

On both pathways, states and ruling classes in the periphery used the removal of social protections and the privatisation of public assets to bolster their position in global markets.

Neoliberalism almost everywhere has been introduced by male elites, who have rolled back institutional protections and cultural gains by women, while promoting women's labour force participation and a notionally de-gendered ideology of individual advancement. Gender segregation and gendered exploitation flourish in new forms in the factories of the 'south China miracle', the *maquilas* of the Mexican borderlands, the huge expatriate workforce of the oil industry in the Persian Gulf states, and among migrant domestic workers such as the *baomu* of capitalist China (Yan 2008).

Neoliberalism has had contradictory effects for masculinity formation. For large numbers of men, 'structural adjustment' meant unemployment or casualization. Mara Viveros (2001) notes the impact across Latin America, especially the growing difficulty for working-class men in sustaining a breadwinner model of masculinity. South Africa has a similar experience (Hunter 2004), where the transition from apartheid to neoliberalism led to the collapse of secondary industry, with mass unemployment and an increasingly desperate situation for young Black men.

On the other hand, as neoliberal regimes concentrated the profits of development, they created conditions for the growth of entrepreneurial masculinities. The most spectacular examples are in China and India, where elite businessmen now control fortunes comparable to the great fortunes in the US/European metropole. Neoliberal development is also producing masculinized business elites in smaller countries such as Vietnam. In Kimberly Hoang's (2014) vivid study in Ho Chi Minh City, we see how the hierarchy of wealth and status among businessmen is displayed by socializing in high-end drinking and sex venues.

Yet the money and power of these new elites may not easily translate into achieved hegemony. Writing from post-communist Serbia, Marina Blagojevic (2013) notes how the pressures of the neoliberal era divide masculinities in the eastern European 'semi-periphery'. The dismantling of the state-centred economy, and dependence on western Europe, threatened men who were bearers of old forms of hegemonic masculinity. Others, who have marketable assets or skills, position themselves in the neoliberal economy and attempt to develop an international-style entrepreneurial masculinity. This split between hegemonic projects is not easily resolved locally.

Neoliberal development may also create, unexpectedly, local conditions for more egalitarian gender relations rather than more hierarchical ones. The violent neoliberal turn in Chile, for instance, created an export fruit industry that drew many women for the first time into wage-earning labour, and eroded patriarchal relations in rural families (Tinsman 2000).

Neoliberal development strategies in the periphery depend on the growth of global markets, global finance, and global communications. The consequence has been the creation of new social arenas in transnational rather than local space. These are powerfully gendered, though in new ways. Transnational manufacturing involves, as Juanita Elias (2008) has shown, a structure of relations between the professionalized masculinities of global corporate managements, local patriarchies in state and factory management, and gender-divided, often feminized, local workforces.

In such a context, the process of constructing masculinity takes new shapes. Fernando Huerta (2006) provides a notable example from his ethnography of a motor plant in México: the corporatization of football, and professional football's global role as a link between popular masculinities and the ethos of neoliberalism. The link is made in the training of bodies and the televised spectacle of embodied sport, both helping to naturalize a sharp division between men and women. Huerta sees in corporate football a mechanism for the international circulation of a generic hegemonic masculinity. That has yet to be confirmed; but his argument certainly dramatizes the world scale on which hegemony in gender relations is now pursued.

Global hegemony and contestation today

The offshore metropole and masculinity

The growth of European empire in past centuries depended on certain social conditions in the metropole: strong states organized for sustained warfare; ideologies of supremacy, first religious and then racial; population growth able to sustain a flow of bodies to the colonies; and a mercantile capitalism searching for unlimited profits. I will call the complex of institutions, cultural patterns and practices that enabled metropolitan societies to sustain empire the *metropole-apparatus*. The historical continuity of the metropole-apparatus underlies the coloniality of power and its persistence in the postcolonial world.

In the neoliberal era of globalization, the metropole-apparatus has, to a certain extent, broken free from the territorial states where it was originally based. The capacity to exercise global power is still connected to the wealth of Europe and north America and the military power of the United States. But metropolitan power increasingly operates offshore, through transnational institutions and spaces of a historically new kind: transnational corporations; global markets (especially finance markets, symbolized by the 24-hour operation of stock exchanges); international electronic media, including television and the Internet; and an international state, including both the United Nations complex and the linked-up military, intelligence and security apparatuses of NATO and other alliances.

The gender research in the metropole most relevant to understanding the contemporary metropole-apparatus concerns managerial masculinities. There is persuasive empirical work documenting power-oriented gender practices in both states and companies (Mulholland 1996; Wajcman 1999). Michael Roper's (1994) excellent history of managerial masculinities in British engineering firms traced changes in a local hegemonic masculinity, as managers' concerns shifted from the workforce and the production process to a neoliberal focus on finance and short-term profit. Richard Collier's (2010) careful study of corporate lawyers in Britain shows professional masculinities close to the patterns of corporate management—with possibilities of change, especially in the younger generation, held back by competitive pressures and the conservatism of their seniors.

Some recent studies have traced the gendered character of markets themselves as social institutions. An aggressive, misogynist occupational culture appears in arenas such as commodity and currency trading and financial manipulation generally (Levin 2001; McDowell 2010; Connell 2010a).

Top corporate management in the global economy is overwhelmingly the business of men. Of the 500 biggest international corporations listed in *Fortune* magazine's 'Global 500' in 2014, 95.2% had a man as CEO. In many ways the social world of these men resembles the managerial masculinities documented in the old metropole—competitive and power-oriented. Elite managers persistently construct hierarchical relationships with women, whether wives, employees, or sex workers. A striking confirmation emerges from an international bank merger in Scandinavia, a region whose gender orders are among the most egalitarian on earth. Janne Tienari and colleagues (2005) conducted interviews with the top executives after the merger. The senior managers were almost all men, and did not want to hear about gender equality problems. They took management to be naturally men's business, 'constructed according to the core family and male-breadwinner model'.

But transnational business masculinity cannot simply reproduce historic bourgeois masculinity. The labour of TNC management is secularized, mobile, and highly technologised, being closely integrated with corporate intranets and high-technology communications (Connell 2010b). This is not a 'geek' masculinity but it requires interaction with the changing masculinities of the ICT industries (Poster 2013). Because TNC management involves negotiations with local patriarchies (Elias 2008), it requires a degree of tolerance for differences in culture; and there are indications this also applies to sexuality. A professionalization of management has been attempted through the US-style MBA, and elite business schools in the metropole take pride in having an international intake of students. Firms from relatively affluent countries in the periphery, such as Chile and Australia, mostly follow transnational managerial practice though they participate in global business on unequal terms (Olavarría 2009; Connell 2010a).

There seems, then, to be a changed hegemonic project of masculinity formation within the global corporate economy. This is not producing a kinder, more inclusive or more feminized capitalism; a closer look at the masculinities of the main powerholding elites in the contemporary world shows the huge task still ahead for the project of gender equality (Connell 2016). But we do see hegemonic projects responding to the turbulence faced by global management and the impossibility of imposing any single gender template.

Contemporary hegemonic projects

As metropolitan power moves offshore into the complex of transnational institutions, the need for mechanisms of consent that produce hegemony at a local or national level declines. Are we now producing, on the scale of global society, the situation that Guha diagnosed in colonial India: hegemony an illusion and coercion the reality? Only in a few parts of the world do state or economic elites now rely on custom or claim old-established authority, and even where they do (e.g. in Thailand) the claim is fragile. Gone too is the old-style paternalism of improving public services or guaranteeing welfare to subaltern groups. The opposition to 'Obamacare' from the political right in the United States is a striking example.

But a more limited and complex form of hegemony may be found on the world scale. Three conditions would be sufficient to sustain the position of transnational corporate masculinity:

1) The institutional complex—private property and state authority—currently delivering control of the global economy, remains socially accepted within the most powerful states. Though there is widespread discontent, seen in the 2016 Brexit vote and the Sanders campaign, no organized alternative has much traction in the United States or the European Union. Police-state repression in China, and populist conservatism in India, are currently well entrenched.
2) The self-selecting masculine elites now in power retain their legitimacy and organizational control within the new metropole-apparatus. The corporate recovery from the 2007–08 global financial crisis suggests the capacity for continuing control is there.
3) The metropole-apparatus connects well enough with national power structures in the periphery to allow continued extraction of raw materials, overseas trade and corporate operations, and to sustain compliant states, in the periphery (see Mbeki 2009, for

diagnosis of Africa along these lines; Messerschmidt 2010 for the symbolic projection of masculinities by the US political elite).

Yet these conditions have to be worked on. The incessant busyness of corporate and political management, with its penumbra of bribery and intimidation and its sponsorship of violent interventions, show there is no *automatic* global control. The gender dynamics outlined in this paper show many examples of tension and dis-articulation. The extension of the neoliberal human rights regime to issues of reproduction and sexuality, to take just one example, has been repeatedly opposed by the most patriarchal governments in the periphery (in UN population debates as recently as 2014). The Islamist insurgencies of recent years, from Afghanistan to Nigeria, are if anything more patriarchal than the regimes they confront.

The emerging world gender order is far from being a smoothly-running machine. Rather, it is a scene of conflicting hegemonic projects. It has multiple tiers, where different configurations of masculinity are at work, and come into conflict. Major gains for gender equality have been made in the last half century, notably in state provision of education for girls and the rising participation of women in wage work. Up to now, however, these changes have yielded only a little ground for democratic projects of change in masculinity.

Counter-hegemony

Movements for change in masculinity, nevertheless, keep welling up. South Africa for instance remains a violent and unequal society, where gender inequalities are deeply implicated in the world's heaviest burden of HIV/AIDS (Epstein et al. 2004). But South Africa has also seen intense debates about changing masculinities, accompanied by local projects of change (Sideris 2005; Shefer et al. 2007; Ratele 2014). India too is a highly unequal society, yet has multiple sources of change among men, revealed in Radhika Chopra's books *From Violence to Supportive Practice* (2002) and *Reframing Masculinities* (2007).

Programmes concerned with the reduction of violence or the prevention of AIDS are now widespread. They are found in Latin America (Zingoni 1998), in Africa (e.g. Sonke Gender Justice, *www.genderjustice.org.za*), in South-east Asia and other regions (Lang et al. 2008; United Nations 2013). They have recently been linked internationally through the MenEngage network (*www.menengage.org*), which has sponsored two international conferences of activists, the most recent producing the 'Delhi Declaration' of 2014. These projects represent a historic change, mobilizing men internationally for gender justice.

But to be realistic, they remain relatively small; and mostly follow concepts developed in the global North. As Dowsett (2003) noted in a study of AIDS prevention in Bangladesh, Anglophone categories such as 'MSM', 'identity', 'heterosexuality' and even 'men' may misrepresent local social realities. Over time, a greater concern with distinctive local experience and strategy has been developing. Melissa Meyer and Helen Struthers' media project *[Un]covering Men: Rewriting Masculinity and Health in South Africa* (2012) is an example of the creative work that results.

Abhijit Das and Satish Singh (2014) offer something even more striking. From more than a decade of NGO-based programmes in India, including the well-known Men's Action for Stopping Violence Against Women (MASVAW), they have generated a seven-point theory of change. This theory emphasises the different starting-points in gender reform for men and women, the inevitability of resistance, and the strategies most likely to overcome it.

Do local gender-equality projects among men represent a counter-hegemonic strategy at the societal level? That question was raised by a team leading workshops about masculinity and violence in the very difficult environment of El Salvador, after a brutal civil war (Bird et al. 2007). Part of their answer is that local interventions bring out alternative practices and desires for peace that already exist in the society. Such possibilities can be seen in other places too (Haque 2013; Myrttinen 2012).

However, the NGO format of social action has been problematic for feminists, because of the way it is integrated into neoliberal politics (Alvarez 1999). The NGOs specifically concerned with gender-based violence overwhelmingly depend on corporate charity, international aid programmes, or national states. Published research reveals few connections between masculinity reform efforts and union activism, landless people's movements, environmental activism, or other movements that offer a significant challenge to corporate or state power. They seem, so far, no threat to the corporate masculinity of the new metropole. For such a challenge to develop would require a different structure of politics.

Conclusion

As Rachel Jewkes and colleagues (2015) show in a valuable current review, the concept of hegemonic masculinity informs much anti-violence activism and when carefully used can illuminate problems of strategy. Their argument is consistent with the approach adopted here, of analyzing masculinities in terms of collective hegemonic projects, local, societal and global.

I have argued that the changing structures of imperialism and neoliberal global power are a vital part of our understanding of masculinities. They represent both the structural conditions of hegemonic projects now, and the sedimented consequences of gender projects in the past. Hegemony cannot be presumed in the violent and exploitative social relations that constitute imperial and transnational gender orders. But hegemony is constantly under construction, renovation and contestation.

In this contestation, intellectual struggle is required. Knowledge produced in the majority world, and Southern perspectives on social relations and power, are increasingly important for global gender politics. A notable example is provided by AMEGH, the Mexican

Association for the Study of the Gender of Men, and the Colegio de la Frontera Norte. Their work has recently produced a powerful volume on the gendered violence in northern México, Salvador Cruz Sierra's *Vida, muerte y resistencia en Ciudad Juárez* (2013).

Knowledge is not a substitute for action. But accurate knowledge and theoretical insight are priceless assets for action, when action is concerned with contesting power and achieving social justice. That was our hope in formulating the concept of hegemonic masculinity, and remains the reason to build on it today.

Gender

3

Theorising gender (1985)

BY THE EARLY 1980s the new feminism had a global presence, and gender analysis had become familiar in the academic world. There were undergraduate courses, interdisciplinary programs, conferences, special issues of established journals and new specialist journals. The field was often called 'women's studies', sometimes 'feminist studies', sometimes other names. The boundaries were vague, though the main task was clear: to disrupt the patriarchal monologue in academic life and revolutionise existing disciplines. This was to be achieved by bringing in experience, ideas and perspectives from women—so long excluded from academic authority—and from marginalised groups of men. The driving force came from the women's liberation and gay liberation movements.

My partner Pam Benton was active in the women's movement—she helped to set up a women's health centre in one state and an organisation for older women in another—and gender politics was a constant topic of discussion in our house. It was, too, in academic life: in the new sociology program at Macquarie University we set up courses on gender and sexuality, and these issues became a major theme in our research. However, I was troubled about the concepts in use, especially the most common, the idea of 'sex roles'. This concept was popular, and it offered an alternative to rigid notions of biological determinism. But role theory was logically weak, and its restricted idea of change limited political horizons. What could replace it?

A more powerful social theory of gender was needed, and in the early 1980s I worked on that problem. This led to a new theorisation of masculinity (Chapter 1), which was a happy outcome, but the work also required rethinking the scope of gender analysis and the way feminist theory understood social structure. I wrote 'Theorising Gender' first as a conference paper, then as a journal article. We were staying in London at the time, and I wanted to put the ideas into international circulation. The British journal *Sociology* published the paper in May 1985.

It's an attempt at synthesis, and so has many sources. The critique of biological determinism came from the women's movement, the scope of gender politics from Juliet Mitchell and Gayle Rubin, the concept of practice from Jean-Paul Sartre, the treatment of social structure from Anthony Giddens and Pierre Bourdieu, and the idea of social dynamics from Jill Matthews and Edward Thompson. It also has limits: there is no trace of postcolonial theory here.

The style of writing is a little uncertain: sometimes vigorous, sometimes abstract and a little pompous. Perhaps that reflected my personal uncertainties at the time. But I wasn't unhappy with it: the paper encouraged readers to think about gender in more ambitious ways. It had a brief argument for what was later called 'intersectionality', it tried to weave in philosophy and psychology as well as social science, and it emphasised the dynamics of gender, the capacity of gender relations themselves to produce change. And though its readership was mostly in sociology, it laid the foundations for two books, *Gender and Power* and *Masculinities*, which circulated more widely.

THEORISING GENDER (1985)

Introduction

We are in the middle of the most important change in the social sciences, and Western social thought generally, since the impact of socialist class analysis in the mid-nineteenth century. Questions of sexuality and personality formation were made prominent by psychoanalysis from early in this century, but Freudian doctrines have always been reputed speculative outside a narrow therapeutic context. A sociology of the family and a psychology of sex differences and sex roles have stuttered along for decades as academic specialties of a rather marginal kind. Academic anthropology has given much more attention to kinship, but its interest has tended to create an impression that this is a matter of importance only in 'primitive' societies. That is the view held by contemporary theorists as prominent as Jürgen Habermas. In his reformulation of historical materialism, sex appears as a 'principle of organisation' of pre-class societies only (Habermas 1979).

That view has to be regarded as obsolete, in the strict sense of the word. 'Second wave' feminism and gay liberation have now made inescapable what was already suggested by some theorists of the 1940s. Sexuality, child development, the family, 'sex role' conventions, and kinship are parts of a whole. That whole is a social structure, not a biological one. It is, among other things, a structure of power, inequality and oppression; a structure of great scope, complexity, and consequence in our affairs as well as those of tribal and ancient societies.

In these respects it is fully comparable with the structure of class relations that has been the main concern of social analysis since the 'army of redressers' (Thompson 1968) marched onto the scene and made questions of class inescapable a hundred and fifty years ago. The redressers of sexual oppression are currently producing a critical and analytical literature of an intellectual liveliness and practical relevance unmatched in any other field of social science.

The intention of this paper is not to mount an argument for the importance of gender questions to social analysis. That argument has now been decisively established. My intention, rather, is to explore what kind of social theory of gender is likely to be most adequate, given current knowledge, understandings, and politics.

Scope

The scope of a social theory of gender is not easily defined. There are a number of speculative abstractions that appear to define it, such as the 'dialectic of sex' (Firestone 1970), 'relations of reproduction' (Centre for Contemporary Cultural Studies 1978), and the astonishing new science 'dimorphics' (Strober 1976). But these are more slogans for a particular way of theorising than specifications of what is being theorised.

It is better to accept that the social theory of gender is not a tightly-knit logical system. It is, rather, a network of insights and arguments about connections. For instance, one argument connects the dynamics of industrial capitalism and its sexual division of labour to the structure of the family (e.g. Zaretsky 1976). Another connects the structure of the family to the production of femininity (e.g. Chodorow 1978). The scope of the theory of gender at any given time is defined by the reach of this network of arguments.

We may reasonably say that at present the network firmly connects the following issues: the social subordination of women, and the cultural practices that sustain it; the politics of sexual object-choice, and particularly the oppression of homosexual people; the sexual division of labour; the formation of character and motive, so far as they are organised as femininity and masculinity; the role of the body in social relations, especially the politics of childbirth; and the nature and strategies of sexual liberation movements. The field defined by this network has no name in common use, though terms like 'patriarchy' and 'sexual politics' point to sizeable parts of it. Young et al. (1981) speak of 'the social relations of gender', a precise

THEORISING GENDER (1985)

but somewhat awkward term. 'Gender relations' is perhaps the most practical name for the whole network.

Arguments based on definitions of the field that exclude some significant problems already linked into this network must be regarded as partial and very likely to be distorted. This applies even to good and original work. Dorothy Dinnerstein (1976) for instance gives a delicate and profound analysis of the emotional tangles involved in personal relationships between women and men. She connects these emotions—sometimes very convincingly—on the one side to the sexual division of labour in early child care and on the other to the general oppression of women. But her tacit definition of subject-matter (through a focus on what I will call the 'normative standard case') completely excludes the relationship between heterosexuality and homosexuality, the general oppression of homosexuals, and the currents of homosexual affect (open or repressed) in predominantly heterosexual people. We can fairly say that these matters are known to be involved in the issues Dinnerstein is analysing. Her failure to reckon with them not only narrows but partly subverts her argument. The causal connections she proposes look much less convincing when homosexual paths of emotional development are brought into the picture of family dynamics too.

Of course it is not possible to theorise everything at once, as Dinnerstein fairly observes. But it matters to keep the whole structure in view. Less subtle analysts than Dinnerstein constantly simplify radical politics, and fragment it, by seizing on one part of the structure to the exclusion of the rest.

Broadly, accounts of gender relations that have attempted some synthesis of this field have been of two types. One emphasises the social construction of the categories of gender, the ways they are learned, inhabited, and transmitted. It speaks of 'sex roles', 'stereotypes' and 'socialisation'. In terms of academic social science it stems from the work of Margaret Mead (1950), Talcott Parsons (Parsons & Bales 1953) and Mirra Komarovsky (1946, 1950) in the US. This approach has enjoyed a huge revival in social psychology, sociology and allied trades since about 1970. The other tendency takes men and women for most purposes as already-constituted categories, and focusses on the relations of power and exploitation between them. It speaks of 'sexual politics', 'oppression' and 'patriarchy'. Its intellectual sources are less specific, though a number of the important ideas were crystallised by Simone de Beauvoir (1949). There is much less academic writing in this vein than in the 'sex role' vein, but the ideas are widespread in the movement publications of women's liberation and gay liberation.

Sex role theory

The analysis of gender relations along the lines initially proposed by Mead and Parsons, as a social script which people learn and enact, is attractive in several ways. It gives, on the face of it, full weight to the social character of gender, emphasising the stereotyped expectations ('role norms', etc.) for women's and men's behaviour. It appeals to familiar facts: the colour of a baby's bonnet, the pitch of a Marlboro advertisement, the script of John Wayne westerns, the aunt murmuring do's and don'ts in a schoolgirl's ear. It connects social structure with the formation of personality, via the idea of role learning or internalisation: thus, women become feminine by learning the 'female role'. It can be specific about what 'agencies of socialisation' are responsible for this learning, pointing the finger at parents in the family, teachers in the school, scriptwriters and directors in television and film, etc. And the approach leads straightforwardly to a particular kind of political practice.

Since the 1960s, in fact, these theoretical ideas have underpinned the politics of liberal feminism. This is the strand of feminism most prominently represented by Betty Friedan (1976) and the National Organization for Women in the U.S., though also widely diffused in the reforming feminism of the education systems (teachers, academics, and others) and bureaucracies of the OECD countries generally. Women's disadvantages are attributed mainly to stereotyped customary expectations, held by both women and men, which keep women back from professional advancement and create prejudice and discrimination against them. In principle, then, sex inequalities can be eliminated by measures to break down the stereotypes and redefine the roles. Among them are giving girls better role models, bringing in anti-discrimination laws, establishing equal-opportunity programmes in education and employment, and the like. This freeing-up of social convention may even be to the advantage of men. At least that is argued by the 'men's liberation' off-shoot of liberal feminism. (For this curious story see Carrigan, Connell & Lee 1985; for a notable endorsement see Friedan 1981: 131–67.)

Many of the facts appealed to by sex-role theory are factual enough. No-one who glances at the British popular press could doubt the existence of pervasive sexist stereotypes in the media, for instance. Few who support equality would oppose anti-discrimination and equal opportunity programmes, though there is room for argument about their effects. But as social theory, as a general account of the social dimensions of sexuality and gender, sex-role analysis is drastically inadequate. It has a number of fundamental weaknesses, which have been documented in a number of critiques (Franzway & Low 1978; Connell 1983; Edwards 1983). Two are of special concern here.

The first concerns what many people see as role theory's greatest strength, its emphasis on the social. Role theory is indeed often seen as a form of social determinism, stressing the way people are trapped in stereotypes and expectations. This image dissolves on closer inspection. The 'expectations' are made effective, in role theory, through the idea that other people reward one's conformity to the stereotypes, and punish departures from them. In role jargon, the occupants of counter-positions sanction role performance. Boys are praised for being aggressive, ridiculed for being girlish. But why do the second parties apply the sanctions? It cannot be explained by role expectations on them, or we get into an infinite regress.

It quickly comes down to a question of individual will, of choices to apply sanctions. The 'social' dimension of sex role theory thus ironically dissolves into voluntarism, into a general assumption that people choose to maintain existing customs. This leads to the second problem.

Lacking any way of grasping structural constraint, and hence lacking a means of formulating contradiction, the sex role framework is fundamentally static as social theory. This is not to say that role analysts ignore change. On the contrary. Change has been a leading theme in North American discussion of the 'male sex role' for decades (Hacker 1957; Pleck 1981). Changing definitions of the 'female sex role' have been the central theme in academic social science's response to feminism (for a review see Lipman-Blumen and Tickamyer 1975). The problem is rather that role theory cannot grasp social change as history, that is, as transformation generated in the interplay of social practice and social structure. Change is always something that happens to sex roles, that impinges on them. It comes from outside, as in discussions of how technological and economic changes demand a shift to a 'modern' male role for men. Or it comes from inside the person, from the 'real self' that protests against the artificial restrictions of constraining roles. Sex role theory has no way of grasping change as a dialectic arising within gender relations themselves.

This weakness is inherent in the procedure by which accounts of sex roles are constructed: generalising about norms, and then using the frozen descriptions as boxes into which to pack the events of people's lives. This happens even in the best sex role research. In *Blue Collar Marriage*, for instance, Komarovsky draws a beautiful picture of the politics of constructing a marriage: the emotional and sexual dilemmas of the new couples, the tussles with in-laws over money and independence, and so on. Then without turning a hair she theorises this as 'learning conjugal roles'—as if, in defiance of her own data, the scripts were just sitting there waiting to be read. The logic of role analysis forces role theorists to reify sex roles.

As Franzway and Lowe argue, sex role research highlights the attitudes that create artificially rigid distinctions between women and men, and plays down the circumstances those attitudes are about. Especially, role research plays down the economic, domestic and political power that men exercise over women. The project of feminism becomes a programme of role reform, of loosening social conventions, not of contesting power and overthrowing injustice. And the project of gay liberation becomes ... well, nothing, because you cannot formulate the oppression of homosexuals in role language except through the concept of 'deviance'. Attempting to loosen sex roles to make the deviance disappear would be to undermine the very solidarity of gay people that gay-liberation politics depend on. Gay liberation theory itself has turned in other directions (Plummer 1981).

Power analysis and categoricalism

The analysis of power is, by contrast, a starting point for the second general approach to a theory of gender relations. While Mead and Parsons synthesised the field around the theme of custom and reciprocity, de Beauvoir synthesised it around the theme of the subordination of women. The more radical feminisms that have developed this line of thought since the late 1960s have done so in two main ways. One is to focus on the relation of sexual domination itself as the core of the matter. Shulamith Firestone (1970) offered the first systematic synthesis on these lines, speaking of 'sex class'. Newer versions such as Mary Daly's (1978) picture of global patriarchy sustained by force, fear and collaboration have focussed even more specifically on men's violence towards women as the core of the core. The focus on pornography and rape in much recent feminism (e.g. Dworkin 1981) is closely connected with this. Pornography is regarded as an expression of the violence in male sexuality and as a means of domination of women. Rape is seen as an act of patriarchal violence rather than sexual desire; in Susan Brownmiller's (1975) well-known argument, 'a conscious process of intimidation by which *all men* keep *all women* in a state of fear'.

Other feminists, however, have seen naked force and sexual domination as something less than a prime cause; have seen them, rather, in the context of larger structures and the circumstances they generate. One argument stresses the sexual division of labour, in a now substantial literature about the division between domestic and public spheres of life (Rosaldo & Lamphere 1974), about the effects of women's mothering (Chodorow 1978), and about the dynamics of change in workplaces (Game & Pringle 1983). Another argument focusses on the structure and dynamic of capitalism, and the ideological conditions for its reproduction from day to day and generation to generation (see the literature reviewed by Barrett 1980). Yet another moves out to the general conditions of human culture and the structure of kinship exchange (Mitchell 1975).

In much of this theorising the categories 'women' and 'men' are taken as being in no need of further examination or finer differentiation. Theory operates with the categories as given; it does not concern itself with how they come to be what they are. I will call this habit of thought 'categoricalism'. It is, I think, closely analogous to the categorical thinking that underpins both stratificationism and structuralism in class analysis (Connell 1983).

The most obvious examples are where the categories are presumed to be biological, and the relation of patriarchal power is straightforwardly seen as a relation between the categories as collections of people. Thus 'rape ... all men ... all women' (Brownmiller); 'pornography: men possessing women' (Dworkin); and so on. It is easy to see how this way of thinking would follow from any tendency towards biological reductionism, given the common (if mistaken) assumption that sexual biology divides humans neatly into well-defined and distinct categories.

Yet a very similar *use* of gender categories can be found in the work of many feminists who are emphatically not biological determinists. This is true of arguments about individual psychology, such as

Mitchell's and Chodorow's psychoanalytic accounts of femininity; of arguments about the institution of marriage, like Christine Delphy's (1977) analysis of the exploitation of wives' labour by husbands; and of the marxist–feminist debate over 'domestic labour' and capitalism (Hartmann 1979). Here, the basis of categoricalism is not (or not explicitly) biology, so much as a radically simplified normative model of the family. As in functionalist sex-role theory, the argument is developed by analysis of a normative standard case, or a case presumed to be normative. The results are tacitly generalised to 'women' and 'men' at large.

This is curious, because a great deal of empirical and policy work by other feminists has gone towards exploding the notion of a standard case that underpins so much official welfare and economic policy. There are now detailed criticisms of the assumptions that everyone (or nearly everyone) lives in a nuclear family, that all women have (or should have) a man supporting them, or that having children presupposes a husband (see Baldock & Cass 1983 and Campbell 1984, among many others). Yet the pull of categorical thinking has been very strong. It has been reinforced by other intellectual influences—Lacanian psychoanalysis as a model for the analysis of culture, structuralism generally—as well as by its usefulness as a mobilising rhetoric for various movements in sexual politics.

A major effect of this has been to direct feminist theory away from divisions that cut across, or seriously complicate, the women/men categories: class, race, nationality, age. More strikingly, there is difficulty getting to grips with divisions that arise *within the field of gender relations itself* and hence bear directly on the processes that constitute gender categories. The most notable is the question of heterosexism, straight society's fear and hatred of homosexuals, which must be regarded as one of the crucial patterns in gender relations. It is very difficult to come to grips with this using a categorical model of gender. The point also applies to other types of differentiation among masculinities and femininities.

More: categorical thinking has led a significant body of feminist theory back to positions that contemporary feminism started by rejecting. If 'all men' are seriously to be taken as a political category, about the only things they actually have in common are their penises. The biological fact of maleness thus gets attached to the social fact of power, not by historical analysis but by definition. Conversely, the biological fact of femaleness becomes the central way of defining the experience of women. (See for instance the vulva as the central symbol in Judy Chicago's famous artwork *The Dinner Party*.) The curve of American radical feminism back towards biological determinism has been traced by Hester Eisenstein, who well summarises the 'false universalism' characteristic of categorical thought: 'To some extent, this habit of thought grew inevitably from the need to establish gender as a legitimate intellectual category. But too often it gave rise to analysis that, in spite of its narrow base of white, middle-class experience, purported to speak about and on behalf of all women, black or white, poor or rich.' (Eisenstein 1984: 132.)

The spread of this kind of thinking is indicated by shifts in language. We now often hear phrases like 'male power', 'male violence', 'male culture', 'malestream thought', 'male authority'. In each of these phrases a social fact or process is coupled with, and implicitly attributed to, a biological fact. The result is not only to collapse together a rather heterogeneous group (do gay men suffer from malestream thought, for instance; do boys?). It also, curiously, takes the heat off the open opponents of feminism. The hard-line male chauvinist is now less liable to be thought personally responsible for what he says or does in particular circumstances, since what he says or does is attributable to the general fatality of being male. As feminist thought has increased its recognition of differences among women, it seems—broadly speaking—to have weakened its ability to recognise differences among men. Another nuance of language shows the structure of feeling here. It is remarkable how many passages of contemporary writing about sexual politics talk of women as 'women' and men as 'males'. I have never found the reverse.

That this is a point where argument and emotion have got tangled is not accidental. There is a basic theoretical problem here. The social categories of gender are quite unlike other categories of social analysis, such as class, in being firmly and visibly connected to biological difference and function in a biological process. It is therefore both tempting and easy to fall back on biological explanation of any gender pattern. This naturalisation of social processes is without question the commonest mechanism of sexual ideologies. That biological difference underpins and explains the social supremacy of men over women is the prized belief of enormous numbers of men, and a useful excuse for resisting equality. Academic or pseudo-academic versions of this argument, male-supremacist 'sociobiology' from Lionel Tiger's *Men in Groups* through Steven Goldberg's *The Inevitability of Patriarchy* to the present, find a never-failing audience.

This kind of ideology cannot be overthrown simply by confronting it with another categoricalism with the plus and minus signs reversed. We need a different approach to understanding the relationship between biological process and social structure, which in turn requires a different way of handling social structure itself. What such an approach might be based on is suggested negatively by the viewpoints just discussed. Both patriarchal and anti-patriarchal categoricalism remove the element of practical politics from sexual politics, that is, the element of choice, doubt, strategy, planning, error, transformation. Without this element, sexual politics becomes (like the 'battle of the sexes' of traditional popular culture in which nothing ever changes) not the 'dialectic of sex' that Firestone glimpsed, but an old-fashioned stand-off.

Approaches through practice

We need, then, ways of thinking about sexual politics which develop the understanding of *power* by giving full weight to the *politics*. We need ways of grasping the interweaving of personal lives and social structure without collapsing towards voluntarism and shapeless pluralism on one side, or categoricalism and biological determinism on the other. In modern writing about gender this has perhaps been best done in fiction and autobiography. In books like Doris Lessing's *The Golden Notebook,* Anja Meulenbelt's *The Shame is Over,* Patrick White's *The Twyborn Affair,* Nadine Gordimer's *Burger's Daughter,* there is a strong sense of the constraining power of gender relations (and other structures like class and race), a sense of something that people fetch up against. Yet this 'something' is neither abstract nor simple, being real in other people and their actions, with all their complexities, ambiguities and contradictions. And this reality is constantly being worked on, and—in ways pleasant and unpleasant—transformed.

There are some parallels in the widely-discussed historical writings on sexuality and family by Michel Foucault (1979) and Jacques Donzelot (1979). The focus of this work is the emergence of social apparatuses, based in the professions and the state, which tried to regiment the domestic lives of ordinary people. This work is very clear about the social construction of sexual ideology and gender identities. As Foucault (1980) observes, the very need for everyone to have a clear-cut unchangeable identity as a member of one sex or the other is historically recent. The difficulty is that the history of power/knowledge apparatuses gives no grip on the grass-roots reality that was the *object* of the doctors', judges' and psychiatrists' strategies. There is, indeed, a strong tendency in this work to take it for granted that the strategies succeeded (e.g. Donzelot 1979: 58)—to elide the practices of the powerful and the lives of the oppressed. The history of the social relations of gender as a social structure is a considerably larger enterprise than the 'history of sexuality' as construed by Foucault.

In very general terms, how to build this kind of social theory is known. In principle, categoricalism can be resolved by a theory of practice, focussing on what people do by way of shaping the social relations they live in. In principle, voluntarism can be overcome by an attention to the structure of relations as a condition of all practices.

THEORISING GENDER (1985)

The notion of structure as process, to which Anthony Giddens (1976) gives the awkward but useful name 'structuration', is difficult to formulate abstractly. Abstract formulations of the structure-and-practice problem such as Pierre Bourdieu's (1977) theory of practice slip towards static reproductionism, as I have shown elsewhere (Connell 1983). But the idea of structure as process makes good sense when understood as the principle of analysis of a historical dynamic. Thompson has remarked that class is not the machine but the way the machine works, and the same is true here. The constraining power of gender as a social structure is found not in its geometry so much as its fluid dynamics, the logic of its historical transformations. To analyse a social structure is basically to work out its constraints, its internal pressures, tensions and disruptions, and its potentials for change.

It seems to me that some feminist and gay theorists have made significant beginnings with this kind of analysis, though their work is not recognised as a 'school' and their politics are very diverse. One of the first was Juliet Mitchell. The second section of her now somewhat neglected book *Woman's Estate* (1971) made a sustained attempt to sort out the social position of women in terms of four 'structures': production, reproduction, sexuality, and the socialisation of children. Each of those structures generates its own form of the oppression of women. Each has its own historical trajectory and at different times may change at a faster or slower pace than others. I don't think Mitchell's model of structures stands up; the four are types of practice rather than 'structures' in the full sense. But her recognition of internal differentiation and historical unevenness is very important.

Partly influenced by Mitchell's work, the American anthropologist Gayle Rubin (1975) developed a formal comparative analysis of the 'system of relationships', the 'systematic social apparatus', by which women became the prey of men. She called this the 'sex/gender system'. Though her discussion of it is rather structuralist in the Lévi-Strauss sense, the argument goes a long way to show what it is to have a systematic social theory of gender relations.

Adrienne Rich (1980), pursuing the critique of 'compulsory heterosexuality' that was also stated by Rubin, develops an account of the social relationships constructed by women among themselves in contradistinction to their connections with men. Her concept of a 'lesbian continuum', as Eisenstein (1984: 55–7) notes, drifts towards an ahistorical universalism, and thus a categorical theory of gender. But it need not be so. Certainly the historical analysis of this system of relationships is a major part of an understanding of gender relations.

This is one of the issues taken up in a notable study by Jill Matthews (1984) of 'the historical construction of femininity' in twentieth-century Australia, which uses the records of psychiatric incarceration to study the impact of changing ideals of femininity in the lives of particular women. Matthews stresses the historicity of femininity (and by implication of masculinity) as lived experience, not just imposed regulation. She firmly links the micro-contexts of household relationships to the large-scale patterns of demographic, economic and cultural change.

On a larger scale again, David Fernbach (1981) also offers a social and relational analysis of what is commonly seen as pre-social desire or anti-social behaviour. Focussing on homosexual relationships among men, he sets the modern emergence of homosexual identity (Weeks 1977; Bray 1982) in the long context of the history of gender relations stretching back to the neolithic. This is speculative in many ways, but is more like a real history than the myth-making about 'origins' that passes current in much of the literature about sexual politics.

Biological 'bases', and practical politics

How can a social theory of gender relations, developing along such lines, deal with the question of biological 'bases', the natural differences of sex? There must be, first, a really thorough rejection of the notion that natural difference *is* a 'basis' of gender, that the social patterns are somehow an *elaboration* of natural difference. This idea is enshrined in the very term 'sex role', juxtaposing a biological term with a dramaturgical one. It is extraordinarily pervasive. A useful cure is to read the excellent though little-noticed book by Suzanne Kessler and Wendy McKenna *Gender: An Ethnomethodological Approach,* which goes through the *biological* literature on human sex differences and shows how even that rests on the taken-for-grantedness of social attributions of gender. We always see the 'natural' through social spectacles, especially human 'nature'.

More generally, natural-difference doctrines result in an untenable view of the nature of human life and the relation between the social and the non-social. These doctrines treat natural difference as a passively-suffered condition, like being subject to gravity. If human life were in its basic structures (gender being one) so conditioned, human history would be unthinkable. For history—the full tapestry from Australopithecus to Ronald Reagan—depends on the transcendence of the natural through social practice.

This point holds good without the bland optimism about progress that has generally accompanied it. In an age of rising awareness of environmental and nuclear disaster it is easier to see negativity in the human rupture from the natural; a theme strongly developed, for instance, by 'eco-feminism' and the Greenham Common women's peace movement. It is also possible to see an expanded meaning in the idea central to the work of Gordon Childe (1954), the pioneer of global history as a science, that the relation between nature and human history is one of practical transformation. This means both the transformation of nature by practice that has sustained each stage of human social evolution, and the mutations of practice itself that have made shifts of structure possible. Practical transformation opens up new possibilities, and these are the tissue of human life. But it always does this by piling up new pressures and risks, for which some people, not just some objects, have to pay. Human society has 'exploited nature' by exploiting people, and the oppressions of gender relations are part of this pattern.

To speak of practical transcendence is to speak of practical negation. Here we have arrived at the crucial point about how a social theory of gender relations must handle the question of biological sex. Social gender relations do not *express* natural patterns; they *negate* the biological statute. (There is a very close parallel here with Sartre's (1976) analysis of the negation of the practico-inert in the developed phenomena of group practice.)

This is not an exotic or original idea. Rubin, for instance, observes: 'A kinship system is not a list of biological relatives. It is a system of categories and statuses which often contradict actual genetic relationships.' (1975: 169.) And 'Men and women are, of course, different. But they are not as different as day and night, earth and sky, yin and yang, life and death. In fact, from the standpoint of nature, men and women are closer to each other than either is to anything else—for instance, mountains, kangaroos, or coconut palms. Far from being an expression of natural differences, exclusive gender identity is the suppression of natural similarities.' (1975: 179–80.)

The social is radically un-natural, and its structure can never be deduced from natural structures. What undergoes transformation is genuinely transformed. But this un-naturalness does not mean disconnection, a radical *separation* from nature. Practical negation involves an incorporation of what is negated into the transformed practice. A *practical relevance* is established, rather than a determination, between natural and social structures. That is to say the social process *deals with* the biological patterns given to it. (As, the ecologists remind us, biological processes have to deal with the social forces impinging on them.)

The practices through which this relation is sustained include labour, as marxism tells us. They also include the practices of power and sexuality. An analysis of the way these kinds of practice are organised is, I think, the best path towards a systematic analysis of the sub-structures of gender relations as a social field. I hope to be able to publish a detailed analysis of this kind shortly. [Author's note: the detailed analysis came two years later, in *Gender and Power*.]

THEORISING GENDER (1985)

Don't worry folks, we're nearly home! Voluntarism and sex role theory, it was argued earlier, have a general connection with the politics of liberal feminism. Categorical theories of gender have been associated with the more radical feminisms of women's liberation, and with an increasingly pessimistic assessment of the prospects for immediate reform of gender relations, and a conviction that more total revolution is needed in the future. The kind of practice-based theory of gender relations that now seems possible has not crystallised far enough to acquire a recognised political identity, but it seems to me to have definite political implications.

In particular, this is a line of thought as radical as categoricalism in its formulation of the depth of the issues and the scope of the goal of liberation, but allowing for much more complexity and confusion on the path towards it. It seems to point towards a political strategy of radical alliances between groups constituted around different processes in the general structure of gender relations. Thus, notably, it brings back the question of the relation between women's liberation and gay liberation as a strategic issue. It is also possible to open up questions about the sexual politics of relations among different groups of men, and the ways some of them can become aligned with feminism in ways other than random individual choice.

Abstract theory can often be a diversion from practice, in sexual politics as elsewhere. Yet theory matters. Intellectuals have been of particular importance in women's liberation and gay liberation compared with other social movements, and the subversion of oppressive gender relations in part *is* intellectual work. (It is not an accident that a key technique of early second-wave feminism was 'consciousness raising'.) The importance of theory is sensed by the ideological opponents of feminism and gay liberation. You have only to notice how much airplay has been given in the conservative media to the supposed 'recantations' by Betty Friedan and Germaine Greer. Whether or not the approach to theory proposed in this essay turns out the right one, I am sure that work on these questions is among the most important projects for social scientists currently to undertake.

4

Rethinking gender from the South (2014)

'THEORISING GENDER', WRITTEN in London in 1984, was focused on theory from the United States and western Europe, as if that was all that 'theory' meant. It took many years to break out of that mindset. But in time I learned other feminist histories, met other networks of gender researchers, wrote *Southern Theory*, and collected books and journals published in the global South. Eventually I had a substantial argument about changes needed in gender studies. Of several papers, this is the one that deals most directly with questions of intellectual and political practice.

Some decolonial writing implies there is a monolithic 'Western' viewpoint, imposed by colonialism and starkly opposed to other epistemologies. I don't take that view. Feminist thought in the global North is multi-stranded, has been changing, and usually now does recognise a wider world. Still, this recognition is limited. Theoretical work done in the periphery rarely gains global attention or authority.

Yet there *is* powerful theoretical work being done in the global South. To make the point concrete, the paper describes three notable examinations of gender that deserved global attention, done respectively in

Brasil, México and Chile. Of course there is much more, including work from other continents. The paper then turns to the agenda of change. It discusses the approach of María Lugones, who coined the term 'coloniality of gender'. It considers how imperialism and gender relations became interwoven; the relevance of feminist analyses of the state; and the research role of NGOs, universities, journals and social movements. Bringing these issues together, it asks about the practical value of theory in struggles for gender justice.

In a way, this is theory about theory. But the paper also had two practical purposes. I hoped to persuade readers in the global North to question what they routinely know, and to look for other resources. For that reason I offered the paper to *Feminist Studies*, one of the first US journals founded by the women's liberation movement. They published it in 2014 as 'Rethinking Gender from the South: An argument for re-shaping feminism's theoretical work in world perspective'. Indeed they went one better, and also published links to translations of some of its sources.

I also hoped to encourage readers in the majority world to look for resources from other regions of the South. The article mentions sources from all continents. This should be easier to do now, with the internet. But the internet is biased, since most search tools and databases have been designed in the global North. The bias is now being contested, for instance by the Latin American database SciELO. But the task of moving to a world perspective is still formidable.

Dilemmas of feminism going global

From the time of the first UN World Conference on Women, in Ciudad México in 1975, the hegemony of the global North in feminism was contested. That historical moment, as Chilla Bulbeck showed in *One World Women's Movement* (1988), posed the questions of global solidarity and global inequality at the same time. Ambiguities in the global project of feminism quickly became evident.

The debate has continued, though on changing terms. It's now a familiar story. Within the North, Black feminists challenged the universalized models of women's oppression put forward by White radical and liberal feminist thinkers in the 1970s. The challenge was reinforced by the reception of Gloria Anzaldúa's *Borderlands/La Frontera* in the United States, by the rise of deconstructionist feminism and queer theory in the following years, and by the growing popularity of Kimberlé Crenshaw's concept of 'intersectionality'. Even the numerical expansion of women's and gender studies programmes played a part, creating a more socially diverse audience for feminist scholarship.

Perhaps the most important change in the North, in terms of global feminism, was the work of a generation of expatriate scholars, from Gayatri Spivak to Deniz Kandiyoti, who created a new conceptual space in the metropole's universities. This was epitomized by Chandra Talpade Mohanty's famous essay 'Under Western Eyes', and the collection *Third World Women and the Politics of Feminism* (Mohanty, Russo & Torres 1991) in which that essay finally appeared. Mohanty and her colleagues identified the colonial gaze in Northern gender scholarship and sharply challenged the stereotypes of 'third world women' in Northern feminist thought.

This critique has been heard. In the last twenty years it has become normal for feminist scholarship in the United States and Europe to acknowledge global context and global difference. This is plainly seen in textbooks. To take one example, the valuable US reader *Gender through the Prism of Difference* (Baca Zinn, Hondagneu-Sotelo & Messner 2000) includes items from Bangladesh, México, Spain, Guatemala, indigenous North America, and a good deal about migration and migrants. Thanks to scholars like Mohanty, Kandiyoti and Spivak, and the rise of Black and Latina feminism, postcolonial feminism has become a fixture in North American curricula, and more recently in Europe (Reuter & Villa 2010). Courses on gender now emphasise, rather than elide, diversity.

A shift has occurred in feminist research as well as teaching. Northern journals (including *Feminist Studies*) make a point of including contributions from around the world, and publish special issues on feminism in the Arab world, India, Africa or Latin America. Global surveys of knowledge have become a definite genre of gender studies. Witness *Women's Activism and Globalization* (Naples & Desai 2002), *Handbook of Studies on Men and Masculinities* (Kimmel, Hearn & Connell 2005), and *Global Gender Research: Transnational Perspectives* (Bose & Kim 2009), all published in the North, and all making efforts to think at global or regional level and include material from the global South. Increasingly, globalization has become an object of knowledge within gender studies. In the journals, the number of papers recorded in the ISI *Web of Knowledge* database whose titles or abstracts combined the term 'globalization' with a gender term rose ten-fold between the early 1990s and early 2000s.

This shift has affected theoretical writing. In *Scattered Hegemonies*, Inderpal Grewal and Caren Kaplan (1994) set out an agenda for blending Northern postmodernism with transnational feminism, and this combination has been influential. It has become more usual for feminist thinkers in the metropole, even when they are not postmodernists, to formulate their analyses at a world level. Examples are Spike Peterson's (2003) careful incorporation of gender theory into global political economy; Sandra Harding's (2008) imaginative reformulation of feminist epistemology in the light of postcolonial thought; and Cynthia Cockburn's (2010) worldwide synthesis on gender relations and war.

These changes represent great progress. Yet there is still a fundamental problem about this literature. Almost all the feminist thought that circulates internationally and addresses economic or cultural globalization, is based on concepts and methods developed in the global North. When speaking empirically of *maquiladoras* in México, sexuality in India or human rights in sub-Saharan

Africa, most of the research that circulates widely, and is accessible through mainstream databases, remains deep in the theoretical world of Marx, Foucault, Mead, de Beauvoir, Mitchell, Butler, and Scott. This literature works on the tacit assumption that the global South produces data and politics, but doesn't produce *theory*. (By 'theory' I mean creating agendas of research, critique and action; conceptualizing, classifying and naming; and developing methodology, paradigms of explanation, and epistemology. Theory is the moment in a larger social process of knowledge formation that transforms data or experience, always in some way moving beyond the given.)

In this, feminist gender studies is not alone. That the South doesn't produce theory is the default assumption in almost all fields of organized knowledge, from biomedical science to comparative linguistics.

Many people have sensed the paradox here. The tension between whole-world politics and Eurocentric theory has helped drive contemporary feminism's emphasis on global diversity—whether understood as postmodern fluidity and multiplicity of identities, or as local cultural difference. But those are Eurocentric framings too! They derive ultimately from the historical experience of the global metropole and overseas empire. They are examples of the 'reading from the centre' characteristic of Northern theory (Connell 2007). And they leave us with a dilemma about how to understand the foundations of feminist knowledge and the status of concepts ranging from 'patriarchy' and 'identity' to 'gender' itself.

The mainstream literature on economic and cultural globalization implies a unified epistemology as the basis for building knowledge. It assumes we can speak about the whole world, provided we speak in a conceptual language derived from the most powerful part of it. Classic examples in feminist writing were Robin Morgan's collection *Sisterhood is Global* (1985), and the Zed Books publications dissected by Mohanty (1991). Current examples are the UNDP league tables of gender equality in all the countries of the world, and the categorical treatment of gender in the influential World Health Organization report *Closing the Gap in a Generation* (CSDH 2008) on the social determinants of health.

One response to this situation is to reject outright the universalized Northern understandings of gender. This is done explicitly in the Afrocentric knowledge projects discussed by Obioma Nnaemeka (2005) and the Islamic methodology for feminism proposed by Fatima Mernissi (1991); and sometimes implicitly in discussions of global gender diversity.

Such projects point towards a very different basis for knowledge, which we might call a *mosaic epistemology*. In this conception, separate knowledge systems or projects sit beside each other like tiles in a mosaic. Each is based on a specific culture, religion, language, historical experience or fragment of identity, and therefore has its own terminology and categories. Each has its own claims to validity, and none should be taken as universal, as the master narrative for the whole world.

But this is not a comfortable position either, given imperialism itself. This is exactly the way colonialists saw the world of tribes and cultures, each unique, with only the colonizing power having the integrating view—a bitter paradox in anti-colonial thought, pointed out by Paulin Hountondji (1976). It is reasonable to argue that in the neocolonial world of the present day there are no separate cultures or religions left. It is transnational corporate businessmen rather than local patriarchs who are now the most powerful group in the world. Feminist researchers in different parts of the world urgently need ways to cross-fertilize, rather than to separate, their work. But how can we do this without a shared theoretical language and its Eurocentric epistemology?

The dilemma posed by the choice between two flawed approaches to the making of knowledge—Northern ethnocentrism and mosaic epistemology—is a major difficulty for feminist approaches to global issues. Therefore, given the strategic importance of global issues, it is a problem for feminist thought generally.

In this essay I suggest a way past this dilemma, which has two key steps. The first is recognizing the degree to which feminist thought is embedded in a powerful global economy of knowledge structured by the inequalities of metropole and periphery. The second is recognizing that, despite the operation of this structure, the periphery *does* produce theory, of depth and importance. From these starting points, a range of issues open up about the coloniality of gender, the workforce of feminist knowledge, and counterpublics on a world scale, which offer new perspectives for feminist theory.

[Here followed a section describing the global economy of knowledge in which the global South functions mainly as a giant data mine, while data accumulation and theorising is concentrated in the global North. (See Chapter 11.) Adapting to this situation, feminist scholars in the majority world tend to produce knowledge whose intellectual framing derives from the global metropole even when responding to local issues and using local data.]

Taking Southern theorists seriously

Nevertheless there *is* theoretical work going on in the South, and not all of it is dominated by Northern paradigms. This has been true from the moment of colonization, since colonized societies always attempted to understand what was happening to them. Settler populations did too. This theoretical work frequently moves out beyond the logic of extraversion, producing concepts, methods and agendas that urgently need to be part of feminist knowledge in the metropole, and should circulate globally.

How can I show this urgent need, against the gravitational pull of the global economy of knowledge? I could propose that the most important feminist theorist in the world today is Bina Agarwal, who works mostly in New Delhi, and that the most illuminating single text for understanding gender in our age is *A Field of One's Own* (Agarwal 1994). I could offer a list of the ten ovular books or twenty explosive articles written in the South that every feminist scholar ought to have on her Kindle.

I am half joking; the 'canon' game is deeply problematic, buying into neoliberal hierarchies and hiding the collective dimension of knowledge production. I am not suggesting a radical separateness of Southern theory from Northern, for the reasons already given against mosaic epistemology. Creative feminist work in the South often involves a critical appropriation of Northern ideas, in combination with ideas that come from radically different experiences. But I will take one step in the canon-making direction, because taking Southern theory seriously means reading specific texts with as much care as we might give texts from de Beauvoir, Scott or Butler. I will make comments—all too brief—on three that are highly interesting in their own right and raise general questions about the recognition of gender theory from the South. The three happen to be from Latin America, though examples could come from any region.

In 1969 Heleieth Saffioti's great pioneering work *A Mulher na Sociedade de Classes* [*Woman in Class Society*] was published in São Paulo. The date is worth noticing: it was before landmark Northern books such as Firestone's *Dialectic of Sex*, Morgan's *Sisterhood is Powerful*, or Mitchell's *Woman's Estate*. In fact Saffioti wrote her text in 1966–67. *A Mulher na Sociedade de Classes* contains a sophisticated marxist–feminist theorization of sex as a form of social stratification, and a detailed account, backed with statistics, of the gender division of labour, the political economy of the family, and women's education. It takes a historical approach to women's subordination, and has a brilliant discussion of the sexual economy of colonial society in Brasil.

Saffioti's book was even translated into English, appearing in 1978. It wasn't translated by feminists, but by a US marxist group.

This reflected Saffioti's orthodox socialist politics at the time. Her account of gender stratification highlights capitalist society's need for social control, and women's substantive unemployment, i.e. our role as surplus labour. A structuralist marxism from Paris, very fashionable in the 1960s, was a strong influence, so Saffioti's text bears many marks of extraversion. But she also used arguments from the South American 'dependency' economists such as Celso Furtado; and the book was more novel and more feminist than it seemed to Anglophone readers. The Monthly Review Press translation omitted two chapters that didn't interest North American marxists: one on the women's suffrage movement, and one analyzing the influence of the Catholic church.

Saffioti continued in activism and writing until her recent death. Her later work, though well aware of the stark class inequalities in Brasilian society, is less tinged with marxist sectarianism. For instance *Gênero, patriarcado, violência* (Saffioti 2004) treats gender, class and race as equally basic structures of society. The concept of 'gender' used by Saffioti in this book is abstract, meaning a particular domain of human action. Social relations in this domain have taken the concrete historical form of patriarchy—which can be abolished. Gender-based violence, which about half of all Brasilian women have experienced personally, is the outcome of a broad system of patriarchal power, including economic and political marginalization, taking specific form in different race and class contexts.

My second example is a notable paper published in 1992 in the *Revista Interamericana de Sociología*, called 'Sobre la categoría género. Una introducción teórico-metodológica' [On the category 'gender': a theoretical-methodological introduction]. The author, Teresita de Barbieri, came from Uruguay. She moved to Chile in the heady days of the late 1960s and began feminist research on women's occupational experience. With military coups in both Chile and Uruguay in 1973 ushering in violent right-wing regimes, she went into exile in México, where she began to pull together evidence about women's situation across Latin America.

'Sobre la categoría género' uses this data, but moves immediately to the conceptual level. De Barbieri makes considerable use of metropolitan theory, especially Gayle Rubin's model of the sex-gender system. But, like Saffioti, she makes a critical appropriation of Northern work, generating a distinctive theory of gender that historicizes the structural analysis of gender relations, and challenges the binary models of kinship on which Rubin and others relied. Here too, the timing is worth noticing. De Barbieri's work was contemporary with the emergence of deconstructionist feminism in the United States, and made similar criticisms of binary models of gender and earlier assumptions about women's solidarity under patriarchy. But she developed the critique in a very different direction.

This was possible because de Barbieri was able to draw on a wider range of literature and historical experience, from Black feminist thought in Brasil to the Latin American debt crisis to indigenous child-rearing in Andean societies. At the centre of her analysis is the issue of social control over women's reproductive power, and men's assertion of rights to offspring. So she characterises the figures of the mother and the male head-of-household as the 'nucleus' of Latin America's gender relations.

Given marked differences across the life cycle, the unequal relations among women (notably domestic service) in a stratified society, and the importance of relations among men, this does not yield a binary model. It produces, rather, a historical understanding of gender as social structure, more flexible than Saffioti's, and sensitive to changing regional realities. De Barbieri's work was notable in factoring into a theory of gender the divergent interests, politics and practices among men, and making a case for researching men in order to understand patriarchy. Indeed, a feminist literature on men and masculinity did emerge across Latin America in the decade after this paper (Valdés & Olavarría 1998).

My third example concerns another dimension of theory—methodology. I have mentioned the 'league table' approach to gender equity as done by the UNDP, with universalsed measurements, in which everybody looks discouragingly worse than Sweden. An alternative approach emerged from the work of the Grupo Iniciativa Mujeres, a coalition of NGOs and research institutions that formed in Chile soon after the end of the dictatorship. This Group worked on preparations for the 1995 UN World Conference on Women in Beijing, so it explored both UN statements such as CEDAW and national policies such as the Chilean equal opportunity plan.

From this came the idea of a 'social watch' instrument to measure progress (or lack of it) towards gender equity. As described by Teresa Valdés (2001), the project coordinator, the resulting index would be 'a strategy for citizen monitoring of gender equity'. Valdés had been involved in the very difficult scene of women's activism under the Pinochet dictatorship, and was concerned that feminist research should have both local relevance and political impact.

The ICC—*Indice de compromiso cumplido* [index of achieved commitments]—has two key features, which provide an elegant solution to the problem of abstracted universalism. First, it is not based on a top-down definition of gender equity, but on actual local policy commitments, embedded in national legislation, administrative rules, or adoption of international agreements. Second, it is multidimensional. It has three kinds of indicators: measures of 'political will', such as enactment of gender quota laws; measures of 'process', such as municipal programmes for domestic violence victims; and measures of 'result', such as the ratio between men's and women's incomes. Reflecting the priorities of the Chilean women's movement, three thematic areas are emphasised: citizenship participation and access to power; economic autonomy and employment; and women's health and reproductive rights.

Creating indicators from these starting-points involves some arbitrary weighting, which can be contested; but the individual variables are also documented. As the Chilean report shows, the ICC allows comparison of regions, and tracking over time. It can also be taken beyond Chile. In a second stage of the project, feminists from eighteen Latin American countries, with the aid of UNIFEM, worked on a combined ICC and published a continent-wide report tracing changes over an eight-year period (Valdés, Muñoz & Donoso 2003).

These are only three examples from a very large field. They illustrate both the creativity of theoretical work in the global South and the difficulty of getting it into worldwide circulation. Language is part of this. Texts written in Portuguese and Spanish aren't much read by Anglophone scholars—and texts in Bengali or Bahasa Indonesia even less. English is growing in dominance as the vehicle of neoliberal globalisation, translation is expensive and as Saffioti's story shows, dependent on the interests of Northern publishers.

Beyond the question of language, there is a powerful tendency in the metropole to define feminists in the South as people of *regional* interest only. They will be read by Latin American Studies scholars, or Africanists, or will appear in volumes about 'Arab Feminisms Today'; but will not be taken as important voices in *general* feminist theory. That is the obstacle, both cultural and practical, we now have to overcome.

Towards a more revolutionary future

To move beyond both a Eurocentric and a mosaic epistemology, we have to address this profound problem of recognition in a historical way, understanding the global social processes that have produced centrality and marginality in feminist thought.

A useful term has been proposed by the philosopher María Lugones (2007, 2010), the 'coloniality of gender'. Lugones is a member of the decolonial school, and this phrase adapts the Peruvian sociologist Aníbal Quijano's influential concept of the coloniality of power. Lugones criticizes her male colleagues on familiar feminist grounds for having an essentialist concept of sex, and argues that gender is socially constructed, not ahistorically but *in the processes of colonialism*. The colonial gender system involves a violent inferiorization of women, on the dark side of the colonial race division, and a hegemonic patriarchal family system (the main subject of Northern gender theory) on the light side.

Lugones' argument is decidedly schematic, and like other writing from the decolonial school, seems to draw an absolute opposition between the colonial and the indigenous; she speaks of gender as 'a colonial imposition'. This claim will hardly work for south Asia, east Asia, north Africa, Australia or the Pacific, which had strongly-marked gender orders before the European colonial impact; and it is debatable for sub-Saharan Africa and the Americas too. (For a notable example of a contrasting viewpoint see Bakare-Yusuf 2003.) There is certainly a profound connection between colonialism and modern gender orders, but it is much more complex than Lugones allows. We have to recognize the resilience of precolonial gender orders, the very turbulent gendered history of colonization itself (now being traced by historians in some detail), the influence of the colonized on the colonizers, and the complex structures of gender relations resulting in the postcolonial era—as documented by Agarwal, Saffioti, de Barbieri and others.

But Lugones is right in her major point. Gender analysis has to incorporate, at its most basic level, an understanding of imperialism and neocolonial global power relations. This does not mean a return to the bad old days when gender was seen as a secondary contradiction and capitalism as the deep reality. Rather, imperialism and capitalism now have to be understood as profoundly gendered processes from start to finish.

This is explored by expatriate scholars such as Anne McClintock in *Imperial Leather* (1995), work that has deservedly caught international attention. Yet an awareness of the interplay of gender and imperial power, for at least a century, has been a feature of feminism and other forms of critical thought in colonial and neocolonial situations. Witness the apparently light-hearted but sharp journalism of the pioneering feminist Mabel Dove (2004) in the British colony of the Gold Coast in the 1930s. Witness, more sombrely, Katharine Susannah Prichard's tragedy of Aboriginal woman and White settler man in the prizewinning novel *Coonardoo* (1929), which created a public scandal in 1920s Australia because it described both sexual exploitation and—even worse—interracial love on the frontier of settlement. In a recent volume of gender theory from Colombia, Mara Viveros (2007) notes how colonialism wove together gender and racial hierarchies with peculiar intensity.

The coloniality of gender also concerns contemporary dependency and global power. Postcolonial states almost all inherited patriarchal institutions and laws from the colonial empires, took over masculinized military forces or built them with Northern aid, and now operate under the shadow of superpower wealth and violence. Global corporations with a masculinized managerial elite produce new, geographically dispersed, gender divisions of labour (Odih 2007). The modern economy has little need of slaves, but gendered exploitation in other forms has flourished in settings such as the export factories or *maquilas* of the Mexican borderlands. There it has given rise to terrifying new forms of gender violence, such as the femicide in the city of Ciudad Juárez (Labrecque 2012). The connection between colonial and contemporary gender violence in Africa has been powerfully argued by Amina Mama (1997).

If I am right that analysis of the colonial and neocolonial structuring of gender will mainly come from the global South, then the future of feminist theory depends a good deal on the conditions of knowledge production in the South and on finding ways to support the workforce involved. We need to think about the different sites of knowledge production, if we are to have a conscious strategy of building theoretical capacity.

Though 'the state' has almost disappeared as a topic in feminist theory in the United States, actual states remain a central issue for feminism in most of the world. They are really unavoidable. The imperial state was central to colonialism and postcolonial states are central in social dynamics now. Many feminists work directly for the state (e.g. in health and education), or for international state organizations (e.g. United Nations agencies). The work of femocrats (to use the Australian term: Eisenstein 1996) has had an impact and they have been a key source of policy ideas in human services and employment. Control of the state doesn't just concern elites: Bina Agarwal (2003) argues that the state is particularly important for poor women's politics around land and development.

Of course states differ: the powerful authoritarian patriarchy in China is a vastly different proposition from the micro-states of Pacific islands or the violent but disordered regimes described by Achille Mbembe (2001) in central Africa. And states change: by independence, by coups, by democratization, or by neoliberal restructuring, which in recent decades has undermined the weaker developmental states. As well as re-shaping economies, structural adjustment programs have weakened social justice and welfare agendas, and as Amina Mama (2005) points out for Africa, has disrupted the growth of gender studies. But neoliberalism is contested, most effectively in South America, where the 'pink tide' of the last decade has created new conditions—though not always favourable ones—for feminist politics (Matos & Paradis 2013). And the recent economic expansion of the BRIC countries, though it has produced more inequality, has also meant public sectors better resourced than in other parts of the postcolonial world. For all the difficulties of institutional politics, then, states are a big resource for feminist thinking and it is important to keep alive connections between social movements and the staff of state agencies.

In the neoliberal era, NGOs have proliferated around gender issues and services to women—Marta Lamas (2011) reckons 500 in México alone. Debate has raged from México to Palestine about whether they depoliticize feminism, or sustain opposition and mobilize very marginalized groups of women (Abdo 2010). In terms of knowledge production, NGOs are now a major source, perhaps *the* major source, of research and publications about gender across the global South and especially in the poorest regions. But the type of research that NGOs usually sponsor has short deadlines and is tied to practical issues such as aid targeting and programme evaluation, sometimes using templates directly imported from the North. NGOs employ researchers, but not often in the long-term jobs that encourage reflective work.

Desiree Lewis (2002, 2007) speaks with some sadness of the balkanization of gender research in Africa resulting from the donor-driven agenda, and the 'brittle language about gender' in the development paradigm. Similarly Teresa Valdés (2007) speaks of the 'technification of gender knowledge' in South America's Southern Cone resulting from professionalization—in the context of the state and international agencies—and its contrast with emancipatory knowledge projects. Yet development jargon can be reworked, as Cecilia Sardenberg (2010) shows for the World Bank language of women's 'empowerment', given a more radical twist in activist work in Brasil. NGOs and the international aid machinery are places where theory-building does happen, more often in the interstices and around the edges than as a declared purpose. If intellectual work in the South were seen as a key part of global gender reform, these spaces could surely be expanded.

Universities provide some of the stability for an intellectual workforce that NGOs don't, though they too suffer from casualization and in poor countries hardly provide a living wage. The field of gender studies has grown with the expansion of university systems in Brasil, China, India and South Africa. In Brasil, India and México the feminist academic scene has reached substantial size, with sophisticated journals such as *Cadernos PAGU*, *Estudos Feministas*, *Indian Journal of Gender Studies*, *Debate Feminista*, and more. South Africa has been a regional hub for gender studies in a network of about 30 universities across Africa.

A particular university may provide a local base for gender research in a difficult environment. Examples are Gadjah Mada University in Yogyakarta; and Ahfad University for Women in Omdurman which sustained and expanded a women's studies programme despite an Islamist military government, with the help of upper-class connections and Northern aid (Haripangest 2009; Hale 2009). Universities have also provided a base for journals intended to link theory and activism, such as *Agenda* in South Africa and *al-Raida* (*The Pioneer*) in Lebanon. Universities, however, are socially selective, and have very different resource levels; social inequalities within the South are strongly reflected in higher education systems. Universities are also where pressures of extraversion are concentrated, with Eurocentric knowledge systems entrenched in most academic disciplines. They are perhaps the most contradictory of all sites for feminist work.

Feminist work in states, NGOs and universities ultimately depends on the energy of social movements. Most of the ideas discussed in this paper have grown, directly or indirectly, from women's movements, labour and peasant movements, and anticolonial and indigenous movements. With the continuing rise of women's literacy rates and participation in advanced education—perhaps feminism's greatest success on a world scale—social movements have increasing capacity to articulate and circulate their knowledge, strategies and concepts.

Social movements, however, are divided and fluctuating. Women's activism in Indonesia, suppressed for a generation under Suharto's New Order dictatorship, burst out in the period of *reformasi*, though feminists in many parts of that very diverse country still have to fight attempts to re-domesticate women (Robinson 2009). The women's movement in India has been criticized for the dominance of upper-caste women and marginalization of Muslim, Dalit and tribal women (Kirmani 2011). The women's movement in Brasil has been criticized for inadequate recognition of Black women's needs and politics (Carneiro 2003). The great series of feminist *encuentros* in Latin America that began in Bogotá in 1981 has been marked by tensions between 'institutional' and 'autonomous', working-class and middle-class, academic and popular feminists. It's not surprising that, as Marta Lamas (2011) puts it, 'urgent political needs have relegated theoretical discussion to a secondary status' even within academia, and that some movement activists reject the idea of 'theory' itself as elitist, patriarchal or imperialist.

On this, I agree with Lamas and Saffioti that theory matters greatly for feminist movements. Though it can certainly function in an intimidating, exclusionary and Eurocentric way, theory can be practiced differently, in an inclusive and democratic approach to knowledge-building.

A great deal depends on the audiences and uptake of intellectual work. Millie Thayer (2010) has recently argued, in a discussion of the translation of ideas and language in feminist activism, that a worldwide 'counterpublic', vast and heterogeneous, is constituted by social movement activists, academics, women's organizations, even state and development agency staff. A great skein of formal and informal links, including the transnational feminist networks mentioned above, ties this counterpublic together. Other feminist thinkers have proposed related ideas, such as Mara Viveros' (2007) argument for the importance of South/South alliances in supporting decolonizing practice for feminism.

We can see this counterpublic as providing not only a counterweight to the privilege of Northern institutions, but a context in which theory is generated. It is worth noticing the sheer diversity of forms that concepts and methodologies can take: from Arabic poetic tradition as a vehicle for critique of women's subordination in the Gulf states (Gohar 2008), to the radical art practices of the amazing Bolivian feminist group *Mujeres Creando* (Paredes 2002), to international online discussions among human rights activists (Ackerly 2001).

Theory, at the most basic level, is a way of seeing and speaking beyond the given. In the process of constructing knowledge, theorising is where reality meets imagination. Anyone can speculate, but good theorising is hard to do, because it has to connect solidly with experience and also lead fruitfully beyond it. When it works, theory provides a bridge between realities, both between different contemporary situations and between present reality and future possibility.

Feminist movements are concerned to transform, to revolutionize, unequal gender relations. To do so on a world scale needs theorizing on a world scale; and to do that, absolutely requires postcolonial, decolonial, Southern theory. The goal isn't to write a unified theory of gender, even one compiled from Southern sources. It's to create, within the worldwide counterpublic, processes for mutual learning and interactive thinking about theoretical questions. Using another metaphor, the goal is to create spaces of theoretical discussion with many more voices and wider and deeper agendas. Given the current shape of the global economy of knowledge, the vital need right now is to give recognition, indeed centrality, to theoretical work from the South. In the longer run, we need to create sustainable democratic processes for intellectual work on a world scale.

We are still near the beginning of this path. In this essay I have done little more than wave at problems and texts. But if this waving helps readers to see the shape of the problems, the brilliant resources already available, and the tremendous possibilities open before us, it will be justified. In an interview published in *Agenda*, Amina Mama (2001) spoke beautifully of a feminism rich with ancestors from many places and countries. I believe contemporary feminism will also have a wealth of descendants—the societies of a future where global violence and gender injustice will have passed like a bad dream.

Class

5

The Australian ruling class (1975)

MODERN AUSTRALIA WAS shaped by a British invasion that began with a small penal settlement, which grew into a settler colony, expanded across the continent, and devastated Indigenous societies. The settler colony developed a class structure that copied class distinctions from the imperial homeland, but over time developed its own shape and its own dynamic of change—which Terry Irving and I tried to map in *Class Structure in Australian History*.

In the early part of my academic life, studying class was a central theme. In the late 1960s and early 1970s I worked on the historical project and also on studies of class consciousness, education, public opinion, major companies, right-wing politics and intra-class conflict. The energy amazes me now!

I came to think that understanding elites, power and privilege was the most important project of all. The New Left of the time argued that sociology should be 'studying up', researching the rich and powerful rather than the poor and marginalised. That meant, to a young socialist intellectual, producing knowledge about the ruling class of a capitalist society. I was part of this class, in a broad sense. My father's family had money from colonial times, and sent their children to elite private schools. He and his brothers joined well-paid professions; and so did I. When I was a teenager we lived on the harbourside in a conservative and affluent neighbourhood. There was scope for dissidence, obviously. I marched in my first political demonstration (against capital punishment) as an undergraduate, and by 1966 was involved in Sydney protests against Australian complicity in the US war in Vietnam.

In 1974 I gave a paper to the Sociological Association's annual conference, 'Structure and Structural Change in the Ruling Class', published the next year in a political economy collection. A little later I shortened and rewrote it as a chapter for *Ruling Class, Ruling Culture*, a book that pulled together the different strands of my research about class in Australia.

The text here comes from the first version, to show the argument in its raw state. It originally included an account of structural ideas in the current literature; since the books discussed are no longer familiar, I omit this section and continue with the paper's reinterpretation of the data and its new lines of thought. These are concerned with how power is exercised, with internal conflict, and with how a potentially divided ruling class is held together.

The most important task facing sociologists in Australia is to make an analysis of the nature, operation, impact, and strategic weaknesses of the ruling class. In carrying this out, an essential step is to give an account of its structure.

Discussions of the ruling class in Australia have not, on the whole, paid much attention to questions of structure. They have addressed themselves more to questions of personnel, recruitment and attitudes. Yet 'ruling class' is itself a structural concept, as are the notions of elites, 'upper strata', and so forth, that various sociologists have offered to replace it. It is a logical step to go from analysing the structure of relations between classes to analysing the structure of relations within classes; indeed if the same principles can be shown to apply, the original analysis will be greatly strengthened. Further,

THE AUSTRALIAN RULING CLASS (1975)

an account of structure is necessary if the analyses of personnel, attitudes, etc., are themselves to bear fruit. For only by an account of their situation will the reasons for the actions of the members of the ruling class become intelligible; and only through a grasp of the structure of the situation in which actions occur can we hope to understand their consequences.

A thorough analysis of ruling class structure, even in a small capitalist power like Australia, is clearly a large undertaking. At a rough estimate there are over a million people involved as owners of shares, the commonest form of productive property; though the numbers active in business, political and social leadership are much smaller than that. The purpose of this essay is merely to take two steps towards this analysis: to systematise and criticise the existing literature on the subject; and to offer some hypotheses about the recent structural development of the ruling class, for which I can offer a certain amount of supporting data but not complete proof.

[Here I omit the section that summarised structural ideas in books about Australian companies, elites and capitalism by Ted Wheelwright, Sol Encel and John Playford. These ideas concerned the internal organisation of the business elite (concentration, interlocks and fundamental unity); relationships between business and the state (government support for business, connections and mutual constraint); and the sources of capital (local vs imported) and personnel (privileged family backgrounds).]

Critique and reformulation

Potential and actual power. The discussion of concentration immediately raises the question, concentration of what? Wheelwright, Encel and Playford all speak of domination, control, or power. The evidence, however, is not about this. The evidence is mainly about ownership of shares; and in his original study, Wheelwright was careful to distinguish this from power, in the sense of initiative in decision-making. At most, the study of ownership can yield information about 'ultimate control', meaning 'the power to select or change the management of a company' (1957: 82). To be blunt, what we have here are conclusions based on inferences about what might happen if the shareholders attempted to mobilise. This, clearly, is only one element in an analysis of power, and not necessarily a very important one (given the usual passivity of shareholders). The studies of market concentration also yield, at best, inferences about a potential for control of an industry (or an economy). It is altogether another matter to show that control is in fact exercised.

The same kind of thing can be said about the studies of networks of directors and family ownership. These provide evidence not of organisation itself, but of potential for organisation. From saying that they could function as systems of power within business, it is a long step to saying that they do. Businessmen themselves deny it, so far as it applies within business (though shareholders sometimes become sceptical, as in 1971 when M.R.L. Dowling was forced off the board of Kathleen Investments which another of his companies, Castlereagh Securities, had been trying to control). The activities of management, obviously central to any discussion of the practical use of power in business, are largely ignored in these calculations. And the inferences become very dicey when one moves on to consider the exercise of power outside business. Encel (1970: 347, 411) cites the example of Staniforth Ricketson, scion of the Melbourne stockbroking house of Were, as an example of business influence. But Ricketson's major venture into independent organisations, the 'All For Australia League' in the Depression, was short-lived, and not very independent at that (Matthews 1970). He could exercise effective influence only through the party system; which introduces quite a new element into the picture of power.

Freedom and conflict. Wheelwright argues that the size of companies, their 'domination' of markets, and the managers' independence of sanctions from shareholders, has conferred a great deal of freedom on the managements. He has also suggested that Rolfe's (1967) study of directors yields data more commensurate with the view that management acts in the interests of the propertied class than with the view that it has become separated from it (Wheelwright 1974: 130–1). The latter point is not proven because the data do not in fact bear on executives (apart from managing directors). But note that if the first point is true, the second can be true only by the *choice* of the managers: they are not *constrained* to maximise profit, exploit the workforce, etc. In Wheelwright's formulation there is no structural imperative acting on company managements that determines the use of their power, the direction in which they will act.

It is at precisely this point that the issue of competition becomes important. For there is competition between businessmen, of a much greater variety than simply competitive selling of products in the marketplace. The system of share ownership of public companies makes management in principle vulnerable to rival groups buying up shares and attempting a takeover. (As the TNT–Ansett takeover battle showed, even corporate heavyweights are vulnerable to this.) Managements which do not maintain a high rate of profit on their assets are vulnerable to 'asset stripping' raiders (who buy up a company's shares cheap, take over, and sell off the undervalued assets, like Gordon Barton with Angus & Robertson—see McCarthy 1973). A declining market share and profit performance may provoke a coup within the company (for instance, British Leyland which axed its Australian management).

These observations become more significant in the light of foreign investment in Australian business. To say that there has been increasing foreign investment is, conversely, to say that Australian business has become increasingly integrated into the world capital market. And big capital is highly mobile, between both countries and between industries—as the multi-national conglomerates like ITT (famous *inter alia* for its role in Chile) very clearly show. These competitive forces, we may infer, have increased in the Australian economy, however internal market competition may have declined.

One of the consequences is that managers of the Australian branches of multinationals must try to squeeze growth and profits out of the local firm in order to get on in their international careers (an example is Bill Bourke, late of Ford Australia, who skipped on to higher things just ahead of the Broadmeadows worker–management confrontation).

We may argue, then, that conflict in business has a continuing and systematic importance. It is a constant force on the actions of businessmen, pushing towards profit making, corporate growth, and resistance to working class politics. Note that this applies as forcibly to managers as to directors. We do not have to assume anything about the attitudes of managers, nor even postulate with Playford (1972: 118) 'a basic community of interests' between managers and owners to explain this tendency.

Business and the state. The case argued, particularly by Playford, for a considerable integration of business with the state, is undoubtedly in its main principles correct. The slightest observation of the actual behaviour of companies like BHP, CRA and others, is enough to dispel the view of businessmen argued by Parker (1965), that 'what they want is to be left alone'. But the formulations of the nature of state support of business through tariffs, infrastructure and other measures, leave much to be desired; they are often summary and repetitive (examples: Wheelwright 1974: 120; Playford 1969: 14). This is unfortunate, as some at least of the examples given are arguable. Tariffs, for instance, are repeatedly cited as a prime example of state support of business (cf. also Encel 1970: 319–22, 352–5). But tariff protection to manufacturers disadvantages other businessmen, notably pastoral and mining capitalists. 'Integration' of the state with the one group implies disintegration with the other.

Similarly one might observe that much of the lobbying activity noted by Playford and Encel, and of the bodies which permit and conduct it, is directed against other businessmen, not against labour. There is integration of the state with one lobbying group only to the extent that its rivals have failed; or, to see it from the other side, to the extent that it is in the interests of political and bureaucratic entrepreneurs such as McEwen [Country Party leader] to form stable links with a particular business group. The point is that there is really no lobby that reflects the interests of businessmen in general. To get to the level of the collective interests of businessmen, one has to penetrate to a very basic institutional level: to the level of the institution of private property itself. *At no other level is there unanimity in business:* not even on an issue such as conceding wage demands to the unions, as the repeated conflicts between the metal trades employers and other employer organisations attest.

At that level, there is nothing 'neo' about an integration of business and the state. In white Australian history, business has *always* depended on the state for a guarantee, by force and suasion, of the system of private property. The very foundation of Australia as a penal colony was part of the enforcement system of private property. Again, the international context is vital to an understanding. One of the most important things about the capitalist world order is the international continuity of private law. This has permitted in Australia, since the 1820s, the formation of international (originally English–Australian) companies; and now of course it permits the integration of Australia into the economy of the multinational corporations. In this respect the state itself is internationalised, it is not limited by the boundaries of the so-called 'nation-state'. The multinationals are not so much a threat to the national sovereignty, as a realisation of the original character of the capitalist state.

Reformulations. The concepts of concentration and network are useful, but it is necessary to distinguish between them and the full concept of a structure of power, which by almost any definition includes the effective exercise of command or constraint. Parker (1965) may be wrong in claiming that in Australia power 'plays an unusually restrained role', but at least he is talking about power and not simply a possible base for it. To move from the one to the other it is necessary to work with a concept of *mobilisation,* one of the keys to a historical understanding of the ruling class in Australia. One does not have to suppose a continuing structure of rigid control: one can observe the ruling class mobilising in periods of crisis such as the bank nationalisation campaign of 1947–49 (May 1968; Connell & Irving 1973). And it is noteworthy, in view of the research attention given to directors and owners, that it was *managers* such as McConnan of the National Bank who were politically decisive in this process.

The concept of competition must be brought in as a fundamental structural category for the analysis of the ruling class, but in a wider sense than simply competition in the product market. Competition in the capital market is of major importance—a worldwide capital market—and also competition in what we can describe as the 'person' market, that is competition between businessmen for the control of companies and their assets—which is also now conducted on a worldwide basis. Such a concept is necessary to account for the systematic character of the ruling class's activity in a stronger way than simply postulating attitudinal consensus.

The concept of 'fundamental unity' drops out, in favour of an analysis of the institutional basis of the power of the ruling class; a concept that applies to the structure of the whole society rather than to the ruling class *per se.* The state enters this analysis in a constitutive role, in connection with the system of property. It is necessary to distinguish the state, which evidently has some international continuity, from state organisations (such as the Federal Government) which have a specific personnel and a local boundary. Relationships with state organisations become part of the analysis of faction formation and factional conflict within the ruling class, rather than a characteristic of the ruling class in general.

We are also obliged to attribute an independent significance to members of the state elite as entrepreneurs, as people capable of taking their own line in the factional conflicts just mentioned. The research evidence of common social origins with business entrepreneurs now takes on a new meaning. It demonstrates not the attitudinal convergence of state and business elites (always rather doubtful), but their common class bases. They appear not as masters and puppets, agents and beneficiaries, nor as independent elites, but as alternative leaderships of the same class.

Hypotheses about structural change in the ruling class

The class and its leadership

It is essential to distinguish between the ruling class as a whole, as a class, and those members of it who are active entrepreneurs. The class is constituted by the system of private ownership and its 'generative capacity', its capacity to enter into and structure a wide range of social transactions, as property is used in production and for other collective purposes. Some, but only some, of the owners of property actually employ it in production. They are however able to mobilise the property of others who are not personally involved. One of the most striking features of modem capitalism is the organisational structure that allows this to be done. There is the limited-liability company, which mobilises capital in the form of shares; and in Australia, very prominently, the financial institutions such as the gargantuan insurance firms which, under the guise of mutual protection societies, mobilise capital through insurance premiums and invest it in production. The entrepreneurs who mobilise and direct the use of property through these means are the most active section, the business leadership, of the class that owns it.

This relationship through capital mobilisation has not fundamentally changed since the introduction of limited-liability companies, the formation of insurance firms, and the organisation of local capital markets, which mostly took place in Australia around 1860–1880, during the first 'long boom' (Hall 1968; National Mutual 1969). It has remained remarkably unregulated by the state, as is shown by the absence of a national company regulation body, and the absence of control of the stock market recently demonstrated by the Rae

Committee (Senate 1974); though the state guarantees the basic relationships through the law of property and the fraud provisions in the Companies Acts. The business leadership of the ruling class is self-appointed, consisting of those people who succeed in mobilising capital or in winning or inheriting control of established accumulations of capital. It acts not so much by consent of the bulk of owners, as in default of their non-consent: that is, it acts by its own lights unless in a particular case they mobilise against it. This practically always occurs as mobilisation under the leadership of some rival entrepreneur. Organisation of shareholders simply as shareholders is extremely weak (there is an Australian Shareholders' Association, but it has no more than nuisance value); and recent attempts to organise policyholders to win seats on the boards of such institutions as the National Mutual have failed.

The conducting of business, however, is not the only purpose for which the ruling class needs leadership. The expansion of the union movement in the later nineteenth century, its rise to electoral success in the Labor Parties of the early twentieth century, and the deepening militancy of industrial workers around the time of the first world war (Turner 1965), posed a threat to the entire position of the ruling class. However mild the Labor parties may appear in historical retrospect, they were certainly seen as a wild and dangerous force by the ruling class at the time.

One response, as is well known in the history books, was a closing of the ranks, a 'fusion' of free-traders and protectionists against Labor in parliament. Another response, less well recognised because it developed over a longer time, was the emergence of a new leadership in the ruling class. A specialised political cadre emerged, a group of men who took on the political leadership of the ruling class as distinct from its business leadership. In the nineteenth century, business leadership and political leadership had been so closely intertwined they were often impossible to separate. Now they were prised apart: in the case of men like Bruce and Massy-Greene in the inter-war years, by a temporal division of a business segment from a political segment in the one career (Edwards 1965; Kemp 1964); in the case of men like [Premier] Playford in South Australia, and Menzies nationally, by a full-time specialisation in politics with only the faintest traces of a personal involvement in business.

In the leadership of the Liberal and Country parties, then, we have a group not separate from the ruling class, but separate from its business leadership: the two are now parallel specialisations within the class. Like businessmen, the political leadership is made up of entrepreneurs; but these are entrepreneurs whose field of action is state organisations, and whose success depends on mobilising and using political support rather than capital. In this process, of course, money is necessary; so the collective operations of this leadership draw funds from the business leadership, and individual members of it may have close relationships with individual business entrepreneurs. But there is no need to assume that conservative politicians are typically the agents of particular groups of businessmen: indeed the general situation is that they are not.

This interpretation leads to a quite different view of the bodies articulating business and politics that Playford (1969, 1972) has carefully mapped. These now appear, not as signs of an increasing integration of business and politics, but as consequences of their historical *separation.* The specialisation in the leadership of the ruling class and the growing independence of the political wing has created a need to re-establish co-ordination in political tactics, social and economic planning.

The rise of new capitalists

As the economic historians tell us, the white settlements in Australia have had a few threads of manufacturing in their economic fabric from the earliest convict days (Hainsworth 1971). But it was not until after the Depression of the 1930s that sustained industrialisation began and heavy industry moved into the strategic place it now occupies (Schedvin 1970; Boehm 1971). The first stages of this did not lead to a shift in power within the ruling class, for the companies involved were already powerful groups. BHP's position when it moved into steel-making was based on the massive profits of its silver mine over twenty years, though it still needed to raise new capital for the steelworks. Other heavy industrial companies such as Electrolytic Zinc and Metal Manufactures were set up by the Baillieu interests, also an established fortune. Even new manufacturers had to plug into establishment circuits, as is shown in the case of Frank Beaurepaire who needed a stockbroker to place the original shares in his Olympic Tyre Company in 1933, and within a few years was Lord Mayor of Melbourne (Lomas 1960).

But the continued industrial expansion eventually did lead to a shift in power. Unlike the situation in Japan, re-industrialising at much the same time, old companies did not diversify rapidly to meet the new economic and social demands. In Australia these demands spawned new corporate structures, and as they continued to grow, they launched new entrepreneurs into the top ranks of the ruling class. It was not in heavy industry, which at this stage of world economic development needed large initial capital outlays. Rather it occurred in 'service' industries, notably transport, real estate development and construction, where an entrepreneur could start in a small way and build up rapidly with the growth of the market and with a strategy of amalgamations and takeovers. The classic example is undoubtedly Reg Ansett, who built up from a one-car service at Hamilton in the 1930s, until in the 1950s he could challenge and defeat the moribund controllers of ANA and establish a near monopoly of private air transport. Other well-known 'new capitalists' who have built empires out of transport are Gordon Barton, Ken Thomas and Peter Abeles. In development and construction there are such figures as Leslie Hooker, Alan Bond and Paul Strasser. The mining boom of the late 1960s saw a whole crop of new faces in the business leadership—though not all survived it—and a series of sharp struggles among them for control of the bonanza (Indyk 1974; Connell 1974).

In many cases the operations of the new capitalists have depended on support from establishment sources. Thus the rebuilding of Sydney by Hooker, Strasser, Dusseldorp and their followers has largely been financed by insurance firms, notably the most colossal and established of all, the Australian Mutual Provident. But the sheer size that the leading new companies have reached, and the enormous personal wealth of some of the new capitalists (Lang Hancock, the West Australian mining entrepreneur, is reputedly the richest man in the country), enables them to deal on equal terms with establishment businessmen. They are able to set up systems that bypass the networks of family wealth and family directorships that have characterised the Australian business scene for the last fifty years. (The network of directorships and financial relationships surrounding the stockbroking firm of Patrick Partners, and linking its finance companies with operating firms such as TNT, Soul Pattinson and Pioneer Concrete, is a major example. Its potential was shown in 1972 in the Ansett takeover attempt.) It seems likely, though I have not got the detailed information to test the idea, that the massive inflow of foreign capital since the 1940s has been important in this development, in providing alternatives to the establishment stranglehold on the major financial institutions. The mushroom growth of merchant banking at the end of the 1960s, largely connected with foreign banks, suggests this.

The earlier observations on the leadership of the ruling class make intelligible the political connections that the new capitalists are able to build up. They do not have to break through an establishment control of the conservative parties. They simply have to develop mutual-support relations with successful political entrepreneurs. Again Ansett provides the classic case, with the close relationship with Henry Bolte [Premier of Victoria] that became the key to his defence against Abeles' takeover attempt. (It was touching, in May 1974, to read that Sir Henry had come out of retirement to join the board of Ansett Transport Industries.) In New South Wales the relationships, less dramatic, have been symbolised in the last few years by knighthoods given by the Askin government to Abeles, Strasser, and Tristan Antico (of Pioneer Concrete). Both Bolte and Askin, it may be noted, are distinctly non-establishment in their own origin, and may well have found a closer personal affinity with the new capitalists than with the Fairfaxes, Baillieus, McLennans and their ilk.

The State elite

Encel (1970: 66–70, 268–74) argues that the growth of the public service since 1939 has amounted to a 'bureaucratic revolution': first greatly increasing the size and range of activities of the central administration; then leading to a marked status differentiation within it, with the emergence of the Second Division of the Commonwealth Public Service as an elite corps by the 1960s. The growth of this group, Encel claims, has led to 'a qualitative change in the structure of political power and influence' (1970: 280); notably a centralization in Canberra.

Numbers alone may be misleading: as Neumann (1950) long ago observed, it is a mistake to equate 'a larger number of bureaucrats with increase of their power'. This must be independently shown. Still, one does not have to accept the hyperbole of a 'bureaucratic revolution' to agree that there is a significant change here. It is inadequate to analyse them simply as 'supporters of capitalism', to describe their place in the structure of power essentially in terms of their attitudes (Playford 1972: 133–8).

In an executive sense, the top civil servants in Canberra, along with a few of the more influential ministers, are certainly the most powerful men in the country. Their government is the biggest employer, with the widest range of functions. Though they may only occasionally (for example in the 1972–73 shakeup) have the possibility of making big 'investment decisions' about the application of resources in the public service, their more minor decisions affect the mass of the population in a range of ways unmatched by executives even of companies like BHP and CSR.

Again, it is worth stressing, there is nothing new in this. The top bureaucratic and political leaders have always been the most powerful executives in the country, from the convict period when officials like Governor Arthur exercised almost totalitarian control (Forsyth 1935), through the colonial period when public investment decisions on matters like railway building were the most important social commitments being made (Butlin 1964). The emergence of a recognised elite corps does not necessarily signify a change in importance.

Yet there has been a change in function in the tasks performed by the state organisations—not as dramatic as the supposed 'bureaucratic revolution' and with roots that go further back—but which has certainly come into a kind of flowering in the last generation. Very briefly, what has occurred is a development of (a) non-entrepreneurial welfare activity; (b) central regulation and service activity (in the case of full employment policy this is intimately linked with welfare functions); and (c) a marked expansion of cultural activity, particularly in mass secondary and higher education. (Some other large areas of state activity, such as provision of transport infrastructure and supply of a labour force through immigration, are not included here as they were well developed in the colonial period.)

Except in minor ways these have not involved direct competition with business entrepreneurs, unlike the many ventures into 'state enterprise' earlier in the century. Consequently they have been accepted by the conservative politicians; indeed much of this development has occurred under the government of conservatives. It is tempting to attribute it to the needs of a period of industrialisation, but the welfare and regulatory activities have their main roots earlier than this, in the periods of boom and bust that culminated in the Depression. In this case the expansion of government is a response to entrepreneurial capitalism's inability to regulate itself. The case of cultural activity is more complex. The expansion of education is in part a response to technical demand for a more highly-trained workforce, in part a product of the greater social surplus generated by the second long boom. But it is also a response to cultural problems, to a new situation created by industrialisation and the end of Empire, and has a cultural consequence in the re-establishment of ruling class hegemony in the 1950s.

To a certain extent, the top civil servants can be seen as bureaucratic entrepreneurs parallel to the business and political entrepreneurs already discussed. But though they come from mostly similar social backgrounds (Encel 1970: 275–80), the analogy breaks down in that their power is not based on a mobilisation of the resources of the class from which they arise. It is directly based on the system of command relationships, of coercion and consent, on which the class structure itself is ultimately based through the institution of property. Within the state organisations the bureaucratic entrepreneurs, when mobilising resources, mobilise influence within a fairly narrow group, rather than mobilising capital or support on a mass scale. There are, then, irreducible differences in the underlying situation which makes it impossible simply to equate them, as a comparable elite, or read them off as essentially supporters or agents of the ruling class.

6

Moloch mutates (2002)

THE MODERNISING LABOR government that was in office when I wrote about the structure of the ruling class in 1974 was thrown out when that class flexed its muscles in 1975. A constitutional coup was staged and the old regime returned. When the next Labor government arrived eight years later, under a jovial and popular leader, it first emphasised social collaboration, and then moved sharply to the right. To the astonishment of many supporters Labor began to deregulate business and abolish support for the manufacturing industry. It sold off the national airline, the national bank, the telephone system, and a host of smaller public enterprises and assets.

When the right-wing Coalition returned in 1996 their work was already half done. Union membership was falling, economic inequality was rising and public services were in decline. This was not exactly popular, and the new right-wing government, pushing further along this path, came close to electoral defeat. Just in time, their leaders ramped up racism, border protection, culture wars, anti-feminism and climate denial. I mention two of their vicious stunts at the start of this paper, the *Tampa* affair and the 'children overboard' scandal. This primitive Trumpism—plus strident support from the commercial mass media, and a flow of funds from the corporations—gave them ten years in power.

Radical intellectuals in Australia were, I think it is fair to say, baffled by this sequence of events. Capitalism gone feral? Betrayal of the workers? The end of class? Post-modernity? In July 2002 a conference gathered at Trades Hall in Melbourne, sponsored by the radical magazine *Overland*, to discuss these questions. The occasion was the twenty-fifth anniversary of *Ruling Class, Ruling Culture*, and this chapter is based on my keynote address to that conference. 'Moloch Mutates' is in Nathan Hollier's 2004 book based on the conference, *Ruling Australia*. I have shortened the text, cutting references to news items and individuals now little remembered.

This was not an academic paper, but it did try to build on research such as Michael Pusey's remarkable study of state capture, *Economic Rationalism in Canberra*, and on theory such as the early work of Antonio Negri. As always, I made some mistakes. I recognised the new ideological formation and called it 'neo-liberal', but exaggerated its coherence. I saw that Australia's insertion in the global economy had changed, but did not realise we were following a typical shift in peripheral countries towards a new colonialism, centred on the export of raw materials. The rest of the argument still seems broadly correct.

This essay is being written six months after the *Tampa* triumph and the Howard government's campaign of lies about 'children overboard'. Like Menzies in 1954, the conservative leadership in 2001 turned around a probably lost election by stunningly successful scare tactics. Our masters have not forgotten how to craft a killer combination of xenophobia and social panic.

The moral squalor of our current national government has become painful. Howard's nudges and winks to bigots now add up to a sustained incitement of racism. The government has conducted a stealth redistribution towards the privileged, via a battery of subsidies, sell-offs and tax devices. It has launched increasingly vicious attacks on scapegoats, from homosexuals to single mothers to the unemployed. It continues to trade the environment and public safety to short-term business interests. As the stink grows about ex-ministers paid by lobby groups, we tend to forget what they did while still ministers: leaking lucrative information, colluding in a paramilitary union-smashing campaign, and so forth.

Less commented on, but just as important, is the Howard government's incompetence. Simply considered as an administration, this must be the worst ministry since Federation. The comic opera in foreign affairs, the ham-fisted handling of Aboriginal affairs, four billion dollars lost in foreign exchange dealing, the farce of education policy, are among the highlights but are far from being the full list. There are very few areas, apart from privatisation of public resources, where one could look to the Howard government for a coherent policy direction in public affairs, an intelligent approach to the resolution of a social problem, or even an articulation of ideas or purposes beyond the level of cliché.

I don't think this happens by chance. There are reasons why we have this kind of government, which have to do with the recent history of Australian and world capitalism.

The rise of neo-liberalism, though it has local consequences, is a global event. It was partly driven by new groups entering the political and business leadership in centres such as London. But the ideology has spread worldwide through right-wing think-tanks, the academic world, institutions like the IMF—and through corporations and markets themselves.

Starting with the Eurodollar market of the 1960s, the world economy has seen a massive growth of mobile capital. Local capital markets have been amalgamated, using new communications technology, into an interacting global financial system. At some point in this process the quantitative increase in mobile funds became a qualitative shift in hegemony from industrial capital to finance capital. It is difficult to avoid the conclusion that neo-liberalism has functioned as the ideology of this shift.

Locally, this shift has made obsolete the model of Australian capitalism developed by left-wing critics in the period of the welfare state, which I partly adopted in *Ruling Class, Ruling Culture*. From the 1970s on, an increasing proportion of the business leadership came to reject the 'industrial relations club', the system of class compromise embodied in the centralized regulation of the labour market. Business opted for a higher-risk strategy in dealing with the workforce, a more confrontational logic. And it seems to have worked. There has been a redistribution of income towards capital, without a rise in working-class militancy.

A parallel shift occurred in relation to the social wage. Business became increasingly hostile to the institutional machinery of the welfare state and to the progressive taxation regime that supported it. In the early 1980s business ideologists in Australia, copying US models, began a sustained campaign to stigmatise 'welfare' in particular, and the public sector in general. In effect, they set out to undo the Menzies strategy for Australian conservatism, based on the Keynesian settlement reached in Australia in the 1940s and early 1950s.

This too was successful. As the new approach gained a grip on Australian politics, there has been a steady squeeze in funding for public services and public institutions, from railways to universities. The cumulative effect has degraded the services and damaged the morale of public sector workers, making the surviving welfare state institutions less and less effective.

The neo-liberal triumph has thus ended the vision of Australia as a social laboratory.

Why did this change in the terms of Australian life happen? I don't pretend to understand it in full, but some things are clear. It did not happen as a result of straightforward ruling-class mobilization, the key mechanism in the conservative revival of the late 1940s. Neo-liberalism operated through the labour movement and the bureaucracy as well as through the right-wing parties. And it gained a grip in the labour movement partly because of panic about the position of Australia in world capitalism.

In a truly stunning transition, which makes the late 1980s the most important turning-point in recent Australian history, the cure and the disease became one. The preferred solution to the threat of global competition was to embrace the global competitive forces and try to blend the Australian economy into the international economy.

This meant more than opening the economy by lowering tariff barriers. Through deregulation of the financial system, then through a sustained program of privatisation, the Australian economy was increasingly made to *resemble*, as well as interact with, the US economy and the system of trade and capital movements centered on the United States. Rather than a distinctive unit in a world-system, Australia increasingly became simply a zone of operations for globally-acting economic power.

Nowadays, large multinational firms that operate in Australia typically do not have an independent Australian division. Either they are organized functionally on a global scale; or they include their Australian operations in an Asia/Pacific division. Executives managing such divisions often live in Australia—it's a White nation, after all—but it is the larger space that is the target of the multinational corporation's serious strategy-making.

Australian capitalism is still a dependent capitalism, but in a different way from both the era of colonialism and from the era of dependent industrialization that ended in the 1970s. Neo-liberal globalization has complex effects in culture. Zygmunt Bauman (*Globalization: The Human Consequences*) and Dennis Altman (*Global Sex*) may be right that in civil society there is actually an increase of global diversity. But the same historical process certainly irons out *economic* difference. In economic terms, Australia comes to look more like Illinois, or Bavaria, or Kyushu, or any other substantial chunk of the developed world.

Difference digested: the change of structure

Decades ago, Antonio Negri (1974) argued that capitalism no longer operated on the basis of an economic 'law of value'; value is now determined by political struggle. Negri was right in appreciating the energy that remained in capitalist politics, and also in his prediction of the political re-imposition of the law of value. But like many on the left at the time, he thought capitalism would respond to challenge by direct state power—by a mutation of the Keynesian system in the direction of violence. Something of the sort did happen in Italy, with state repression of the 'working class autonomy' movement; but that proved exceptional.

The originality of neo-liberalism was that it solved this problem by a turn *away from* direct state power. The law of value was re-imposed not by bayonets but by a gigantic growth, a hypertrophy, of the market. State power is certainly used, but used indirectly— to create markets where they did not exist before, and to wreck or corrode public institutions and cooperatives that provided alternatives to market relationships.

Market logic, as commentators on neo-liberalism have long recognized, functions as a meta-policy governing all areas of public life. It overrides the specificity of institutions just as it overrides the specificity of regions. What passes for 'policy' is, generally speaking, the attempt to expand the reach of markets, or to create markets where they did not exist before.

In Australia two of the most striking examples are in education and employment. Neo-liberal 'education' policy is largely an attempt to turn education from a public service into a market-ruled industry. It does this by increasing competition among schools and technical education institutions, turning universities into competitive corporations (a goal now half-achieved), and propping up private schools. Neo-liberal 'employment' policy includes downward pressure on wages, and the demolition of the Commonwealth Employment Service, replaced by competition among contractors— which has turned out a disaster for the long-term unemployed.

Neo-liberal regimes have thus presided over a steady expansion of the role of the commodity as a social form. More and more of the goods and services formerly provided by the public sector, voluntary agencies, and even families, have been turned into commodities sold for profit by entrepreneurs. We not only have fast food sold by franchises. Increasingly we have fast education, fast health, fast welfare, fast prisons, not to mention private freeways, private railways, private electricity, and private water supply. We also have a cloud of 'consultants' around governments, including big firms such as Andersen, KPMG and their ilk who have made a killing out of advising governments to undertake privatisations and then 'managing' the privatisation process. These agencies now do much of the research and policy development, formerly done by government departments, that give the state its steering capacity.

The expansion of markets and the spread of the commodity form means that the institutions producing goods and services are increasingly homogenized. The functions, staff, and even organizational units which used to belong to government departments, local governments, boards, cooperatives, mutuals, clubs and associations, have gone into the digester and have all emerged as companies. Privatisation of public assets and institutions is only part of this. A spectacular example is the de-mutualization of the National Roads and Motorists' Association in NSW, led by the corporate entrepreneur Nick Whitlam. In this case the process of commodification became well-understood because it was bitterly resisted, and remains only half completed. In other big insurance mutuals there was little resistance.

As the corporate form becomes the norm for all social institutions, two significant changes in class structure follow. One has been widely discussed, the other is hardly discussed at all.

The visible change is that *ownership* has spread, as many more people hold shares in some company or other. The sell-off of agencies like Qantas and Telstra has been the main force in lifting the percentage of Australian adults who own shares. This has been trumpeted as a social revolution by our new cultural leaders, the Australian Stock Exchange. (The ASX has itself been de-mutualized, so we now have a listed company presiding over the trade in shares of listed companies; capitalism has become reflexive.)

This growth in the numbers of people owning shares is undoubtedly politically important, though hardly revolutionary in economic terms. Something similar had already occurred through insurance and pension funds. What it means economically is that the fundraising networks of corporate capitalism have been extended more widely. The percentage of people who actually derive a significant proportion of their income from property ownership remains small.

The less visible change is in the ruling class leadership. Privatisations and de-mutualizations, as well as the general swelling of the corporate economy, have increased the mass of corporate executives. Corporate managers, despite attempts to constitute management as a 'profession', are in no sense a social group distinct from the owners of capital. Managers are that part of the ruling class who appropriate property-based incomes in the form of 'packages' and extremely high salaries more than in the form of dividends. At the very top level of management, this appropriation reverts to the old property form, as a large percentage of top executive 'compensation' now consists of shares and share options, or—as illustrated by One.Tel—outright gifts of part of the capital, called 'bonuses'.

At the same time, the upper levels of the state have been restructured to resemble the upper levels of the corporate economy. Senior public servants, and executives of corporatised public agencies (including universities), now work in conditions modelled on those of business executives. They are employed on contracts, at greatly increased salaries, with individually-negotiated and often secret packages, and are subject to performance audits and restructures. They are markedly more vulnerable to the displeasure of their political masters, while at the same time the rewards for compliance with the neo-liberal agenda have rocketed.

There has been some change in recruitment to the business leadership of the ruling class. More paths, and more various paths, lead into the corporate elite, and this means a somewhat more diverse group climbing up the hill. More migrants, and more women, have entered middle management. More corporate executives have a background in the public service, or in the professions, or in academia. Deregulation, globalization and the rise of finance capital, together with the rise of some new industries, created spaces for new men such as the corporate manipulators of the 1980s.

We should not exaggerate this change. When the Congressional 'Glass Ceiling Commission' researched the US corporate elite in the 1990s, it found the top executives of the top corporations were 97% white and 95% to 97% men. In Australia there are still very few women CEOs or soon-to-be CEOs. But the trend towards diversification creates at least a potential problem of integration among the capitalist leadership. And this problem may be sharpened, rather than eased, by the cultural change that has come with neo-liberalism.

The change of culture

As public services have been turned into commodities, citizens have been redefined as customers. I first noticed this on a government bus in Sydney about fifteen years ago, when I read a notice addressed to 'customers' that made me blink—I had thought I was a passenger. A few days ago I discovered that my local council no longer gives information to residents or ratepayers. Instead it has a 'customer help desk'.

More and more, people have been encouraged to think of their relationship with the collective processes of society as that of a purchaser in a market, or an owner seeking profit. In both cases the fundamental imperative is to improve one's private return at the expense of others.

In one of the most dazzling deceptions in contemporary history, this huge expansion of the logic of greed has been sold as a moral triumph. The growth of the market is presented to us as a growth of individual freedom, an attack on rigid bureaucracy and stifling regulation, an expansion of choice, even—in some of the more shameless propaganda for privatisation—as economic democracy, a return of property to 'the public'.

But the freedom promoted is freedom to do one thing: make money. For all the trumpeting of 'values' from right-wing politicians, there is no valuing of human beings here except as a source of advantage. Therefore there is nothing fundamental to restrain the tactics through which one gains advantage. Any competitive edge is a good edge. Even if it means lying to the people, cooking the corporate books, slandering targets of opportunity, or building concentration camps.

Of course there has been resistance to this transvaluation. Teachers continue to value education, nurses continue to value health, academics continue to value knowledge. This, however, is countered by the attack on 'provider capture', a key aspect of neo-liberal social politics. Trading on popular frustrations with bureaucratic systems, this attack has generated an elaborate discourse of accountability. New systems of surveillance and performance indicators now dominate life in the remains of the public sector.

These systems institutionalise distrust of the professional workforce. Just as the industrial systems studied by Harry Braverman (*Labor and Monopoly Capital*) a generation ago concentrated technical knowledge in the hands of management, so the new surveillance systems concentrate knowledge about professional practice in the hands of managers and accountants. This knowledge can be used, and is used, to control events silently through funding structures rather than openly through formal policy-making and public debate.

In almost every area of public life the result has been a decline of democracy, a retreat from policy-making in public arenas, a greater concentration of authority in the hands of a managerial and entrepreneurial elite. The complex structures of representation and social compromise that had been growing up around the welfare state from the 1960s to the 1980s have been flattened, wherever neo-liberal governments have come to power. The Kennett government in Victoria provides the most dramatic illustration in Australia of the disruption of public institutions and democratic processes. But the loss of morale in the public sector, the voluntary sector, and the workforce of the private sector—a sense of exhaustion, hopelessness, and loss of purpose—is nationwide, and is very striking.

Apart from a heavily intimidated ABC, we have no mass media left that are not controlled by corporate capital and funded by advertising. Most of the corporate-owned media are now assimilated to the cultural world of neo-liberalism—though there remain some centres of media professionalism, as there remain some academic centres that have resisted the corporatisation of universities.

Neo-liberal media presuppose the market logic in the way they interpret the social world to their audiences. It was, I think, in the 1980s that share market prices became a routine item in the daily TV news. But the penetration of market logic goes much deeper than that. For instance, the market logic in education, the idea that the worth of a school is measured by competitive exam results, has been presupposed in scandalously bad reporting that attacks government schools in poverty-blighted suburbs for their poor results in public exams. Much more airplay has been given to 'welfare cheats' and 'dole bludgers' than to the institutional failures of the marketized employment and welfare services.

The language of the outspoken rebel, in the world of corporate media, is appropriated by the right-wing shock jocks—who actually lead the charge in scapegoating the weak. The now evident corruption of talkback radio (sanitised by the media's own term, 'cash-for-comment') does not seem to have reduced its appeal, or its usefulness, by an ounce. The merging with global capitalism extends even to the language of neo-liberalism. The terminology is almost wholly imported: the attacks on 'political correctness', 'welfare dependency' and 'provider capture', the exaltation of 'the market', 'the culture of enterprise', 'incentive', and so on.

Howard adopted this language prematurely in the 1980s, when his trumpeting of 'incentivation' was greeted with some laughter. No-one is laughing any more. In Australian cities we now have shops entirely devoted to selling motivational posters, plaques and the like, with pictures of bald eagles in flight and slogans encouraging the office workforce to work harder (achieve), conform (teamwork), and believe in the corporate ethos. Bald eagles come from America, and smell of fish, but you can't tell that from the posters.

There is absolutely no reason why the new ruling-class leadership should be interested in the local production of ideas. It has no interest in sponsoring a local intelligentsia or a vibrant higher education system. It understands research as a matter of helping corporations make profits from new inventions, and woe betide any Vice-Chancellor who does not fall in with this agenda.

The cultural barrenness of neo-liberalism is striking. In twenty years of hegemony in Australian government, the new conservatism has attracted only one intellectual figure of any weight. That is the poet Les Murray, and the best the government could do with Murray was use him as bait to attract support for a purely cosmetic change to the constitution.

The second team in power

Conservative acceptance of the welfare state in the 1940s, and conservative administration of welfare states up to the 1970s, in political terms were a response to working-class strength. In cultural terms, however, they reflected an old ethos of government and public service.

In the ideology of the imperial ruling class, from which the ideology of Australian capitalism historically came, the right to rule flowed from the rulers' care for the public weal, their capacity to represent the common interest of society. In the functional division of ruling-class leadership between the business elite and the political elite, this ideology gave the political leadership the upper hand. It gave bright and energetic young bourgeois a reason for choosing politics as a vocation, and gave a rationale for older bourgeois to mentor those on the way up. Further, it created a moral standard in their use of power.

The neo-liberal attack on the welfare state in the 1980s did more than end the social compromises of the post-war decades. It also fatally weakened the ethos of public service in the capitalist class. First, it promoted a radical egocentrism (preferring to call it individualism) which denied the primacy of the common good. Second, it promoted a cult of the market as the only legitimate steering mechanism for society—thus undermining policymaking, social negotiation, and any conception of politics as long-term thinking. Third, by attacking the state as such, and discrediting bureaucracy, redistribution, planning and regulation, neo-liberalism undermined the institutional machinery through which decision-making in the public interest could actually operate on the world.

How this doctrine became dominant in the ruling class is still not entirely clear. No-one in Australian politics played the Menzies role, though Thatcher played such a role in Britain. Michael Pusey (*Economic Rationalism in Canberra*) has traced the rise of neo-liberalism within the federal bureaucracy. The hegemony of finance capital must be part of the explanation for its spread in business. Also relevant are events in the expanded system of higher education characteristic of developed capitalism, such as the rise of the MBA and the model of the generic manager, and the successful propagation of Chicago-school monetarism among economists. One way or another, the cultural rationale for an autonomous, ethically driven capitalist politics was destroyed.

The relative autonomy of the state, to use a famous phrase from the late days of the welfare state, was thus demolished. Not by a reversion to direct rule by capitalists, rather by the digestion of politics, along with other institutions, by the market. Politics becomes just another business, another route to profit. This is why complaining about the Howard government's lack of ministerial responsibility and violations of Westminster conventions is wasted breath. Of course you don't resign unless you are forced to. That would amount to giving away the profits you have earned in your business, and what businessman is mad enough to do that?

The problem is that politics is not the best business. The profits are limited and the costs in time and energy are relatively high.

The real talent, the real energy and creativeness in a neo-liberal generation of young bourgeois, would be likely to go where the real money and adventure lie: into businesses like real property, the new communications industries, global finance. It is noticeable that since the rise of neo-liberalism, there has been a sharp decline in the quality of the leadership of the conservative parties, and the quality of their recruits. Politics now gets the second team.

This is, I think, the underlying reason for the character of Howard's ministry. Talent, energy and commitment, so far as they emerge in the social groups from which the Coalition is recruited, are increasingly unlikely to go into politics. The ideology that provided cohesion and direction for political cadres of the ruling class has been destroyed. The result is the triumph of short-term thinking, philistinism and self-interest. That is enough to produce clever electoral manipulation. It may not produce much more.

This is, of course, not the only change in the ruling-class leadership. The familiar dynasties of Australian business are struggling, if not dying, in the new environment. The Fairfax dynasty went down when its scion decided he was a neo-liberal lion, tried to re-privatise the public company, and got eaten by the real predators of the 1980s. The Packer and Murdoch scions have done their best to be egotists and entrepreneurs, and have succeeded in acquiring trophy girlfriends and wives. But they got burnt in the new telecommunications market.

New groups are appearing in the business leadership, as I have suggested above. But so far they have failed to establish any political presence in Australia, beyond a spreading disquiet at the divisiveness of the Howard government. This may in time grow into an alternative, but it has certainly not done so yet.

Support, vulnerability, opposition

If the structure and politics of capitalism has been changing, it follows that the conditions of opposition have been changing too.

MOLOCH MUTATES (2002)

With the rise of market ideology, the issue of consent takes a new form. There is a great secret about neo-liberalism, which can only be whispered, but which at some level everyone knows: neo-liberalism does not have popular support.

There has *never* been popular demand for privatisation of public institutions, for deregulation, for the run-down of public services, for indirect taxation, for globalization, for more markets and wider commodification. New right leaders, from Thatcher and Reagan to Howard, Kennett and Bush, have come to power because they seemed strong or tapped into nationalism and racism, or because previous governments imploded and became vulnerable to electoral manipulation. But in power, these leaders have had to introduce neo-liberal policies without popular backing, as have Labor neo-liberals.

The implementation of the new ruling class agenda, therefore, has depended crucially on two things. One is the ability of the political and business leadership to accomplish structural changes by essentially administrative means, or by controllable mechanisms of assent.

Thus the big privatisations have been carried through by legislation in a party-controlled parliament, and the creation (by consultants) of a business consortium to market and underwrite the shares. This process is declared a success when the issue of shares is fully subscribed. This validation involves an appeal to people with money, the share price being pitched to encourage subscription. In a successful privatisation the initial investors are, in effect, bribed—with public assets. People without money to buy shares, i.e. the majority of the population, are nowhere involved. Had there been a plebiscite about privatising Telstra, the public telecommunications system, it would probably have been lost.

The other condition for the adoption of the market agenda is the absence of an alternative. That there was no alternative to the neo-liberal direction was frequently proclaimed by Thatcher, Keating and Douglas in the 1980s, and has become in a sense true.

The collapse of the Soviet Union, and the steady restoration of private enterprise in China, eliminated the external alternative to capitalism—even if that alternative mainly consisted of a military dictatorship with pretensions. The decline of late social democracy, and the shift of labour parties to neo-liberal positions, has eliminated the internal political alternative. Finally the absorption of most public sector management into the corporate elite, by the combination of intimidation and bribery that neo-liberalism blandly justifies as incentives for performance, has neutralized the institutional alternative represented by the public sector.

These factors have created an *appearance* of total triumph which is important in current politics. But the neo-liberal settlement is not fireproof. There are a number of points of vulnerability.

First, the political leadership is vulnerable. The Kennett state government in Victoria lost legitimacy, the Howard government seems in the process of losing legitimacy now. A muted social democracy is making a comeback in Europe, and it is striking that Labor (admittedly half neo-liberal now) keeps winning state elections in Australia. At a somewhat deeper level, the neo-liberal 'reforms' that have stripped the state apparatus of much of its steering capacity, have also reduced the political leadership's capacity to determine major events and set the continuing agenda. The political initiatives that set the terms of day-to-day politics increasingly have the character of stunts. In time, people see through the stunts. A consequence is the current almost universal contempt for politicians. Governments become more vulnerable to long-term crisis tendencies which they have less capacity to deal with.

Naomi Klein's bestseller *No Logo* documents the scale of cultural manipulation by contemporary business, and the growing intrusiveness of advertising. As more and more cultural space is occupied by spin doctors and advertisers, the audiences come to believe that they are always being manipulated. A simmering distrust results, well illustrated by the current helpless bitterness against the most visible part of finance capital, the banks.

Underlying this, again, is the spread of market relations, and the digestion of other organizational forms into the corporation. The necessary consequence of this change is that more and more of social life takes the alienated form of commodity exchange, governed by a calculus of self-interest. Deepening alienation probably makes, in the short term, for political passivity. But the long term may be different. An increasingly angry, turbulent and violent population seems quite likely.

Finally, the corrosion of democracy, while necessary to force through the redistributive agenda that lowers the social wage and increases the concentration of wealth, carries long-term dangers. The institutional system becomes less stable as the process goes on. Companies collapse. The new managerialism is less restrained than the old system but the managers are no smarter. When workers and residents are excluded from social decision-making, so is their knowledge and inventiveness.

Where is the social force through which the system might be transformed? Socialist discussion has always focussed on the working class, and in this country, on the role of the Labor Party as a mass expression of the working class. The ALP's capacity to serve as a vehicle of working-class mobilization has now been declining over a long period. It is remarkable how persistent the class roots of the party have been—they are still reflected in the geography of the vote, in the trade union connection, and in Labor's electoral successes at state level. But in terms of articulating working-class consciousness and social identity, the Labor Party has now reached a zero point.

Labor would, however, fracture its electoral support by a naked commitment to the interests of finance capital. Hence the attractiveness to the Labor leadership of 'third way' politics, which quietly accept the expansion of the market and abandon socialist (or even interventionist) economic policies, while attempting to build a non-market alternative in civil society by community development processes. Social-democratic parties pursuing this approach gain an electoral advantage by remaining more inclusive and tolerant than the conservative parties on non-economic issues.

The vision of society implicit in 'third way' politics is one of social diversity without social structure. Society consists of a formless agglomeration of individuals and groups pursuing diverse lifestyles. Presiding over the scene is a benevolent elite who strive to manage conflicts, moderate the most scandalous inequalities by a scaled-down welfare state, ensure each group has a place in society (combating 'social exclusion' is a key task), and facilitate the smooth working of the market. There is no place in this vision for class struggle.

Yet the working class is still there. Greatly changed over the last half-century—double the size, ethnically diverse, changed in gender relations and industrial composition. And now without a political voice. One of the most frightening features of the current era in Australian politics is that a good half of the population have essentially no political representation at all.

Strange things are happening in this political and cultural vacuum. The most vocal working-class revolt in recent years was the campaign by South Sydney rugby league supporters against the exclusion of their team by the corporate managers of this (now completely commercialized) sport. In terms of formal politics, it was Howard who presented himself as the friend of the 'battlers' against the 'elites'. Hanson [leader of the small racist One Nation party] gained some urban working-class support, as well as rural support, for her campaigns against aborigines and migrants. If One Nation had been a little more competent we might now have a racist political movement on the scale of Austria or France. Yet to everyone's astonishment, the most openly racist government on the continent was thrown out in the last Northern Territory election.

There are, of course, other articulations of opposition than the traditional forms of working-class politics. Among them are Midnight Oil, Mardi Gras, *Good News Week*, the Ernies, poststructuralism, the Sea of Hands, Blues & Roots at Byron Bay, home schooling, home birth, the movement against genetically modified crops, alternative health, Greenpeace, queer theory, self-publishing, ethical investment, support groups for refugees, the campaign for the ordination of women, Napster (until it was nobbled), and, of course, *Overland*.

The fact of such diverse and culturally lively oppositions is surely important. What is deeply problematic is that many, perhaps most, of these groups and movements have little connection, not just with the labour movement, but more broadly with working-class people. Few of them have a significant presence in ethnic minority communities, and few of them have much connection with country people. Without those links the opposition remains interesting but not formidable.

I think the dynamics of contemporary capitalism will make those connections possible. The union movement has declined, in terms of its workforce coverage, as the arbitration system was dismantled; but it has become more socially diverse and representative. The neo-liberal assault on the welfare state has produced, for society as a whole, not more freedom but more inequality. The spread of the corporate form and the market may produce more entrepreneurs, but it also produces more alienation. So does the collapse of the ethos of public service in some of the remaining structures of the state. There are, then, continuing—and in some respects growing—bases for class anger against the contemporary ruling class, however muted or indirect its current expressions may be.

Finding constructive directions for that anger, and making connections with the many new articulations of opposition just mentioned, is in part a cultural task. It requires validating, rather than de-legitimizing, struggle—even when the struggle takes unfamiliar forms such as culture-jamming, movements for Internet democracy, and refugee support groups. It requires exploration of alternative visions of society and of our possible future, working in the dimension of utopian thinking, which both neo-liberals and third-wayers have been at pains to discredit.

In this work, intellectuals have an important, though not exclusive, role. To repeat a thought from 25 years ago, which still seems true: in both critique and construction, socialist intellectuals have a great deal of work to do. Understanding the changing structures of power and privilege in this country is a central part of this work. For this reason I believe that this initiative by *Overland*, far from being an exercise in nostalgia, will help us chart paths forward.

Education

7

Poverty and education (1994)

EDUCATION IS A paradoxical field for researchers. In public opinion polls asking voters what are the most important issues, 'education' always comes at or near the top of the list. But in the actual politics of government, the Education portfolio is rarely a powerful one. Similarly in the academic world, education schools and educational researchers have no great prestige. Nevertheless, teaching is my family trade, and it's not surprising that I became a university teacher nor that education became a subject of my research.

In 1977 I shared a grant from the short-lived Education Research and Development Committee to make a study of inequalities in Australian schools. The project proved one of the most intensive and productive I have known. From it came two books, a raft of journal articles, an illustrated booklet, a documentary video, and many talks for schools, parents, teachers' organisations, academic conferences and media. Our book *Making the Difference* was, for a while, widely used in teacher education across Australia.

In 1987 I was invited to conduct, as a 'project of national significance', a study of the Disadvantaged Schools Programme, Australia's main compensatory education initiative. This, too, became a big effort, using multiple methods that included a documentary study, a quantitative survey with teachers, oral history interviews, school-level case studies, a special study of assessment, and more. It took members of the research team into every school system in every state and territory in Australia.

We wrote ten reports, hoping for a big policy impact. That didn't happen. By the time the project was finished, the federal department that had paid for the study was under new management with a new ideology (see Chapter 6). Our reports were simply shelved.

We looked for other ways to get the findings out. Colleagues at Deakin University in Victoria, bless them, published a set of our reports as a textbook in 'policy development and analysis', called *Running Twice as Hard*. Much of my own thinking about the issues went into a short book called *Schools and Social Justice*. We also tried to get the story to readers overseas via global-North journals. In 1991–92 I was at Harvard University as professor-for-a-year of Australian Studies, and while there I visited their school of education. This paper resulted, published in the *Harvard Educational Review* in 1994.

Speaking mainly to a North American audience, I didn't want to offer just an exotic case from the colonies. I wanted to engage with their problems too. The paper reviewed the history of compensatory education and the concept of poverty, arguing that mainstream policy had worked with a false map of the problem. I tried to spell out the rethinking needed, and ended with some proposals about a strategy for change.

It's a long and complex paper, much too long to include here in full. I have selected parts of the introduction, the section describing the false map of the problem, the section on re-mapping the problem, and those parts of the concluding section that seem to have weathered best.

POVERTY AND EDUCATION (1994)

How schools address poverty is an important test of an education system. Children from poor families are, generally speaking, the least successful by conventional measures and the hardest to teach by traditional methods. They are the least powerful of the schools' clients, the least able to enforce their claims or insist their needs be met, yet the most dependent on schools for their educational resources.

Since modern school systems persistently do fail children in poverty, a sense of outrage runs through much educational writing about disadvantage. Several authors have recently added a note of urgency to this discussion. Natriello, McDill and Pallas (1990) give their survey of U.S. practice the subtitle 'Racing against Catastrophe'. Kozol's (1991) book *Savage Inequalities* presents an even bleaker portrait of willful neglect and deepening tragedy. Korbin (1992) speaks of the 'devastation' of children in the United States. This note has also been heard outside education in discussions of the urban 'underclass' and is given strength by the 1992 violence in Los Angeles and the rise of neo-fascism in Europe.

There is a need to rethink the underlying logic of compensatory programs, which have not changed in their basic design and political justification, either in the United States or in other countries, since the 1960s. Meanwhile, child poverty has grown dramatically, and the difficulties faced by some parts of the school system have reached crisis proportions.

The purposes of this article are to question the social and educational assumptions behind the general design of compensatory programs; to propose an alternative way of thinking about the education of children in poverty, drawn from current practice and social research; and to explore some broad questions about the strategy of reform this rethinking implies. My focus is on the educational systems of industrialized, predominantly English-speaking, liberal-capitalist states (Australia, Britain, Canada, and the United States), though in broad outline the argument should also apply to other countries with comparable economic and political systems.

The false map of the problem

The circumstances of the birth of compensatory programs and the political means by which some have survived—not all did—produced a false map of the problem. By this I mean a set of assumptions that govern policy and public discussion but are factually wrong, doubtful, or profoundly misleading. Three are central: that the problem concerns only a disadvantaged minority; that the poor are distinct from the majority in culture or attitudes; and that correcting disadvantage in education is a technical problem requiring, above all, the application of research-based expertise.

The disadvantaged minority

The image of a disadvantaged minority is built into compensatory education via the poverty line by which target groups are identified. Whatever the formulae used to measure disadvantage (they vary from country to country, from state to state, and from time to time, with a running controversy over the method), the procedure always involves drawing a cut-off line at some point on a dimension of advantage and disadvantage. Where the cut-off comes is fundamentally arbitrary. This is a familiar problem with defining poverty lines. In compensatory programs, determining the cut-off point leads to unending dispute over which children or schools should be on the list for funds. The procedure could label 50 percent of the population 'disadvantaged' as logically as it could 10 percent or 20 percent. In practice, however, the cut-off point is always placed so as to indicate a modest-sized minority. This demarcation is credible because of the already existing political imagery of poverty, in which the poor are pictured as a minority outside mainstream society. The policy implication is that the other 80 or 90 percent, the mainstream, are all on the same footing.

However, this is not what the evidence shows. Regardless of which measures of class inequality and educational outcomes are used, gradients of advantage and disadvantage typically appear across the school population as a whole (for one example among hundreds, see Williams 1987). We can identify an exceptionally advantaged minority as well as an exceptionally disadvantaged one, but focusing on either extreme is insufficient. The fundamental point is that class inequality is a problem that concerns the school system *as a whole*. Poor children are not facing a separate problem. They face the worst effects of a larger pattern.

The distinctiveness of the poor

That the poor are not like the rest of us is a traditional belief of the affluent. This belief affected the design of compensatory education mainly through the 'culture of poverty' thesis, where the reproduction of poverty from one generation to another was attributed to the cultural adaptations poor people made to their circumstances (Lewis 1968; for a later review see Hoyles 1977).

Though framed within the discourse of anthropology, this idea was immediately given a psychological twist. Cultural difference in the group meant psychological deficit in the individual; that is, a lack of the traits needed to succeed in school. With this twist, a very wide range of research could be read as demonstrating cultural deprivation, from studies of linguistic codes to occupational expectations to achievement motivation to IQ, and so on. In the 1960s and 1970s, the cultural deficit concept became folklore among teachers as well as policymakers (Interim Committee for the Australian Schools Commission 1973; Ryan 1971).

It was this tendency to reduce arguments about different situations to the idea of a cultural deficit that Bernstein (1974) protested against in a famous critique of compensatory education. Culture-of-poverty ideas were strongly criticized by anthropologists, linguists, and teachers, not to mention poor people themselves, yet these ideas have had tremendous resilience, persisting through two decades of changing rhetoric, as Griffin (1993) has recently shown in a detailed survey of youth research. The ideas survive partly because they have become the organic ideology of compensatory and special education programs. The very existence of such programs now evokes the rationale of deficit, as Casanova (1990) illustrates in heartbreaking case studies of two Latino children in a U.S. school system. Battered by the system's languages policy; inserted into 'special education' programs—with mandated, rigid, teacher-centered methods—these children's education was massively disrupted and their social selves assaulted with labels like 'learning-disabled'. More broadly, deficit ideas also survive because they fit comfortably into wider ideologies of race and class difference.

But the facts of the matter do not require us to adopt cultural deficit concepts. The bulk of evidence points to cultural *similarity* between the poorest groups and the less poor. This might be expected from facts about the demography of poverty not widely known to educators. Studies such as the U.S. Panel Study of Income Dynamics (PSID), which has followed the same families since 1968, show large numbers of families moving into and out of poverty (as measured by the poverty-line approach). Over a twenty-year period, nearly 40 percent of the families in the PSID spent some period in poverty, when the rate of poverty in any one year was only 11 percent to 15 percent (Devine & Wright 1993). We should, then, expect those in poverty at any one time to have a lot in common with the broader working class, including their relations with schools. For example, attitude surveys produce little evidence that the poor lack other people's interest in education or in children (for a recent example in England, see Heath 1992).

In the United States, the argument over cultural deficit has been refocused by the concept of the 'underclass', which is defined as inhabitants of urban centers marked by massive unemployment, environmental decay, high numbers of births to single mothers, community violence, and the presence of the drug trade. It is clear that the most severe concentrations of poverty have the most severe impact on education (for statistical evidence, see Orland 1990). Ethnographies in inner-city settings (Anderson 1991) and in communities of the rural poor (Heath 1983) show ways of life that do not mesh with the practices of mainstream schooling. Ogbu's (1988) argument that this bad mesh has roots in the history of imperialism, with 'involuntary minorities' such as conquered indigenous peoples and enslaved labor forces resisting the institutions of White supremacy, is attractive.

But ethnography may not be the best guide to this issue. As a research method, it assumes the coherence of the group being studied, and ethnographic writing understandably tends to emphasize what is unique or distinctive about its subjects' way of life. We must counter-balance this by considering the interplay and interconnection of poor people with other groups. The cultural inventiveness of poor people (including the American 'underclass'), and their interplay with wider popular culture, is hardly to be denied—witness music from jazz to rap, new wave rock, punk fashion, contemporary street styles, and so on. And further, close-focus research on schooling, using interviews and participant observation, documents a vigorous desire for education among poor people and ethnic minorities (for example, Wexler 1992, from the United States; Angus 1993, from Australia). Yet there is massive educational failure. Something is malfunctioning, but hardly the culture of the poor.

The nature of reform

The belief that educational reform is, above all, a technical question, a matter of assembling the research and deducing the best interventions, is embedded in the education world through the very hierarchy of teaching institutions. At the apex of this hierarchy are the universities, which both produce education research and train administrators for the schools in education studies programs. The dominant ideology in education studies is positivist. The 1966

Coleman Report (Coleman 1990) was a monument to technocratic policy research, and the 'effective schools' and national testing movements continue to promote the belief that quantitative research will generate good policy more or less automatically. Teachers are defined within this framework as receiving guidance from educational science, rather than as producing fundamental knowledge themselves. The structure of educational funding in federal systems, where local institutions provide bread-and-butter school finance while higher level institutions fund policy innovation, further encourages a view of school reform as based on outside expertise.

While these are general conditions in educational policymaking, their effect on policy about poverty is especially strong. The poor are precisely the group with the least resources and the least capacity to contest the views of policymaking elites. Social movements of the poor can win concessions, but only by widespread mobilization and social disruption, as shown in the classic study by Piven and Cloward (1979). Mobilization and disruption do not generally develop around the education of the poor.

As a consequence, policy discussions about education and poverty have frequently been conducted in the absence of the two groups most likely to understand the issues: poor people themselves, and the teachers in their schools. A striking example is the 1986 conference held by the U.S. Department of Education to reconsider Chapter I programs, which was entirely composed of academics, administrators, and policy analysts (Doyle & Cooper 1988). Teachers are expected to implement policies, but not to make them, while poor people are defined as the objects of policy interventions rather than as the authors of social change.

The broad effect of this 'map' of the issues has been to locate the problem in the heads of the poor and in the errors of the particular schools serving them. Meanwhile, the virtues of other schools are taken for granted. The consequences of this policy, as Natriello et al. (1990) have perceptively pointed out, has been an oscillation among strategies of intervention that are mostly technocratic, all narrowly focused, all within a context of massive under funding, and none making a great difference to the situation.

Re-mapping the issues

What can we offer instead? 'We' meaning researchers, teacher educators, students, and administrators, the typical audience for academic journals in education. We cannot continue to offer what we usually do: proposals for fresh, expert interventions and for more research to support them. The exemplary research by Snow, Barnes, Chandler, Goodman and Hemphill (1991) shows the limits that have been reached by this approach. This careful and compassionate study, which sought practical lessons for literacy teaching by comparing good and bad readers among poor children in a U.S. city, found on returning four years later that hopeful differences were overwhelmed by what one can only read as the structural consequences of poverty. The enrichments these researchers proposed certainly improved the children's quality of life, but they were not capable of altering the forces shaping the children's educational fates.

There are no great surprises in the research on poverty and education, no secret keys that will unlock the solution. If there is a mystery, it is the kind that Sartre (1958) called a 'mystery in broad daylight', an un-knowing created by the way we frame and use our knowledge. Descriptive research on poor children by psychologists, sociologists, and educators will certainly continue—spiced by occasional claims from biologists to have found the gene for school failure. But that kind of research is no longer decisive. What we need, above all, is a rethinking of the pattern of policy, a re-examination of the way the issues have been configured.

This rethinking should start with the theme that comes through insistently when poor people talk about education: power. This issue leads to the institutional form of mass education, the politics of the curriculum, and the character of teachers' work. I develop each of these themes in the discussion that follows.

Power

Educators are uncomfortable with the language of power; to talk of 'disadvantage' is easier. But schools are literally power-full institutions. Public schools exercise power, both in the general compulsion to attend and in the particular decisions they make. School grades, for instance, are not just aids to teaching. They are also tiny judicial decisions with legal status, which cumulate into large authoritative decisions about people's lives—progression in school, selection into higher education, employment prospects.

Poor people, like the rest of the working class, by and large understand this feature of schools. It is central to their more dire experiences of education. An example is Wexler's (1992) description of students' experiences at Washington High, where tardiness is policed by an intrusive patrolling of corridors, leading to the bureaucratic processing of students for expulsion.

Once again we must recognize that what students in poverty experience is not unique. Mass schooling systems were created in the nineteenth century as state intervention into working-class life, to regulate and partly take over the rearing of children. Legal compulsion was needed because this intervention was widely resisted.

From this history, public schools and their working-class clientele inherit a deeply ambivalent relationship. On the one hand, the school embodies state power; hence the most common complaint from parents and students is about teachers who 'don't care' but cannot be made to change. On the other hand, the school system has become the main bearer of working-class hopes for a better future, especially where the hopes of unionism or socialism have died. Hence the dilemma, poignantly described by Lareau (1987), of working-class parents who want educational advancement for their children but cannot deploy the techniques or resources called for by the school. The extent to which school routines presuppose a gender pattern based on a certain level of affluence, the unpaid labor of a mother/housewife, is particularly noteworthy.

POVERTY AND EDUCATION (1994)

To deal with powerful institutions requires power. Some of the resources that families need to handle contemporary schools are the bread and butter of positivist research on children: adequate food, physical security, attention from helpful adults, books in the home, scholastic know-how in the family, and so on. Generally absent from positivist research (because they are hard to quantify as attributes of a person) are the collective resources that produce the kind of school system that favors a particular home environment for success. These resources are put into play when property owners cap taxes supporting public schools; or when university faculty dominate curriculum boards and corporations create textbooks; or when the professional parents at an upper income school meet with routine responsiveness from principal and teachers.

In the false map already discussed, poverty is constantly taken as the sign of something else, such as cultural difference, or psychological or genetic deficit. Educators need to be more blunt and see poverty as poverty. Poor people are short of resources, individually and jointly, including many of the resources that are deployed in education. The scale of material shortages is easily shown. For instance, an Australian study of household expenditure in families with dependent children found high-income couples spending an average of $8.82 per week on books and periodicals, while sole-parent pensioners (roughly equivalent to AFDC [Aid to Families with Dependent Children] recipients in the United States) spent $2.06 (Whiteford, Bradbury & Saunders 1989).

Such differences in income and expenditure, not to mention the greater inequalities of wealth, mean both shortages of resources in the home and vulnerability to institutional power—such as derogatory labelling in the welfare system, and streaming or tracking in the education system. There is no mystery about this to poor people. As an activist in a Canadian immigrant women's group put it:

> Streaming of low income, immigrant children is obvious. More well-to-do parents make sure their children are directed in the

proper direction, they have much more pro-active involvement in the school system. Poor working-class families don't have the time or the wherewithal to fight. (quoted in Curtis et al. 1992: 23)

Poverty and alienation are likely to mean material disruptions of life, one of the points emphatically made in the 'underclass' discussion. Disruptions can also be seen outside the United States: witness Robins and Cohen's *Knuckle Sandwich* (1978), about youth and violence in England, and Embling's look at *Fragmented Lives* (1986) in Australia. We do not need to assume cultural difference to understand the damaging effects of poverty on young people's lives. We certainly need to think carefully about power in order to understand the violence that has long been an undercurrent in schools for the urban poor, and which has taken a dramatic turn with the advent of guns in U.S. high schools.

Serious violence is more common from boys than from girls, not because of their hormones, but because Western masculinities are socially constructed around claims to power. Where this claim is made with few resources except physical force, and where boys have been habitually disciplined by force, 'trouble' in the form of violence is eminently likely. A familiar course of events frequently develops where boys' masculinity comes to be defined or tested in their conflict with the state power embodied in the school, a conflict that can turn violent. Losing this conflict, which is inevitable, is likely to end the boys' formal education. The power relations of gender thus play out paradoxically in a context of poverty. To grapple with such a process means directly addressing the politics of masculinity—an issue, as Yates (1993) notes at the end of her review of the education of girls, still absent from educational agendas.

The school as an institution

The young people who fight the school and find themselves bounced out on the street are meeting more than the anger of particular teachers and principals. They are facing the logic of an institution embodying the power of the state and the cultural authority of the dominant class. Fine's (1991) study of a New York inner-city school shows the dull bureaucratic rationality of encouraging students to drop out. In a school facing great difficulties in teaching and establishing its legitimacy, and with no prospect of the resources it needs or a change in its working methods, 'discharge' of a student becomes the routine solution to a wide range of problems.

The role of institutional power in shaping pupil-teacher interactions has been clear in close-focus studies of schools for some time. It was vividly portrayed, for instance, in Corrigan's (1979) study of the struggle for control in two schools in a declining industrial area of England. What 'school ethnographies' cannot show, however, is the institutional shape of the education system as a whole. Selectiveness at upper levels (selection cuts in at different ages in different countries) means a narrowing offer of learning that forces unequal outcomes, whether or not the system attempts to equalize opportunity. For instance, if a university system trains only one in ten of a particular age group, which is the current average for industrial countries (United Nations Development Programme 1992), then nine must go without degrees. If unequal outcomes are forced, a struggle for advantage results, and the political and economic resources that can be mobilized in that struggle become important. The poor are precisely those with the least resources.

Policies to increase competitive pressures within the school system—including mandatory objective testing, parental choice plans, and 'gifted and talented' programs—have a transparent class meaning, reinforcing the advantages of the privileged and confirming the exclusion of the poor. The fact that such policies deliver class advantages is not new knowledge; similar observations on the class meaning of testing programs have been made for half a century (for example, Davis 1948). It seems to be a fact that has to be constantly rediscovered.

The legitimacy of educational competitions depends on some belief in level playing fields. Economic facts have been marginal in discussions of educational disadvantage, though educators periodically justify compensatory programs as contributing to a well-trained work force. In the United States, however, Kozol (1991) has recently made an issue of differences in school funding. Taylor and Piche (1991), in a study of per-pupil expenditure by U.S. school boards, found a range from $11,752 in the richest district to $1,324 in the poorest, with many states having a 2.5-to-1 or 3-to-1 ratio between high-expenditure and low-expenditure groups of districts. Further, current per-capita spending is likely to understate differences, because background capital expenditure has also been unequal. And beyond public finance, as already noted, there are stark inequalities in what can be privately spent on educational resources.

Other wealthy countries have more centralized, and thus more uniform, funding of schools than the United States, but a more exclusive system of student selection for higher education. This, being more costly, weights overall per-capita expenditure back in favor of advantaged groups who enter higher education in greater proportions. On the face of it, differences in the total social investment in the education of rich children and poor children appear to be much larger than any redistributive effect of compensatory education funds.

Curriculum

The importance of curriculum for issues of educational inequality has long been argued by Apple (1982, 1993), and the point is highly relevant to strategy about poverty. Compensatory programs were intended to lever disadvantaged children back into mainstream schooling. The success of these programs is conventionally measured by pupil progress in the established curriculum, especially as evidenced by the closing of gaps to system norms. This logic has been taken to a startling extreme in a program in Cleveland, Ohio, which consists of awarding pupils $40 for getting an A, $20 for a B, and $10 for a C (Natriello et al. 1990). When progress in the mainstream curriculum is taken as the goal of intervention, that curriculum is exempted from criticism. However, the experience of teachers in disadvantaged schools has persistently led them to question the curriculum. Conventional subject matter and texts and traditional teaching methods and assessment techniques turn out to be sources of systematic difficulty. They persistently produce boredom. Enforcing them heightens the problem of discipline, and so far as they are successfully enforced, they divide pupils between an academically successful minority and an academically discredited majority (Connell, Johnston & White 1992; Wexler 1992).

To teach well in disadvantaged schools requires a shift in pedagogy and in the way content is determined. A shift towards more negotiated curriculum and more participatory classroom practice can be seen in compensatory education in Australia, where it is a broad tendency in disadvantaged schools, not just a matter of isolated initiatives (Connell, White & Johnston 1991). The effectiveness of similar practice in U.S. elementary classrooms is demonstrated by Knapp, Shields, and Turnbull (1992). However, such practices do not seem to be the main tendency in the United States. A survey of U.S. middle schools by Maciver and Epstein (1990) suggests a more conventional pedagogy, with less commitment to active learning methods and exploratory courses in disadvantaged schools than in advantaged schools. The push for 'standards' and 'basic skills' has fostered a rigid, teacher-centered pedagogy in compensatory and special education programs (for a striking illustration, see Griswold, Cotton & Hansen 1986).

To see 'mainstream' curriculum as a key source of educational inequality raises the question of where it comes from. We are beginning to get an answer from the new social history of the curriculum produced by Goodson (1985, 1988) and others. The very concept of 'mainstream' must be called into question, as it suggests reasoned consensus. What we are dealing with, rather, is a dominant, or hegemonic, curriculum, derived historically from the educational practices of European upper class men. The competitive academic curriculum sits alongside other kinds of curriculum in the schools—such as practical knowledge in music or in manual arts—but remains hegemonic in the sense that it defines 'real' knowledge, is linked to teacher professionalism, and determines promotion in the education system (Connell, Ashenden, Kessler & Dowsett 1982).

The apparently remote discipline of curriculum history has made a key contribution to rethinking the issues of poverty and education. It has de-mythologized the hegemonic curriculum and shown it to be only one among a number of ways knowledge could have been organized for the schools (Whitty 1985; Whitty & Young 1976). Without this historical perspective, proposals for alternative curricula are easily discredited as abandoning real knowledge and educational quality. Different versions of this claim were made in turn by the 'Black Papers' neoconservatives in England in the 1960s and 1970s, cultural literacy entrepreneurs in the United States in the 1980s, and professors attacking assessment reform in Australia in the 1990s. We can now see that the work of teachers in disadvantaged schools implies not a shift to different content (though there will be some of that), but, more decisively, a different organization of the field of knowledge as a whole.

Teachers' work

Teachers are strikingly absent from much of the policy debate about schooling and poverty (so much so that a recent book reviewing the subject does not even list teachers in its index). This absence is an important consequence of the deficit interpretation of disadvantage and the technocratic style of policymaking.

But teachers are the front-line workers in schools. If exclusion is accomplished by schools, it is certainly in large measure through what teachers do. We may not wish to blame teachers, but we also cannot ignore them. Education as a cultural enterprise is constituted in and through their labor. Their work is the arena where the great contradictions around education and social justice condense.

Teachers' work has been studied in an international literature (surveyed by Ginsburg 1994; Seddon 1994), which, like curriculum history, has been little noticed in discussions of poverty. Nevertheless, its significance is clear. Lawn (1993), for example, shows the complexity of teachers' relationships to state power and the importance of teacher professionalism as a system of indirect control. Professionalism is an important factor attaching teachers to the hegemonic curriculum. The question of the 'de-skilling' of teachers through tighter management control and packaged curricula is highly relevant to the prospects for good teaching in disadvantaged schools, which requires maximum flexibility and imagination.

Some activities included under the name 'compensatory education' expand teachers' options and call for higher levels of skill. Others, as a condition of funding, constrict methods and de-skill teachers, generally pushing them towards more authoritarian styles. Where compensatory programs are accompanied by an active testing program, for example, a familiar pressure is created to teach to the test and thus narrow the curriculum. 'Pull-out' classes are likely to disrupt the supportive classroom dynamics that good teachers try to establish. The whole model of expert intervention tends to disempower teachers. Given all these effects, it is likely that some compensatory interventions have worsened the educational situation in disadvantaged schools, not improved it. It is almost impossible for embattled schools to resist offers of resources, but the consequences are not always beneficial. (See the uneasy discussions in Doyle & Cooper 1988; Knapp, Shields & Turnbull 1992; Savage 1987; Scheerens 1987.)

Teaching practice is governed mainly by the institutional constraints of the school as a workplace. Compensatory interventions are generally far too small to change these constraints, a point that has been made throughout their history (see, for example, Halsey 1972; Natriello et al. 1990). Accordingly, most educational practice in disadvantaged schools is routinely like practice in other schools (for evidence, see Connell 1991), and produces the usual socially selective effects. Those programs that do produce changes happen to have found one of the variety of ways—which may be situational and temporary—of bolstering teachers' agency, increasing their capacity to maneuver around constraints and grapple with the contradictions of the relationship between poor children and schools.

Towards a strategy of change

Formulating goals: curricular justice

Most statements of purpose for educational reform treat justice in distributional terms. That is, they treat education in much the way arguments about economic justice treat money: as a social good of standard character that needs to be shared more fairly. Even if the criteria for fair shares vary from one policy sphere to another, as in Walzer's (1983) sophisticated model of justice, the distributional approach governs the discussion of education.

If we have learned one thing from research on the interaction of curriculum and social context, it is that educational processes are not standard in this sense. Distributing equal amounts of the hegemonic curriculum to girls and boys, to poor children and rich children, to Black children and White children, to immigrants and native-born, to indigenous people and their colonizers, does not do the same thing for them—or to them. In education, the 'how much' and the 'who' cannot be separated from the 'what'.

The concept of distributive justice certainly applies to material resources for education, such as school funds and equipment. But we need something more to deal with the content and process of education: a concept of curricular justice (Connell 1993). This idea is closely connected to the lesson curriculum history teaches: that there are always multiple ways to organize the knowledge content of schooling.

Each particular way of constructing the curriculum (i.e., organizing the field of knowledge and defining how it is to be taught and learned) carries social effects. Curriculum empowers and disempowers, authorizes and de-authorizes, recognizes and mis-recognizes different social groups and their knowledge and identities. For instance, curriculum developed from academic institutions controlled by men has, in a variety of ways, authorized the practices and experiences of men and marginalized those of women. Curriculum defined by representatives of a dominant ethnic group is liable to exclude or de-authorize the knowledge and experience of dominated groups, or to incorporate them on terms that suit the dominant group. Curricular justice concerns the organization of knowledge, and, through it, the justice of the social relations being produced through education.

There is nothing exotic about this idea. It is implied in a great deal of practical teaching that goes on in disadvantaged schools, teaching that contests the disempowering effects of the hegemonic curriculum and authorizes locally produced knowledge. This is the kind of 'good teaching' Haberman (1991) has recently contrasted with the 'pedagogy of poverty'. As he observes, the challenge is how to institutionalize 'good teaching' in disadvantaged schools. Initiatives of this kind remain marginal and are easily dismantled, unless they can be linked to larger purposes.

I think a concept of curricular justice makes the link to larger purposes possible and should be at the heart of strategic thinking on education and disadvantage. It requires us to think through curriculum-making from the point of view of the least advantaged, not from the standpoint of what is currently authorized. It requires us to think about how to generalize the point of view of the least advantaged as a program for the organization and production of knowledge in general.

Taking an *educational* view of poverty and education thus pushes us beyond the goal of 'compensation' and towards the goal of reorganizing the cultural content of education as a whole. This goal is intimidating, given the difficulties encountered with much more limited goals. Yet clear thinking is helped if we put local initiatives in the perspective of the larger agenda they imply.

The workforce of reform

Given the institutional and cultural forces that make for inequality in education, the case can be made that more can be done outside schools than inside them. This seems to be implied by postmodernist readings of educational politics by authors such as Giroux (1992). Acknowledging the cultural changes to which this reading responds, I would nevertheless argue that the profoundly ambivalent relationship between working-class people and educational institutions is central to contemporary cultural politics in industrial countries. This relationship has grown in importance with the growing weight of education as a part of the economy and the culture. Teachers in schools are the workers most strategically placed to affect the relationship. I have argued already for bringing teachers' work to the center of discussions of disadvantage. If the education of children in poverty is to be changed, teachers will be the workforce of reform. This conclusion has two important corollaries.

First, teachers should be centrally involved in the design of reform strategies. Giroux (1988) earlier called our attention to the sense in which teachers are intellectuals. A capacity for strategic thinking certainly exists among the teachers of the poor. The Disadvantaged Schools Program in Australia, partly because of its decentralized design, encouraged the growth of an activist network that included teachers' unions and a group of experienced teachers in poor districts. This informal network, more than any formal agency, has transmitted experience and provided the forum for intense policy debates (White & Johnston 1993). Such groups exist in other countries, too. A notable example is the network around the magazine *Our Schools/Our Selves,* which has brought teachers across Canada into a series of debates about educational reform. An intelligent approach to policymaking would regard such teacher networks as a key asset.

Second, a reform agenda must concern the shaping of this workforce: the recruitment, training, in-service education, and career structures of teachers in disadvantaged schools. The 1966 Coleman report, to its credit, raised this issue and collected data on teacher training, but the issue almost vanished from later discussions of disadvantage. In a recession, where education budgets are under pressure, funds for teacher preparation, and especially for in-service training, are likely to be cut. To an extent, compensatory programs themselves function as teacher educators. A potentially cost-effective reform would be to expand these programs' capacities to train teachers, to circulate information, to pool knowledge, and to pass on expertise.

The workforce is not static. Families move into and out of poverty, and teachers move into and out of disadvantaged schools. For both reasons, issues about poverty *should* concern teachers in all parts of a school system. I would argue that these issues should be major themes in initial teacher training, and that competence in work with disadvantaged groups should be central to the idea of professionalism in teaching.

8

The neoliberal cascade and education (2013)

THE COMPENSATORY EDUCATION programs discussed in Chapter 7 were products of a time when education was understood as a collective, social responsibility, and when most governments around the world invested in expanding public education systems. But public education came under attack in the shift to 'market' agendas discussed in Chapter 6. Neoliberal thought imagined education as a private, not a public, good. In the 1980s and 1990s Australian schools, colleges and universities were reimagined as competitive firms, fees were introduced or greatly increased, corporate-style management was wheeled in, and much of education was directly or indirectly privatised.

In the new century I was working in the Faculty of Education and Social Work at the University of Sydney. A group of colleagues organised a series of public lectures on current issues; I gave one of the lectures, and this paper is the result. It was published in 2013 in *Critical Studies in Education*, the lively successor to the staid *Melbourne Studies in Education*. It does not present new research but tries to synthesise knowledge in the field and reflect on what has happened. I have condensed the early sections of the paper, which recite what is now a well-known story. I have kept in full the argument about the nature of education and the tensions and injustices created by attempts to commodify education.

Introduction

In the last few decades, education systems all over the world have been impacted by the rise of neoliberal ideology and practices of government. Education is not alone: business-friendly governments and market-driven agendas have re-shaped all areas of public life and many areas of private life too (Braedley & Luxton 2010). Education is, however—for reasons I hope to make clear—particularly troubled by this impact.

We now have a valuable body of research on neoliberal changes in school systems and higher education, and their consequences for teachers' working conditions and subjectivity, pupils' experience and family education strategies. We have not yet, however, fully assimilated the profound consequences of the neoliberal turn for the basic project of education.

The dynamics of neoliberalism

'Neoliberalism' broadly means the agenda of economic and social transformation under the sign of the free market. It also means the institutional arrangements to implement this project that have been installed, step by step, in every society under neoliberal control (Connell 2010, Harvey 2005).

Neoliberal governments have set about 'freeing' businesses in many ways. Controls over banking, currency exchange, and capital movement were all loosened or abolished. Gradually a fast-moving global arena of financial transactions was brought into being, a network of national and international markets in shares, bonds, financial derivatives and currency. This arena is the core of what corporate executives and financial journalists mean by 'globalization'.

Through its linkages, the Wall Street financial crisis of 2007 was turned into a global slump.

Neoliberalism seeks to make existing markets wider, and to create new markets where they did not exist before. Needs formerly met by public agencies on a principle of citizen rights, or through personal relationships in communities and families, are now to be met by companies selling services in a market. Many public assets have been privatised—in Australia including the national airline, the national bank and the national telecommunications system. Neoliberals have had astonishing success in creating markets for things whose commodification was once almost unimaginable: drinking water, body parts and social welfare among them. Welfare is commodified by putting the provision of services up for tender, and forcing the public agencies that formerly provided them to compete with NGOs, churches and companies to win the tenders. Many other functions formerly routine within public sector organizations—such as the printing of official documents—are now outsourced to profit-making companies.

The expansion of market relations allows, at least in principle, a lower level of public spending, and therefore a lower level of taxation. Alongside de-regulation, cutting taxes was one of the first neoliberal policies to be put into practice. The passing of Proposition 13 in California in 1978, a referendum to cap property taxes which eventually caused a massive funding crisis in Californian public education, is one of the historic markers of the neoliberal turn in the global North. Tax cutting has remained a banner cause for neoliberals. In cold fact, the overall tax take of OECD governments has fallen little. But there has certainly been a shift from direct to indirect taxation, and a marked reduction of taxes on wealth and on high incomes—a shift to a more regressive tax system.

It was in the global South, however, that neoliberalism first gained political power. This was in Chile under the right-wing Pinochet dictatorship which came to power by violence in 1973 (Silva 1996). This regime replaced the previous agenda of democratisation and state-led industrialisation, with a new strategy of economic development based on corporations pursuing comparative advantage within the world capitalist economy. Opening to the world market, and privatizing the ownership of social assets, were closely linked.

Other Latin American regimes began a turn towards neoliberalism about the same time, though with less consistency; and were soon followed by policymakers in other developing countries such as Turkey. The new-right regimes of Thatcher and Reagan enabled a neoliberal takeover of the IMF and World Bank in the 1980s, and the creation of Structural Adjustment Programmes. The result of a global shift towards de-regulated markets and the search for comparative advantage was a huge growth in the volume of international trade (Dados & Connell 2014). Former industrialized economies were de-industrialized as manufacturing moved rapidly to low-wage regimes such as China.

Neoliberalism has its central dynamic not within the metropole, but in the *relation* between metropole and periphery. It has roots in a long history of international capitalism (Amin 1997). Neoliberalism is the latest mutation in a sprawling world-wide regime, which forged a new settlement between military, political and business elites in the global periphery, and their counterparts in the metropole. The most dramatic expressions of this changed relationship were the Structural Adjustment Programs of the 1980s and 1990s. These were imposed by the World Bank, IMF and transnational finance capital, on those countries of the global periphery which had got into trouble servicing loans. The price of rescheduling loan repayments was enforcing neoliberal economic policies, putting inflation control and debt servicing as the top priorities.

The commodification of services and the privatisation of public sector agencies demands institutional and cultural change. The profit-seeking corporation is promoted as the admired model for the public sector, and for much of civil society too. Schemes of organization and control are imported from business to public institutions. In an 'audit society', public institutions have to make themselves auditable, on a model imported from business accountancy (Power 1997). The discussions in the 1970s about representative bureaucracy and industrial democracy came to a sudden halt, displaced by a new ethos of managerialism. A clear measure of the new scale of managerial power is that managers' salaries and bonuses have risen, in both the private and the public sector, to unprecedented levels. The top corporate managers in Australia now are paid around $10 million per year, each. This is publicly defended on the grounds that US managers are paid even more.

At the same time, an emphasis on labour market flexibility produces a growing workforce of part-time and casual and contract labour at the bottom of the heap. Applying market discipline to the labour force has meant sustained pressure against unions. There has been an irregular but insistent roll-back of entitlements and security which the organized part of the working class had historically won.

Thus neoliberalism succeeded in changing the connection between politics and economy in much of the world. In the global metropole, i.e. North America and Europe, neoliberalism has gone far to dismantle the Keynesian welfare state, the system of regulated capitalism and state-supplied services that was dominant in the generation from 1945 to 1980. In the global periphery, neoliberalism thoroughly dismantled the strategy of autonomous economic development, and broke up the social alliances around it.

The Australian case: the neoliberal cascade in education

Though the first steps in a neoliberal direction were taken in Australia in the 1970s (tariff cuts, abandoning a long-held policy of protection for local manufacturing), the main shift came in the 1980s. A pioneering study by the sociologist Michael Pusey traced the strengthening hegemony of market ideology in the federal public service as well as among the politicians (Pusey 1991).

Australian neoliberalism, typically for a country of the global periphery, turned away from local industrialization towards primary export industries, especially mining. The local economy has again come to resemble the colonial economy of the late 19th century. In the search for 'comparative advantage' in world markets, Australian wages are not low enough to compete in manufactured goods with Mexico, Vietnam, Sri Lanka and especially China. This has undermined skilled trades and working-class youth employment, with effects clearly visible in TAFE and public schools.

Once a neoliberal policy regime had been established, around the mid-1980s, a cascade of 'reforms' followed which brought every institutional sector under the sway of market logic. Education is a major example. Increasingly education has been defined as an industry and educational institutions have been forced to conduct themselves more and more like profit-seeking firms.

Some of these changes are highly visible to people working in universities (for an excellent short survey see Marginson 2009). The re-introduction of university fees in 1988–89 was a key starting point, because that action redefined higher education as a commodity not a citizen right. It was soon followed by the redefinition of higher education as an *export* industry, extracting income from overseas students, rather than educating them for free as development aid by a rich country.

Funding mechanisms in Canberra have been repeatedly adjusted since the 1980s to force universities to compete with each other, for budget funds as well as student fees. These are little-publicised moves with powerful effects, driving the growth of managerialism in universities. The growth of managerialism in turn has undermined academic democracy (power of central managers and deans rising, departmental decision-making declining, students redefined simply as customers). Management's search for a cheap and flexible labour force has had a dramatic educational effect: though universities do not advertise this fact, around half of the undergraduate teaching in Australia is now done by casual labour (Hil 2012).

Even more drastic are the changes in the technical and further education sector. Here, as Australia de-industrialized and the old apprenticeship system crumbled, the conditions for extensive marketization were created: corporatization of public sector TAFE institutions, a growth of managerial power, and a ruthless restructuring of the teaching workforce, followed (Clark 2003). A sustained attempt to create competitive markets in modularized training services meant that both public and private institutions became simply 'providers', competing for fees and subsidies.

As technical education too was integrated into a global market and became, from the Australian policy perspective, another export industry, a lucrative and substantially unregulated market in training overseas students emerged. Plagued by scandals, student complaints, and accusations of being a backdoor visa mill, the private college sector was then rocked by a series of corporate collapses in 2009–2011. Sterling College, Melbourne International College, the Meridian Group colleges, GEOS language school, and others suddenly closed their doors when profitability fell or the authorities made belated audits.

Schools have been more resistant to the excesses of managerialism, but the school system too has been re-shaped by the market agenda (Campbell, Proctor & Sherington 2009). At the state level, de-zoning of public schools and the expansion of state selective schools have undermined the comprehensive public schools of the previous generation (Campbell & Sherington 2006). The right-wing Kennett government's 'Schools for the Future' programme in Victoria is the classic case. The effect is to define each school as a firm competing with all others for students, marks and money, in markets where parents are consumers expected to exercise 'choice' between different firms/schools.

These changes at state level were given bite by the federal government's policy of expanding the private school system. 'State aid' for religious schools was introduced by the Liberal [i.e. conservative] Party in the 1960s in a bid for the Catholic vote. It was expanded in the 1970s by the Labor Party, on the grounds of providing for disadvantaged children, many of whom were in Catholic schools.

Since then, the federal subsidies to private schools have grown enormously, and changed in rationale. They now support a mass market in privately-controlled schooling that is effectively secular, and whose main clientele now is middle-class families 'choosing' for their own advantage (Campbell, Proctor & Sherington 2009). Working-class children mostly go to public schools, but the public schools are increasingly residualized. The main exception is selective public schools, which now function as cheap private schools for families able to win at the competitive-examination game.

The cascade has also reached the pre-school sector, with a policy change allowing public funds to go to for-profit providers (Brennan 2002). The more aggressive proceeded to buy out cooperatives and other local groups in a splendid display of predatory entrepreneurship. Eventually there was just one corporate empire as Australia's major actor in pre-school provision—ABC Learning, led by the entrepreneur Eddy Groves. This firm collapsed in 2007–2008 producing chaos in the sector. The major parties have studiously avoided responsibility for the disaster.

This is a bare outline; the full story is complex and multi-layered. Nevertheless we can say that in the basic logic of policy, there is now no difference between Labor and Liberal/National parties. The unchallenged assumption of national and state policy is that whatever problem exists, market logic can fix it.

The concept of education

Neoliberalism has a definite view of education, understanding it as human capital formation. It is the business of forming the skills and attitudes needed by a productive workforce—productive in the precise sense of producing an ever-growing mass of profits for the market economy. 'Human capital' is a metaphor, and in itself too narrow. But this economistic idea does catch an important feature of education, that it is a creative process oriented to the future.

In this respect the neoliberal model is superior to the view widespread in other areas of social science, including the sociology of education, that education is a process of social reproduction. There are both bland and critical versions of this idea. The bland version is that society's existence requires training up the young in the values and languages of their elders, and then sorting them into appropriate social roles; and that school systems have been created to do these jobs. The critical version observes that the sorting is an exercise of power that reproduces the privileges of dominant social groups through time. This is an important observation, and one of the keys to what has been happening in Australian education.

But without another dimension, any concept of social reproduction is static, and leads either to complacency or despair. The missing dimension is history, the creative development of social practice through time. Bringing history more centrally into the frame, we arrive at an understanding of education as the social process in which we nurture and develop capacities for practice. That may be done in a way that re-generates privilege and poverty, or even increases privilege and poverty. But it need not be.

To say that education involves nurture is important. Education involves encounter between persons, and that encounter involves care. Learning from a computer isn't education; the machine doesn't care. Learning from a person behaving like a machine isn't education; that person's capacity for care is being suppressed. It is care that is the basis of the creativity in teaching, at all levels from Kindergarten to PhD supervision, as the teacher's practice evolves in response to the learner's development and needs.

Encounter between persons implies people capable of encounter; that is, people with significant autonomy. The more that power relations impinge on a situation, the less scope there is for encounter and therefore for education. Military training is not education. Power of course exists in many forms, and one of the tasks of educational research is to explore the many ways power in and around educational relations can be diagnosed and contested.

THE NEOLIBERAL CASCADE AND EDUCATION (2013)

Encounter implies respect and reciprocity, a degree of mutual engagement by learner and teacher. And despite the distinction between learners and teachers, that mutual engagement requires a strong kind of equality, an equal citizenship in the educational situation. Mutual respect is required for the complex communication through which complex learning occurs. Trust is easily damaged, indeed easily stopped—by violence, by threats, by arbitrariness, by privilege and by economic exploitation.

Considerable work, then, is needed to institutionalize education, to create learning-and-teaching settings where equal citizenship is normative and where trust is sustained. This work is *social* labour, in real-life situations involving large numbers of people in the institutional settings where education is hoped for. The conventional models of education as human capital formation and social reproduction absurdly over-simplify these settings. The complexity of school teachers' daily work is well documented in the research literature on teaching.

Educational encounter is always multiple, in terms of the numbers and diversity of people involved and the number of structures shaping educational relationships: not only class structures but also gender structures, ethnic and race relations, connections with region and land, generational relations, and more. Trust and citizenship cannot be limited, cannot be made a privilege of specific groups. Education is inherently socially inclusive; any failure of inclusion signals the presence of power. An exclusive education is a corrupted education.

To think of education as the development of capacities for practice is also to put a strong requirement on educational relationships. They must be calibrated to reality. We are not free to teach lies to children and call the result 'education'. That is propaganda, and a violation of trust. We are not free to *imply* lies, for instance by omission—denying an encounter with reality that learners need, and could have. (A sad example: the refusal of knowledge about contraception and abortion that is needed by teenagers and young adults.)

To say that educational encounters are calibrated to reality is to emphasise the cognitive side of education, alongside the emotional—the dimension of intellectual excitement, at every level from basic language learning onwards. Learning involves discovery, realization, and engagement with truth. The inner fire of education is the same as the inner fire of culture in general; education does not involve a watered-down reality.

At the same time, anyone who has been involved with research, whether in the natural or human sciences, knows that establishing truth is not easy, and that our collective knowledge is constantly in a process of transformation and growth. Because of this, respect for the learners requires that the curriculum must itself be historical, always be open to debate and change, rather than fossilized by institutional mechanisms.

Commodifying the education world

In human services, to create a market you have to restrict the service in some way. What you sell, then, is a privilege—something that other people can't get. (The argument in this section draws on the pioneering work of Marginson 1997.)

Provided there is a rationing of educational resources it is possible to commodify access to schools or colleges, and to particular services within them. Importantly, the rationing itself can be marketed. The marketing brochures of private schools, and mass media advertising by richer schools, create images of an orderly, disciplined, clean and uniformed little world, which parents are invited to contrast with the undisciplined, dirty and dangerous world outside. 'Outside' being understood to include the public schools.

There need to be known losers, if people are to be persuaded to pay to become winners. A spectacular example was the vilification of a public high school in a very poor community, Mount Druitt, in 1997 by the Sydney newspaper the *Daily Telegraph*, on the grounds of its students' failure in the Higher School Certificate. It is not by accident that the newspaper that conducted this campaign is owned by a subsidiary of Rupert Murdoch's News Corp, Murdoch being one of the international promoters of neoliberal politics.

The losing has to be legitimated, and not appear a matter of unfair discrimination or pure bad luck. The neoliberal takeover of education has been accompanied by a revival of competitive testing. Not too long ago, competitive testing itself was in disrepute, because it was socially biassed, and of little use in classroom teaching. This has been forgotten. Australia now has not only state-level competitive testing (e.g. for entry to selective schools and then at high school graduation) but also national competitive testing, the NAPLAN system. The results are duly displayed on the *MySchool* website, in fact they are the central feature of *MySchool*. These displays in turn are processed by the mass media into league tables (e.g. *Sydney Morning Herald* 2012). International league tables are compiled from the PISA testing system administered through the OECD. Australia's competitive position vis-a-vis Finland, Singapore etc. is the subject of media exposures and policy angst. Meanwhile universities are named and shamed according to their annual rankings in international league tables, which have even shakier methodological bases, but seem to be regarded as holy writ in public discourse.

This elaborate system of sorting sheep from goats, winners from losers, is deeply corrosive of education. Social exclusion is antithetical to the inclusive character of educational relationships. Respect and trust are undermined by the jockeying for position in competitive markets. Educational institutions—this includes universities, who are supposed to be beacons of truth and critical thinking—become purveyors of spin, image-making, manipulative marketing, organized boasting, and sometimes more toxic forms of deceit. The education system as a whole comes to stand, not for the common interest and self-knowledge of the society, but for ways to extract private advantage at the expense of others.

Consequences for teachers

The market agenda implies an insecure workforce. Neoliberal politics weakens employee unions and tries to turn employer/employee relationships into individual contracts—for employees. The strategy is international, as teacher unions have found (Compton and Weiner 2008). In the name of flexibility—for employers—casual, part-time and temporary employment has increased.

Insecurity has been growing in some parts of the teaching workforce. Technical and further education programmes, which previously had a lot of secure part-time work, are now mainly taught by casual or fixed-term contract labour. University teaching, which has always had a minority of casuals and fixed-term appointments—tutors, demonstrators, etc.—who were mainly young people doing higher degrees and beginning an academic career, is now evolving strongly towards a two-tier system. There is a growing casualized teaching-only sector, doing work that used to be done by tenured lecturers, plus a privileged sector with tenure (itself increasingly precarious), research opportunities and promotion paths.

Casualization has not yet greatly affected the school teaching workforce, though there is constant talk about it as a policy option. What has emerged is a push towards a more strongly tiered system of employment. The capstone is performance pay for an elite of teachers. This policy was promoted by the Business Council of Australia (2008) and was embraced by the Gillard Labor government in its election campaign in 2010.

Above the elite of teachers are the principals and deputy principals, who are being re-shaped in the neoliberal imagination as a managerial class, exactly parallel to corporate managers in the private sector. With schools being redefined as firms competing with each other in a market, of course the firms need entrepreneurial managers to run them—not educators. They need managers who control a budget, hire and fire staff, attract corporate funding, market their product through advertising, and so on. Exactly this package was promoted in the 2012 education measures of the O'Farrell Liberal government in NSW (Stevenson & Robins 2012).

A gradual change in relationships between classroom teachers and school executives is thus under way, with public schools being reshaped on the model of private schools. This re-engineering, to use a business term, does not stop at the classroom door. Teachers' relations with their pupils are also being re-shaped. High-stakes competitive testing produces formidable pressure to teach to the test: narrowing the curriculum to the knowledge and skills being tested, and drilling the specific performance that pupils have to emit during the test. This is a familiar effect of competitive examinations, for instance for entry to university or to selective schools.

Theoretically, the national testing regime (NAPLAN) does not have consequences for the pupils. But the policy changes that turn schools into firms competing with each other, and assess teachers' performance by the test results of their pupils, have made the national testing regime a high-stakes enterprise for the schools and teachers. Witness the league tables that commercial mass media immediately constructed from the *MySchool* data—a result which the government pretends was unintended. The level of hypocrisy around education policy now is impressive.

The pressure on teachers is publicly acknowledged: it is called, in an interesting slide into business language, 'accountability' (Kleinhenz & Ingvarson 2004). The neoliberal audit society (Power 1997) is made very visible here. With the pressure growing for teachers to narrow their efforts, to focus on what is testable, teachers' capacity to develop curricula appropriate to their actual pupils is undermined.

Since the system of tests and examinations measures a set of skills and performances defined within the dominant Anglo upper-middle-class practices of living, the school system's capacity for cultural and class diversity is quietly but powerfully constricted. Working-class children, not surprisingly, generally do worse at the tests than middle-class children. Thus the hierarchy of success and failure solidifies, and schools serving mainly working-class, migrant and indigenous communities, who collectively occupy the bottom layers of the league tables, are collectively re-defined as failures.

The neoliberal policy claim that public schools are being freed from stifling bureaucracy and heavy-handed state control, is essentially a sham. Schools are being tied more tightly into a system of *remote* control, operated by funding mechanisms, testing systems, and certification, audit and surveillance mechanisms. In this environment there is an inevitable de-professionalization of teachers. Teachers' capacity to make autonomous judgment about curriculum and pedagogy in the interests of their actual pupils is undermined by the system of remote control.

These developments have created unavoidable tensions for teachers. Teachers want to act in the interests of their students; but the current institutional system creates contradictions between short-term results and long-term effects. A rhetoric of teacher professionalism contradicts the emerging industrial and technical realities of teachers' work. Australia has seen a mushroom growth of official teacher accreditation bodies in the last decade. These Institutes are simultaneously a vehicle of surveillance (especially for teacher education and early-career teachers) tied in to the market regime, and a repository of practical know-how and occupational identity with quite different bases.

Effects on the knowledge base of education

Parts of the knowledge system on which contemporary education depends has already been strongly commodified. Public sector funding for research intended for the advancement of knowledge has been increasingly replaced by market-oriented private sector funding. This is especially true of biomedical research, a sector now largely funded by drug and medical-equipment corporations. This connection has already produced a series of corruption scandals in the research world.

Biomedical research does not affect a large part of the school curriculum, though its potential to colonize school life is revealed by the growth of ADHD (attention deficit/hyperactivity disorder) diagnoses and the immense profitability of the drug Ritalin. But biomedical science is a large part of the university curriculum, for allied health professions as well as medicine and nursing. The focus on profitable interventions rather than public health and prevention (which implies a different kind of knowledge, combining biology with social science) does affect practice: commercial distortion of the knowledge base does matter. The expansion of this style of biomedical research has a more general ideological effect that matters for education, through thousands of mass media stories about medical breakthroughs, brain science, and more. Individually-targeted expert treatment is presented again and again as the solution to problems, rather than collective action to change the conditions from which the problems arise.

That points to the wider effect of neoliberalism on the knowledge base: an increasing technicization of knowledge and knowledge production. What can be most readily marketed is patentable knowledge: the design of new equipment or new drugs, or techniques for which access can be restricted and therefore charged for. It's not surprising that Intellectual Property has become an active concern of university managements in Australia as overseas, and that many universities have set up offices to patent and sell discoveries by university staff or to market the expertise of university staff. There is a stark irony that universities which were set up for the advancement of knowledge now seek to *restrict* knowledge to extract a commercial benefit from it.

In school education, the technicization of knowledge is partly expressed in the testing system itself. The ability to administer and interpret standardized tests has been seen as part of teachers' professional knowledge since the 1930s, so neoliberalism has not changed the principle here. What is novel is the scale, as the testing system has been institutionalized nationally, and its persistent use to create league tables. Something else, too, is new: the idea that teachers should learn and use evidence-based best practice, and be held accountable for it, under the system of indirect surveillance. The evidence base appealed to is provided by the testing system, via an international literature (now very large) of correlational studies on what variables are associated with improved test results. The abstracted 'teacher effectiveness' literature is a striking example of the technicization of knowledge, and the gradual absorption of business language (such as 'best practice') into education. One is not surprised to find a teacher-effectiveness policy agenda being pushed by the rich countries' neoliberal economic think-tank, the OECD (Organisation for Economic Co-operation and Development 2005).

In this way, the neoliberal policy regime produces its own knowledge base, in a closed loop that does not allow other kinds of knowledge to enter policy debate. As it happens, there is a considerable amount of other research on the powerfully divisive social consequences of the market agenda in education, tracing which groups are advantaged and which are disadvantaged. Indeed we have had this information for years, from different countries and indeed different continents (e.g. Reay 2001, Ball 2003, Teese & Polesel 2003, Chisholm 2004). It is ignored by policymakers; they do not want to know.

Neoliberal politicians, businessmen, measurement experts, economists and education system managers now form the arena in which education policy is made. In Australia, the last vestige of an alternative was eliminated when the statutory Schools Commission was abolished in 1988, and its weakened replacement, the Schools Council, was allowed to die later. The neoliberal policy community find their technicized knowledge base eminently satisfying, because nothing coming out of it can possibly question the framework in which they are acting or the social interests they represent.

But this knowledge base is so impoverished that it cannot meet the social need for discourse about educational problems. So around it, there has grown up a gaudy arena of pseudo-science, fads and fakery about education, much of it promoted by the entrepreneurial consultants who have multiplied in the neoliberal world. Different consultants market brain science, boys' special learning styles, parent training, computer solutions, gifted-and-talented programmes, boot camps for troublesome kids, direct instruction, tough love, patent reading schemes, zero tolerance, charter schools, and many, many more slogans, programmes and devices. Since Australia is a small market, much of this is copied from the USA, or directly imported.

This arena of pseudo-knowledge in education can only flourish because wider social processes have supported it. The instrumentalization of knowledge in universities has led to a decline of critical disciplines such as philosophy—you cannot easily commodify deep reflection, nor patent its results, and philosophers don't seem to have the art of attracting million-dollar grants. Corporate interests globally have mounted a fierce and well-funded attack on science when scientific findings challenge profit-making: the tobacco companies' decades-long assault on cancer research, and the current corporate assault on climate science, in Australia promoted especially by mining interests, are notable cases. In the cultural climate created by the spread of market logic throughout society, the encounter with truth that is a central feature of education is increasingly difficult to achieve.

Though educators must be concerned about the penumbra of spin and distortion around the market in education, the main ideological effect may be produced by the expanding market itself. Back in 1996, one of Australia's neo-conservative, corporate-funded think tanks published a pamphlet proposing 'A private schooling for everyone'. A voucher system—a favourite project of the Chicago-school economist Milton Friedman—would do it. And we are approaching that, in current school funding models.

The market is, in a sense, its own teacher. We learn more by doing than by being told, as all teachers know. So the best way to learn the market outlook is by being made to live in a market system. With markets all around, what else are people likely to learn?

The national news now routinely includes the stock market quotations on the same level as the weather. The Federal Government puts every local school in a competitive frame on *MySchool*. The Australian Council for Educational Research—the main supplier of standardized tests—promotes performance pay. The newspapers publish advertorials for the private schools, and then publish the league tables for schools, and then publish the international league tables for universities. The cumulative effect is formidable.

In conclusion

Totalitarianism of the market is not yet an established fact in Australia, nor in most of the world. A public sector survives, and an ethos of public service survives within it (Connell 2011). Commitments to knowledge, and to principles of justice and equality, are still found widely, however much they struggle for institutional presence. Yet the slide towards market dominance is well advanced. The Australian Labor Party, which lost its mass membership in the 1980s and 1990s, is now part of the neoliberal coalition, not part of the resistance to the corporate takeover. The public school system is still large, but has been under attack by right-wing ideologues for about thirty years and is significantly eroded and residualized. The universities are now controlled by a thoroughly neoliberal managerial regime.

The organized groups most likely to push for alternatives, the public sector teacher unions, were certainly in the midst of educational invention and debate in the 1970s. Since then, they have been organizationally on the defensive—unions being one of the prime targets of neoliberal politics, given the need for an insecure workforce—and have been frozen out of the educational policy-making milieu.

Under neoliberal rule, education is displaced by competitive training, competition for privilege, social conformity, fear and corruption, while protest and rational alternatives are marginalized.

THE NEOLIBERAL CASCADE AND EDUCATION (2013)

It is easy to despair about the current scene. But education itself has a resilience, has a grounding in social needs, that cannot be suppressed—and that will be heard. As Shakespeare put it, in the direst time, stones have been known to move and trees to speak.

Resources can be found. Education needs invention, and there are certainly enough lively minds in the teaching workforce to be confident that invention will come. Education needs coalitions of social groups able to create the spaces in which educational invention will work. Those requirements are clear enough. How they can be turned into practice, we still have to discover.

Fieldwork

9

Fieldwork (2006, 2010)

THIS CHAPTER OFFERS three examples of the empirical work that has constantly gone together with my theoretical and policy writing. These projects have used a variety of methods: field interviews, clinical interviews, questionnaires, telephone and face-to-face surveys, documentary history, field observation, policy analysis, and more. I've chosen, from the past two decades of my research, three studies that used field interviews, the method I have used more than any other. In two, the method is specifically life-history interviewing, a labour-intensive, slow but very illuminating approach that maximises the scope for participants to give their own accounts of events and experiences.

1. Gender in organizational life (2006)

This picture of workplaces comes from a large study of gender equity policy and its effects undertaken for the NSW state government. As well as collecting statistics and studying documents, the research group conducted interviews in ten public sector workplaces, in both service-delivery and policy-making units. We wrote an anonymised case study for each workplace, and these informed our general reports to the government and our papers for journals. The extracts come from my article 'The Experience of Gender Change in Public Sector Organizations' in the journal *Gender, Work and Organization*, published in 2006.

Participants from all sites expressed a consciousness of living in a time of gender change. Older staff especially had a strong sense of 'then' and 'now' in the broad gender patterns of society. ...

Many participants described a change in public sector workplaces that corresponded to this larger picture of social change. They observed that women's employment is now diverse, job ghettoes such as the typing pool have disappeared, women are now present in management, dress codes are more relaxed and 'boys' clubs' are in decline. Many worksites in the New South Wales public sector have been, to a significant degree, de-gendered. Old occupational barriers have been removed, the physical segregation of men and women has ended.

In some cases this de-gendering is clearly associated with a change in the labour process and organizational structure. The study's Sites 1 and 2, for instance, are located in an infrastructure agency where a traditional form of blue-collar men's work has been largely automated over the last decade. This agency's workforce has been drastically downsized. With a new labour process centering on computer control systems, old occupational divisions have collapsed and a new, integrated occupational category has been created which is open to women as well as to men. At the same time, a multilayered bureaucratic hierarchy has been simplified into a 'flat' structure, with the basis of authority shifting from seniority to professional qualifications. Both changes have undermined the organizational predominance of particular kinds of masculinity which are familiar in the research literature on engineering and heavy industry.

A change almost as profound has occurred in mainstream office work. Since all public sector agencies have 'offices', this change is documented in interviews from all participating agencies and the majority of specific worksites. The earlier labour process centred on the production and storage of paper documents—letters, file cards and so on. A category of workers who were mostly women (typists, secretaries) produced, filed and retrieved documents on the instructions of managers and professionals who were mostly men.

The advent of word processing, databanks and e-mail since the 1970s has changed much of this. The typing pool has gone. The secretary and the filing clerk have mostly gone (partly replaced by the 'personal assistant', but this is likely to be a young person getting experience rather than a woman in a life-time job). Managers and professionals do much of their own keyboard work. In Site 9, part of a central agency, the researcher conducted fieldwork in a room where a group of administrators spent much of their time staring at their individual computer screens. This is, in a sense, a gender-blending scene. Labour that was formerly coded masculine (bureaucratic administration) has been combined with labour formerly coded feminine (secretarial) in the one job. ...

In other respects too, the picture of growing gender integration must be qualified. In Sites 1 and 2 mentioned above, some participants explicitly cautioned us not to exaggerate the picture of change. For all the formal changes, this agency still mainly employs men. While most men in managerial and professional occupations have learnt enough keyboard skills to do e-mail and drafting, there were a few who have not, and who still give this work to women. In Site 5, in a human service agency, the researchers encountered a group of workers doing routine keyboard work, data entry and retrieval from a database. All were women, and this was one of the most gender-segregated workplaces in the whole study. In both these cases a pattern of gender segregation has survived the technical transformation of the labour process. This is a useful warning not to overestimate the direct impact of 'technology' in transforming gender.

In other sites, women participants point to continuing workplace sexism, both inside and outside the public sector, and mention arrogant and oppressive men remaining in management. For many public sector workers, family divisions of labour have changed very little. Women still provide the bulk of childcare and domestic services and men consume the services. ...

Gender as a problem in organizational life— and as a non-problem

The situation addressed by the 'equal employment opportunity' reforms of 20 years ago has therefore changed, but not enough to make such policy irrelevant. In thinking about new directions for gender equity policy, it becomes important to know how, and to what extent, gender becomes recognized as a problem that public sector organizations still need to address. In some study sites there was evidence of overt gender difficulties, such as organizational problems that were clearly thematized as gender issues. Most fall into three types.

The first is a pattern familiar in organizational gender research. It concerns men, either as individuals or groups, who have difficulty accepting the gender changes that are occurring in their workplaces. They had particular difficulty with the arrival of women in the workplace in roles other than traditional support roles. In one service delivery site there had been considerable conflict of this kind: management had banned pornography, brought women into all-male workplaces, banned harassment and so on. In some units of this agency a marked change towards co-operative gender relations had occurred. In other units little change had occurred. In these cases the men evidently saw the work as inappropriate for women, or saw women as intruders in a masculine domain. Women were seen as creating embarrassment and difficulty, disrupting the solidarity of work units and not having the skills, strength or commitment needed for the work. Even in units where women and men now combined successfully as a group, some individual men maintained their opposition.

The second issue concerns women managers. Though the principle of women holding managerial authority is now accepted across the public sector, in practice women's authority may be contested, challenged, ignored or doubted in many ways. For instance, a female manager in Site 2 was treated with scorn by a male colleague of equal rank. He belittled her proposals in meetings and behind her back, and refused to communicate with her until obliged to go into a mediation process. A male worker in Site 6 would not accept direction from a female supervisor, always going over her head to get instructions confirmed by a male superior. In Site 8, a much-restructured site in a regulatory agency, women are now prominent in senior management. But they are thought by some of the workforce, especially men, to have been promoted too fast, and therefore to lack skill and background. The emotion in these remarks is significant. It is difficult to quote examples within the participating agencies, because specific people may be identifiable, but the tone is conveyed by a Site 8 man's story about another agency:

> I notice that especially women who get into senior positions, the first thing they want to do is to exert their authority. They've appointed a woman over there as the director of [Unit], now she has gone totally feral. She has told him to, you know, 'Get fucked, you're useless, I have been carrying you since I got here'. And it just degenerated. Luckily she said it in front of another person ... and that was the culmination of about six or eight months of just abuse and bullying.

There are enough such comments—some more hostile than that—to indicate a continuing problem in establishing women's authority in management. At the same time, we encountered a number of situations, sometimes in the same agencies, where women managers were accepted and respected by their workforces.

The third issue concerns respondents in a number of sites who feel they or their colleagues have suffered gender discrimination.

This claim is made by men as well as by women. There is, however, a difference in the character of their complaints. The women who feel discriminated against are complaining about old-fashioned sexist put-downs. Examples are repeated jokes against women (updated in one respect: they are now circulated by e-mail), being felt up, being stared at, their bodies and appearance commented upon, and not being taken seriously as co-workers. The men who complain of discrimination seem to feel they are up against something new and even sinister. They believe that their manager is a feminist who has something to prove against men, that there is an organized push to get women into top jobs, that they are *'victims of the sisterhood'*, as a male respondent (who distanced himself from these claims) put it. These complaints are noticeably less specific than the women's complaints, but strong feelings are clearly involved.

It was easy for the researchers to name gender problems of these three types. Yet when asked what current gender problems existed in their workplace, most participants in most sites reported that there were few or none. In some cases the answer went further and respondents praised the workplace for gender sensitivity and positive relations between women and men. Other sites were characterized as peaceful workplaces with no open conflicts and no sexual harassment. This also seems an important finding. For much of the time, across much of the public sector, gender is regarded as a non-problem.

This was not because participants were unable to 'see' gender issues. The same people often did comment on gender problems—but located them elsewhere. Gender conflicts were often located in the past, in an organizational history that has now been transcended. Or they were located somewhere else in the present—in other units, other agencies, or other sectors of society. Here, for instance, is a woman from Site 10 at the policy-advice level in a central agency:

> Not in this workplace, it is obvious, you just have to look around, there is so many women. So I can't see any problem. I get along well with— it their knowledge and their experience, whether

male or female. So I have never encountered any chauvinism, if I can put it that way, you know, where you are locked out. I have experienced it in the past. When you're developing policy, gender doesn't really have a role to play, in my view.

We were also told of many episodes that were seen as gender problems, but were not seen as *organizational* gender problems. For instance, sexist comments from a man are often discussed by a woman as a problem about a prejudiced individual. Here is an example from Site 1 in an infrastructure agency:

There is a few people here, a few men here, who still have that, you know, real sort of, 'How are you darling?', 'How is it going?', pat on the bum, really male chauvinistic, sexual overtones in everything they say. And it is just a pain in the arse. They're not senior managers or anything like that, it is just the staff.

A good deal of gender trouble is handled informally at an individual level. In this site, for instance, women express confidence in their ability to handle sexist behaviour from such men, now that the gross sexism of the old work culture has mostly been eliminated. The woman just quoted went on to describe how she dealt with criticism from a male manager about participating in a women's staff development programme:

I wouldn't take any crap: when he made a comment, I told him where to go with it—not quite that way, but you know, I pretty much set him straight. And it is funny, because he has never said anything to me since.

The fact that gender equity and anti-discrimination are now official policy may result, ironically, in a degree of unwillingness to articulate gender problems within the organization. A sexist comment from a man may be judged by a woman far too small an issue to call the anti-discrimination machinery into play. Few people want to make their agency look bad in public and few people want to damage their careers by opposing established policy.

When this is put together with a tendency to play down the gender dimension of problems, to speak of gender-related issues as personal 'choices' (especially work–life balance issues) and to step cautiously in personal interactions lest relationships be misinterpreted—we get a picture of an almost subterranean gender politics occurring in organizational life. Indeed a thoughtful participant in Site 3 spoke of gender being 'increasingly disguised' in the life of this agency, despite having real effects. To the extent this is true, gender problems may become increasingly difficult to deal with, because they are expressed only indirectly.

2. Managers as business intellectuals (2010)

In the late 1990s I began several studies of intellectual workers, using both surveys and life-history interviews. Among those interviewed were some senior managers in Australia, from both public and private sectors, and these interviews were so interesting that they called for separate analysis. They cast an unexpected light on recent changes in class relations and what was happening in organisational leadership.

These extracts come from my paper 'Building the Neoliberal World: Managers as Intellectuals in a Peripheral Economy', published in *Critical Sociology* in 2010.

Our interviews were rich in detail about the labor process of management, and we were able to tease out a substantial element of intellectual work in conventional managerial positions—gathering data, interpreting it, creating agendas and plans, communicating.

There are also niches in the managerial/professional world for people performing a more overtly intellectual function. Toni, a senior public sector manager, defines her role through a contrast with line management:

This is a kind of, the strategic leadership of the organization, and so it's actually one of the more thinking jobs in an organization like this one. Rather than, you know—and I've had many operational jobs where your in-tray drives what your framework is, or if you're project managing something huge, [that is] very operationally, tactically, focused. If I were to look at broadly an average week of mine, two to three days are spent traveling, visiting offices, or giving speeches external to the organization.

Toni's 'thinking job' includes planning the organization's trajectory and scanning the organization's environment. She was a central figure in the corporatization of her agency. She was responsible not only for planning the transition from government department to corporation, but also for selling the transition to the staff. She does have a sense of herself as an intellectual, performing a conceptual function:

Look, my job is to really understand where the trends are going, and to understand how trends in different areas of activity all come together and re-shape. If you're involved in strategy, you're involved about the future, and you're involved in what the whole picture looks like.

The most important way the pressures of management and the needs of intellectual work are reconciled is through the collectivization of the labor process itself. The labor process of management is now merged with information and communication technology [ICT]. As the scale of business grows, managers may be engaged in scanning markets, calculating risks, managing client relationships, tendering, arbitraging, making prices, studying competitors, and more. All of this is beyond any individual manager, indeed beyond any office. It therefore has to be automated. The data compilation and the continuous calculation are built into computer systems within the firm, or are bought in from more specialized firms. In a multinational corporation, the computer systems of the global firm become the intellectual environment for any individual manager.

In one of our interviews we saw a system of this kind in its moment of construction. Aged about 60 at the time of interview, Christopher is a senior manager who had a central role in the technological restructuring of his whole industry. He came to Australia as a young man, married, made good connections and found himself in the heartland of Australian business about the time computers were coming in. He thus became involved in 'pioneering times', gained competence, and moved quickly up the ladder: programmer, systems analyst, to manager in six or seven years. He then had a managerial career moving among finance, accountancy and legal companies, converting them to advanced computer systems. This was pleasure as well as business:

> I've enjoyed it, it's very exciting, it's very project driven and the project is fun, it's a bit hairy, it's exciting. It involves a team of people, it involves panics, highs and lows, risks and rewards. And I've been very lucky, I've really had a terrific run.

Many scientists might say the same. But in Christopher's case, the technical thrill was interwoven with increasing his organization's revenue, restructuring, marketing, streamlining and downsizing.

A decade ago he became the senior manager at an important finance company which was on the brink of a major amalgamation—a 'forced merger', as Christopher put it, in the face of global competition. This involved a massive transformation of the labor process, information processing, and personnel arrangements, including heavy job losses. Christopher has driven the change and is proud of his achievement. He is particularly proud of the creation of a computerized transaction system, in which he considers the Australian firm led the world. But he is ironically aware of the way ICT can shake up the established hierarchies of business: 'I'm the MD [Managing Director] and I'm the least competent on the PC here!'

He is aware of the impact on staff whom his work had made obsolete; he took care to get 'absolutely every last dollar that is available' for redundancy payments. There is sadness but, ultimately, downsizing is good for everybody. The story is a notable example of the interweaving of technical knowledge, ideology, and profit. Christopher's work in this restructuring duly won a business journal award for excellence.

'It's here, it's inevitable, it's happening, more and more of it.' That is Rachel's summary on globalization, and that is the general view. 'Globalization' ranks even ahead of 'technology' as a pressure for change. Often the two are woven together, as in these comments by Emerson, a private sector personnel manager:

> We act local and think global. I think the world is now a global environment. The communications revolution has hit us. We'll look back in two or three decades to the 1990s and see that it was akin to the Industrial Revolution. There's no more borders any more, there's no more passports. The internet has done away with all of those things. And all of our children are just so familiar with it, it's like waking up every day and cleaning their teeth.

In fact, 'thinking global' mainly means thinking about the global metropole. The USA and Europe come first, and other parts of the world a long way behind. Allowing for this bias, our respondents' picture of globalization is detailed and sophisticated. Christopher gives a well-informed account of the new volatility of international finance markets, where information flows are crucial, and different strategies are possible. Globalization is seen as a pervasive and unstoppable process but not a catastrophe. It is a field of opportunities for smart, modern players. And in this way, globalization is not only an external force, an environment for local managers and businesses. It is, in specific ways, *created* by their operations.

The active creation of a neoliberal world is most obvious in the privatization of public sector institutions. The general superiority of market provision and market decisions was assumed by all the managers we interviewed, and taken for granted in Australian public discourse. Both major parties, and practically all the mass media, are strongly neoliberal in outlook. Yet the ascendancy of the market agenda in Australia is recent, and required hard work by business ideologists, and detailed work to realize as institutional fact. In another of our cases, this process is particularly clear.

Aged about 45 when we interviewed her, Catherine came from a middle-class family, did well at university, and then joined an elite branch of the public service. She was bitterly disillusioned in her first job, and transferred to a major service agency in the public sector.

Here she was recruited by an ambitious manager into a 'hunt and destroy' team bent on controlling and privatizing this agency. As Catherine tells the story, they ran 'an open agenda and a hidden agenda'. The goal was to persuade people in the agency, and their political masters, of the need for the agency to become a market player. They were highly successful: the agency was fully privatized.

So, in a sense, was Catherine. Her experience at the interface of government and business made her an asset; her corporate employers initially used this expertise for lobbying. However, she rose through a series of appointments, with both Australian and multinational firms, and shifted over to line management. She was brilliantly successful, winding up as CEO of the overseas operations of a large Australian firm.

Catherine recalls the exact moment when the excitement and rewards of this path in life became clear to her. She had just been employed by a multinational firm, and was sent on a round-the-world trip:

> It was my first time in the United States. I had a boss at the time who I think appreciated the good life, and I didn't know anything about anything ... [He] arranged where to stay, and I mean it turned out to be, for example I'd go to New York and I'd stay in the X Hotel, I'd go to London and I'd stay in Y. To me it was just

wonderfully exciting. I can remember sitting on the windowsill, it was the June long weekend, Memorial Day or something in the States, and so it was a public holiday. It was a lovely summer day, and sitting on the windowsill at the X Hotel, looking over Central Park, and thinking, you know, 'Fuck, this is great!' So it wasn't prestige ... it was just my own inner excitement.

Catherine is one of the people who make 'globalization' real. She gives chapter and verse of the huge managerial labor involved in taking an Australian firm offshore. She worked 5 am to 10 pm, 'ridiculous hours'—and wondered, how can we do this to ourselves? But it worked for her, and she learnt her outlook from the ideological effort that many businesses make. Catherine went to work for a well-known multinational corporation and admired the very professional management there:

> not so much under the original Managing Director who was a bit of an old style guy ... but the subsequent two Chief Executives were really really good in their business philosophy. You knew that the answer to any business question at [the multinational firm] was 'What would the free-market solution be?' So I became a very very dry person economically there. You know, no government assistance, no government picking errors, don't ever ask government for handouts, do it all on your own. But equally don't let government rip you off, and charge you ... royalties just because you can afford to pay, sort of thing.

There are of course different emphases. Emerson, the personnel manager quoted above, has a slightly old-fashioned emphasis on personal effort: 'no one's ever died of hard work, in this modern era anyway.' He believes in giving value, achievement, living up to one's standards. He feels his company should not only serve its staff, its clients and its shareholders but should also do something for the community: 'the more you put back into the community, the more you'll get out of it.' So he helps raise money for various charities. He thinks, probably rightly, that this attitude is a 'radical view'.

3. A gender transition (2010)

One of the most remarkable interviews I have done came quite unexpectedly. In the late 1980s I was working on a life-history project with four groups of Australian men—the reports are in my book *Masculinities*. A newspaper ran a story about my project, and soon afterwards I had a letter from a woman who wanted to be interviewed, because she used to be a man. Though it was a little outside the sampling plan, it was an invitation I could not refuse. So one evening I climbed the stairs of Robyn's inner-city flat, and spent a fascinating few hours hearing her story and being shown through her photograph albums. And then I did not know what to do with the information. Robyn invited me to publish her story, saying 'I want people to realize that transsexuals are just normal people'. But I could not see how to do so without the report being read as a clinical 'case', as transsexual stories usually were in the 1980s. That was a reading I very much resisted. It was only after my own transition, more than fifteen years later, that I could see how to do what Robyn asked.

This is an extract from 'Two Cans of Paint: A Transsexual Life Story, with Reflections on Gender Change and History', published in 2010 in the journal *Sexualities*. The first sections described the interview and told of Robyn's life before transition: the story of a working-class child growing up as a boy between the wars, a career in heavy industry, marriage and family life, breakdown of the marriage, moving out and working as a taxi owner/driver. Then we arrive at the gender transition.

Around this point in the interview there is a change in the style of Robyn's narration. There is less of detailed chronological history, more repetition and circling-back, and more passages with many strands seeming to compete for attention. That is to say, Robyn does not give a single narrative of gender transition. Rather than try to reconstruct one, I will follow the strands that lead out from a characteristic passage.

> And so when my marriage fell flat on its face, all of a sudden [1] I wanted to do what I started doing [2], cross-dressing, gradually dressed and gradually dressed fully [3]. I was lucky I had the taxi. And I was dressing [and] wasn't dressing, I was still dressing as a guy in—my hair was growing, my facial features were changing [4]. I got three boys in the cab one day [5], and they said 'Are you a queen or something?'... I realized then that I was changing and it was becoming obvious. The taxi industry saw me as an engineer, and then saw me changing, they called me a homosexual, they called me a poofter, they called me everything [6]. And I couldn't handle it. But I couldn't do anything about it. My body said [7] you have got to be a woman, whether you like it or not.

I will outline what Robyn further said on each of the numbered themes.

[1] *All of a sudden*. Robyn repeatedly describes the transition as something that came on without warning, that began suddenly. This is consistent with the structure of the whole interview, starting with a long narrative of being a man and then changing abruptly into an account of becoming a woman. Abrupt change is clearly an important part of how Robyn sees events.

At the same time, Robyn is well aware that the full change was a long process—ten years from the aftermath of the divorce to the genital reconstruction surgery, and then three or four more for the effects to settle. During the second half of the interview she gave many details of the events of those years, and it is clear that she worked long and hard to make the change happen.

Her effort involved a partial change of occupation, becoming a part-time masseur (not a prostitute). She borrowed money, buying and setting up her flat. She made a major change of social milieu, from suburban fringe to the counter-cultural inner-city scene; and there explored transvestite and transsexual venues, such as a conservative TV club and gay/transgender bars. She undertook a major effort to learn how to dress and present herself as a woman. And she developed a new network of friends who were comfortable with transsexuality and were in some cases transsexual themselves. This is at one level an example of 'doing gender' in the sense of ethnomethodology. At another level, it is an economic and political practice.

[2] *I wanted to do what I started doing.* Robyn describes the onset of the change as the arrival of an acute, overwhelming desire. She is quite pungent about this: 'I just had to dress, you know. As I say, if you have got to go to the toilet, you have got to go to the toilet. I had to dress.'

At times she talks about the pleasures of femininity. She likes colourful clothes, for instance, and a good many of her photographs show herself in glamour poses suggesting an enjoyment of emphasised femininity. But equally often, the feminine practices seem to be an obligation. Robyn wore skirts even when driving the taxi— 'I can't dress in slacks today even, I find them uncomfortable ... I have got to dress in a dress and I have got to wear women's shoes'. She painted her nails despite having medical problems with them, and is trying to get back onto heels despite the hip trouble.

Robyn acknowledges a desire to be a woman, but she pictures desire as imperative need, not as a search for pleasure. When eventually she saw a surgeon, he at first demurred because of her age. 'I said, if you can cut a nerve and stop me from wanting to be a woman that will suit me fine. But if you can't, I said, would you do the operation.'

[3] *Gradually dressed fully.* Robyn gives detail about learning to dress and present herself as a woman. She first did this in concealment, then wore some women's garments in public, then oscillated between women's clothes and men's clothes, then went full-time. That this was a learning process, she wryly acknowledges: 'when I first

started to go through it, before I had surgery, I was over-dressing, I was blustering, I was throwing myself around—expensive, it cost me a fortune to dress.'

Her photographs and commentary show her wearing a wig early in the transition in order to appear as a woman. She oscillated about that too, and eventually grew her own hair long and went to a hairdresser 'who was training it to be woman's hair'. She learned how to put on plastic nails, and has now managed to grow her own nails, despite some damage, 'so they are coming good'. In sum, she put herself through a comprehensive training in grooming, and developed a routine practice of self-presentation as a woman.

[4] *My facial features were changing.* The physical changes resulting from oestrogen therapy were important to her, as they are to most women in transition—especially, for Robyn, facial changes and the growth of breasts. In running through the photographs of the transition, these changes were a major theme:

> That is me as a woman. That is me as a woman, my own hair, in my swimming costume, you can see my breasts, I have got cleavage—this was taken a few years back. And there I am as a woman again, see, all of a sudden I am getting older, and you can see my changes.

In fact she recalls that her breasts began to grow before she started taking hormones. But the cleavage still needed help, and Robyn had breast implants well before she had genital reconstruction surgery.

[5] *In the cab one day.* Robyn several times expresses her gratitude (to an unspecified god) for having the taxi business before the gender change began. Owning a taxi, which she could either drive herself or employ someone else to drive, gave her economic independence—there was no boss to give her the sack—and flexibility. She was never wealthy, lost most of her assets in the divorce, and speaks of declining income now (the taxi business having finally been sold).

But at least she had no need for desperate measures to finance the transition.

The taxi is a public space, but a space where interaction is limited. It seems to have served Robyn as a trial ground for the transition. She wore a skirt while driving, and seems to have discussed gender issues quite freely with her passengers.

[6] *They called me everything.* Robyn had no problems about gender identity. The situation was always clear—first she was a man, then she turned into a woman, end of story. For her there is nothing fluid, ambiguous or playful about gender. The queer current of transgender theory, as it emerged in the 1990s in the United States, gives no grip on her story.

But other people did have problems about her identity, and these turned into problems of misrecognition for Robyn. Both the boys in the cab, and her colleagues in the taxi business, at first read her as homosexual, relying on the stereotype of homosexual men as effeminate. Others were in doubt as to whether she was a man or a woman, like the immigrant lady in her eighties with limited eyesight whom Robyn picked up as a fare. 'She said, are you a man or a woman', being concerned about the voice she heard. When told that Robyn was a woman who used to be a man, 'She said, gees, we have often talked about you people, and it is interesting to have met you, she said, but I would love to be a man'.

Recognition matters to Robyn, but it is recognition as a real woman she wants now. She is not concealing her history, nor trying to pass for something she is not. 'I am very lucky that I have had a lot of backing from the womenfolk.' She notes with pleasure that the taxi industry has been 'educated' by seeing her transition, and that the men now accept her:

> Now the guy that walked away from the table has come back to me and said 'Darling, how are you?' He has accepted it and everyone else in the industry has accepted it.

[7] *My body said.* One of the most striking themes in Robyn's narration is the agency of the body. I asked her to explain the statement 'my body said', and she went on:

> Physically I felt as though I had a girl in me and I had to show a woman exterior. It was demanding of me I had to get rid of the sexual organs. I tried every trick in the book. As a matter of fact if I could have cut it off, I would have cut it off. Lots of kids have unfortunately cut them off, and they've crucified themselves, bled to death, and are in dreadful trouble. So I used to wear tight pants ...

Later in the interview she came back to the theme:

> I didn't change from a man to a woman because I said 'Oh bugger it, I want to be a woman now'. I was happy [as a man]. When I was divorced, I said to myself, 'Well, this is fine, I am now going for trips overseas ... I am going to enjoy life.' I didn't have the chance. All of a sudden my body said 'You are not going there, you are going to be a bloody woman, you have got to be a woman.'

Obviously this experience is hard to express, and Robyn uses multiple metaphors: her body containing the body of a woman, her body talking to her and issuing warnings and instructions, her breasts growing of their own accord. Other transsexual narratives also struggle to convey the experience of contradictory embodiment.

The crucial point in Robyn's account is that the impulse to change was strongly embodied from the start. It wasn't a matter of first developing a feminine identity and then shaping the body to match. Robyn experienced the process the other way round, with the demand coming forth from her body.

Social science and
Southern theory

10

Why is classical theory classical? (1997)

THERE IS NOW a vigorous discussion of how we might de-colonise knowledge. Historians have traced how empire and racism have, over the past few centuries, shaped the human sciences and the natural sciences. Global inequalities in higher education, research institutions, and intellectual recognition and authority have been mapped. Indigenous methodologies have been asserted, and attempts made to reshape curricula and knowledge institutions.

It is hard to tell when exactly I became concerned with these questions. Perhaps in 1970, when I travelled to the United States for a postdoctoral year and fetched up against the world centre of sociology. Perhaps in 1988, when I was invited to speak at the American Sociological Association's annual conference and boldly talked about 'American Sociology and American Power'. Certainly no later than 1992, when I took a job at the University of California in Santa Cruz. US sociology departments almost all had courses presenting Marx, Durkheim and Weber as the foundational classics. I regarded this story as a myth, but now I had to teach the course. So I offered my students a deal: they would write for me an essay about the bundle of Weber's manuscripts published after his death as *Economy and Society*, and I would write for them an essay about why they should not be doing this. The essay I gave them was the first draft of 'Why is classical theory classical?'

That required a deep dive into the historical archive, reading the textbooks, journals and teaching programs from the decades when sociology was being formed as a discipline. It was a dusty project, along library shelves where no reader had wandered for decades, but it was fascinating. I found not only gems from forgotten authors, but forgotten writing by famous ones, such as the amazing *L'Année sociologique*, the one major work of Durkheim that has never been translated. A very different picture of the early years of sociology began to emerge. At a certain point I felt this was a major story that needed to be told. Taking a deep breath, I sent the much-revised paper to a journal that survived from the foundation period, the *American Journal of Sociology*. And after taking a deep breath too—and asking for more evidence, which I supplied—they published it in 1997.

The aftermath has been fascinating. The first response came from the *AJS* editors themselves, who published, in the same issue as my paper, a vigorous attack on it by Randall Collins. Perhaps in regret, they then declined to publish rebuttals of Collins that other colleagues sent. Nevertheless my paper did get around. It appeared, charmingly, in 'classical theory' course reading lists. It provoked a discussion of sociology's connections with empire and colonialism that has produced some very helpful research. It was the starting point for *Southern Theory*. And that sent me on the next stage of my project, which will be described in Chapter 11.

Here we reprint the 1997 article, minus its bibliographical appendix, and omitting the not-very-satisfactory section that sketched the interlude before the classical 'canon' was created.

Origin stories

Open any Introduction to Sociology textbook and you will probably find, in the first few pages, a discussion of founding fathers focused on Marx, Durkheim and Weber. The introductory chapter may also cite Comte, Spencer, Tönnies and Simmel, and perhaps a few others. In the view normally presented to students, these men created sociology in response to dramatic changes in European society: the industrial revolution, class conflict, secularization, alienation and the modern state. This curriculum is backed by histories such as Alan Swingewood's *A Short History of Sociological Thought*. This well-regarded British text presents a two-part narrative of 'Foundations: Classical Sociology' (centering on Durkheim, Weber and Marx), and 'Modern Sociology', tied together by the belief that 'Marx, Weber and Durkheim have remained at the core of modern sociology' (Swingewood 2000: x).

The idea of classical theory embodies a canon, in the sense of literary theory: a privileged set of texts, whose interpretation and re-interpretation defines a field (Seidman 1994). This particular canon embeds an internalist doctrine of sociology's history as a social science. The story consists of a foundational moment arising from the internal transformation of European society; classic discipline-defining texts written by a small group of brilliant authors; and a direct line of descent from them to us.

But sociologists in the classical period itself did not have this origin story. When Franklin Giddings (1896), the first professor of sociology at Columbia University, published *The Principles of Sociology*, he named as the founding father—Adam Smith. Victor Branford (1904), expounding 'the founders of sociology' to a meeting in London, named as the central figure—Condorcet.

Turn-of-the-century sociology had no list of classic texts in the modern sense. Writers expounding the new science would commonly refer to Comte as the inventor of the term, to Darwin as the key figure in the theory of evolution, and then to any of a wide range of figures in the landscape of evolutionary speculation. Witness the account of the discipline in the second edition of *Dynamic Sociology* (1897) by Lester Ward, later the founding president of the American Sociological Society. At the time of the first edition in 1883, Ward observed, the term 'sociology' had not been in popular use. But in the intervening decade a series of brilliant scientific contributions had established sociology as a popular concept. There were now research journals, university courses, societies; and sociology 'bids fair to become the leading science of the twentieth century, as biology has been that of the nineteenth'. Ward listed thirty-seven notable contributors to the new science. The list included Durkheim and Tönnies but not Marx nor Weber.

The list of notables became a common feature in the textbooks of sociology that multiplied in the United States from the 1890s, Giddings' *Principles* being one of the first. (Ward had included Giddings in his list, and Giddings politely included Ward in his.) The famous 'Green Bible' of the Chicago School, Park and Burgess's (1924) *Introduction to the Science of Sociology*, listed twenty-three 'representative works in systematic sociology'. Simmel and Durkheim were among them but not Marx, Weber or Pareto. Only one work by Weber was mentioned in this thousand-page volume, and only in the notes.

As late as the 1920s, then, there was no sense that certain texts were discipline-defining classics demanding special study. Rather, there was a sense of a broad, almost impersonal advance of scientific knowledge; the notables being simply leading members of the pioneering crew. Sociologists accepted the view, articulated early in the history of the discipline by Charles Letourneau (1881: vi), who was to hold the first chair of sociology in the world, that: 'The commencement of any science, however simple, is always a collective work. It requires the constant labour of many patient workmen ...'

We have, therefore, strong reasons to doubt the conventional picture of the creation of sociology. This is not just to question the influence of certain individuals. We must examine the history of sociology as a collective product—the shared concerns, assumptions and practices making up the discipline at various times, and the shape given that history by the changing social forces that constructed the new science.

WHY IS CLASSICAL THEORY CLASSICAL? (1997)

Global difference and empire

Sociology as a teaching discipline and a public discourse was constructed in the final two decades of the nineteenth century and the first decade of the twentieth, in the great cities and university towns of France, the United States, Britain, Germany, and a little later, Russia. The internalist foundation story interprets these places as the site of a process of modernization, or capitalist industrialization, with sociology an attempt to interpret what was emerging here. 'It was above all a science of the new industrial society' (Bottomore 1987: 7).

The main difficulty with this view is that it does not square with the most relevant evidence—what sociologists at the time were writing. Most general textbooks of sociology, up to the First World War, did not have a great deal to say about the modernization of the society the authors lived in. Giddings' *Readings in Descriptive and Historical Sociology* (1906), typical in this respect, ranged from polyandry in Ceylon via matrilineal survivals among the Tartars to the mining camps of California. It was so little focussed on modernity that it took as its reading on 'sovereignty' a medieval rendering of the legend of King Arthur.

What is in college textbooks need not correspond to the research focus of sociology; but on this too we have abundant evidence. Between 1898 and 1913 Émile Durkheim and his hardworking collaborators produced twelve issues of *L'Année sociologique*, an extraordinarily detailed international survey of each year's publications in, or relevant to, sociology. In these twelve issues nearly 2400 reviews were published. [I have counted only the reviews in large type, whatever their length; not the brief notices in small type in the early issues, nor the listings of titles without reviews.] The reviews concerning Western/Northern Europe and modern North America increase with time: they average 24% of all reviews in the first six issues, 28% in the next five issues, and 32% in the bumper issue of the year before the War.

Modern industrial society was included: the journal published reviews about the American worker, the European middle class, technology in German industries, books by the Webbs and by Sombart, Booth on London poverty, even a work by Ramsay Macdonald, later Labour prime minister of Britain. But works focussed on the recent or contemporary societies of Europe and North America made up only a fraction of the content of *L'Année sociologique*: about 28% of all reviews. Even fewer were focussed on 'the new industrial society', since the reviews on Europe included treatises on peasant folk-tales, witchcraft in Scotland, crime in Asturias, and the measurements of skulls.

Twice as many of the reviews concerned ancient and medieval societies, colonial or remote societies, or global surveys of human history. Studies of holy war in ancient Israel, Malay magic, Buddhist India, technical points of Roman law, medieval vengeance, Aboriginal kinship in central Australia, and the legal systems of primitive societies, were more characteristic of sociology as seen in *L'Année sociologique* than studies of new technology or bureaucracy.

The enormous spectrum of human history that the sociologists took as their domain was organized by a central idea: difference between the civilization of the metropole and other cultures whose main feature was their primitiveness. I will call this the idea of global difference. Presented in many different forms, this contrast pervades the sociology of the late nineteenth and early twentieth centuries.

The idea of global difference was often conveyed by a discussion of 'origins'. In this genre of writing, sociologists would posit an original state of society, then speculate on the process of evolution that must have led from then to now. The bulk of the three volumes of Herbert Spencer's *Principles of Sociology*, first issued in the 1870s, told such a story for every type of institution that Spencer could think of: domestic institutions, political institutions, ecclesiastical institutions, and so on. Spencer acted as if the proof of social evolution was not complete without an evolutionary narrative, from origins to the contemporary form, for each and every case.

WHY IS CLASSICAL THEORY CLASSICAL? (1997)

The formula of development from a primitive origin to an advanced form was widespread in Victorian thought (Burrow 1966). Sociologists simply applied a logic that their audience would find familiar. The same architecture is found in works as well known as Durkheim's *The Division of Labor in Society* (1893) and as obscure as Fairbanks' *Introduction to Sociology* (1896).

In none of these works was the idea of an origin taken as a concrete historical question. It could have been, because knowledge of early societies was growing dramatically in these decades. Troy, Mycenae and Knossos were excavated by Schliemann and Evans. Flinders Petrie systematised the archaeology of Egypt, and the first evidence of Sumerian culture was uncovered at Lagash and Nippur (Stiebing 1993). But sociologists were not interested in where and when a particular originating event occurred, nor when the major changes actually happened. Time functioned in sociological thought mainly as a sign of global difference.

Durkheim did not have to find a precise time in the past for 'segmentary societies'; they existed in his own day. Durkheim used the example of the Kabyle of Algeria as well as the ancient Hebrews, and made no conceptual distinction between the two. He knew about the Hebrews because the ancient texts were in his library. How did he know about Kabylia? Because the French had conquered Algeria earlier in the century, and at the time Durkheim wrote, French colonists were evicting the local population from the best land (Bennoune 1988). Given the recent history of conquest, peasant rebellion, and debate over colonization, no French intellectual could fail to know something about the Kabyle. Indeed, the social life of France's North African subjects was being documented in great detail by a series of private and official enquiries (Burke 1980).

Algeria was not an isolated case. In the dozen years before *Division of Labour* was published, the armies of the French republic had moved out from Algeria to conquer Tunisia; had fought a war in Indo-China, conquered Annam and Tonkin (modern Vietnam) and seized control of Laos and Cambodia; and had established a protectorate over Madagascar. Under the Berlin Treaty of 1885, French trading-posts in central and western Africa became the basis of a whole new empire. While Durkheim was writing and publishing *The Division of Labor* and *The Rules of Sociological Method* (1895), French colonial armies were engaged in a spectacular series of campaigns against the Muslim regimes of inland north and west Africa which produced vast conquests from the Atlantic almost to the Nile.

All this was part of a larger process. The British empire, also a maritime empire with a pre-industrial history, similarly gained a new dynamism and grew to vast size in the nineteenth century (Cain & Hopkins 1993). The 13-colony United States became one of the most dynamic imperial powers of the nineteenth century, with about eighty years of overland conquest and settlement (the 'westward expansion'), followed by a shorter period of overseas conquest. The Tsarist overland conquests, begun in earlier centuries, were extended to north-east and central Asia. In the later part of the nineteenth century they were consolidated by Russian settlement. Prussia's expansion as an imperial power began with conquest within Europe—in the process, setting up a relationship between dominant and conquered races in the East which became the subject of the young Weber's first sociological research (Weber 1894). German overseas colonies in Africa and the Pacific followed the formation of the Reich in 1871. By the time the system of rival empires reached its crisis in the Great War of 1914–18, the expansion of Western power to a global scale had reached its climax.

In this light, the making of sociology takes a new significance. The places where the discipline was created were the urban and cultural centres of the major imperial powers at the high tide of modern imperialism. They were the 'metropole', in the useful French term, to the larger colonial world. The intellectuals who created sociology were very much aware of this.

Since Kiernan's (1969) remarkable survey *The Lords of Human Kind*, historians have begun to grasp the immense impact that the global expansion of North Atlantic power had on popular culture

(MacDonald 1994) and intellectual life (Said 1993) in the metropole, as well as in the colonies. It would be astonishing if the new science of society had escaped the impact of the greatest social change in the world at the time. In fact the relationship was intimate. Sociology was formed within the culture of imperialism, and embodied an intellectual response to the colonized world. This fact is crucial in understanding the content and method of sociology, as well as the discipline's wider cultural significance.

The content and method of sociology

As remarked by the civilized Arthur Todd (the first, and perhaps still the only, professor of sociology to introduce Japanese cherry-blossom paintings into a discussion of social theory):

> From Comte onward sociologists have pretty generally agreed that the only justification for a Science of Society is its contributions to a workable theory of progress. (Todd 1918: vii)

John Stuart Mill, the sharpest mind among all whose idea of social science was shaped by Comte, had cautioned against equating historical change with improvement (Mill 1843: 596). Few of the sociologists took heed. Spencer's first attempt at social theory, in *Social Statics* (1850), made moral improvement the touchstone of analysis of 'the social state'. Discovering and expounding laws of progress was the core of what sociology meant for the next two generations.

In Auguste Comte's writings the idea mostly had to do with the ancient-medieval-modern sequence within Western culture. Critics in the later nineteenth century rejected the arbitrariness of Comte's system and demanded an empirical base for the concept of progress.

This was the common ground between Spencer and Letourneau, and it is a fact of the greatest significance that both of these authors turned to the ethnographical dividend of empire as their main source of sociological data. Spencer's *Principles of Sociology* documented its evolutionary stories from the writings of European travellers, missionaries, settlers and colonial officials, as well as historians. For instance, Spencer's reference list for the section on 'Political Institutions' ranged from the journals of the north American explorers Lewis and Clarke, through the *Journal of the Asiatic Society of Bengal* and *Thirty-three years in Tasmania and Victoria*, to that riveting work, *A Phrenologist amongst the Todas*. Letourneau's *Sociology, Based upon Ethnography* (1881), while setting the facts out in a finer grid, was very similar in its sources.

By the time sociology was institutionalized in the final decade of the century, the central proof of progress, and therefore the main intellectual ground on which the new science rested, was the contrast of metropolitan and colonized societies. Sociologists did not debate the importance of this contrast. Rather, they debated how it should be interpreted—whether through physical evolution from lower to higher human types, or an evolution of mind and social forms; whether competition or cooperation was the motor of progress. In this context Durkheim's *The Division of Labor* was no founding text. It was a late intervention in a long-running debate.

The concern with progress was not a 'value' separable from the science; it was constitutive of sociological knowledge. The arguments of Ward, Hobhouse, Durkheim, Spencer and Comte himself are absurd if one does not presuppose the *reality* of progress. It was as an account of progress that sociology spread beyond the metropole. Spencer's sociology, for instance, was being debated in India well before the turn of the century, and in translation became a significant influence on the intellectuals of Meiji Japan and the Chinese republican movement (Tominaga 1994; Grieder 1981).

The topics addressed by the new discipline are revealing. A social science based on the social relations of empire must deal with race, and a social science concerned with evolutionary progress and hierarchies of populations must deal with gender and sexuality. And in fact, race, gender and sexuality *were* core issues in early sociology.

WHY IS CLASSICAL THEORY CLASSICAL? (1997)

When Du Bois proposed in 1901 that the color line was 'the problem of the twentieth century' he was saying nothing unusual for the time (Du Bois 1950: 281). Global difference was persistently interpreted in terms of race. Letourneau's 'ethnography' meant a science of racial differences, and his *Sociology* opened with an enumeration of the human races, with black, yellow and white distinguished by brain size. Ward (1897) was confident that global race conflict reflected the superiority of the European races and that universal progress was dependent on their universal triumph.

Here sociology reflected, in the most direct way, the social relations of imperialism. This is not to say that all sociologists were outright racists, though some certainly were (see Crozier 1911 for a toxic example). Others, Du Bois and Durkheim among them, suffered the effects of racism. The point is, rather, that racial hierarchy on a world scale was a perception built into the concept of 'progress', and was a central part of what sociology was thought to be about.

Nor was there any question about the importance of gender and sexuality. Comte in his *Système de politique positive* gave considerable prominence to the social role of women, and his famous conflict with Mill included sharp differences over the subjection of women. When Spencer came to write the substantive part of *The Principles of Sociology*, the very first set of institutions he addressed was the 'Domestic'. By this he meant what we now call gender issues: kinship, family, and the status of women. Letourneau treated marriage and the family before, and at greater length than, property. He dealt with sexuality ('the genesic need') near the start of *Sociology*, with an impressive absence of Victorian delicacy. Menstruation, infanticide, prostitution, promiscuity and sodomy were all on his agenda. In the next generation, Ward, Tönnies, Sumner and Thomas all continued the focus on sex and gender.

Some of this can be explained on internalist lines, through the influence of first-wave feminism (Paxton 1991). But the way gender and sexual issues were taken up in sociology was very much affected by evolutionary concerns and the issues of empire. In the imperial context, racial and sexual issues were not separate. In the later nineteenth century, the expansion of the North Atlantic powers was accompanied by a growing fear of miscegenation, a hardening color line, growing contempt of the colonizers for the sexuality or masculinity of the colonized (Sinha 1995), and fears of racial swamping. Echoes are heard even in the most abstract metropolitan texts. Giddings (1896: xiii), expounding his theme of 'consciousness of kind', remarked that 'Living creatures do not commonly mate with individuals of other than their own species', and his first example was: 'White men do not usually marry black women'.

The most striking feature of sociological method was its bold abstraction. Comte offered cultural 'laws' of vast scope; and the inaugural meeting of the American Sociological Society, sixty years later, was still celebrating tremendous 'laws' of social evolution. Durkheim argued convincingly that this approach was the basis of the whole enterprise: 'Comparative sociology is not a particular branch of sociology; it is sociology itself …' (Durkheim 1895: 139). The comparative method meant assembling examples of the particular social 'species' under study, and examining their variations.

This method rested on a one-way flow of information, a capacity to examine a range of societies from the outside, and an ability to move freely from one society to another—features which all map the relation of colonial domination. Letourneau expressed the sociological point of view in a striking image:

> Let us imagine an observer placed somewhere high up in air above our terrestrial equator, far enough from the globe on which we live to take in a whole hemisphere at one glance, and yet close enough to distinguish with the aid, if need be, of a magnifying-glass, the continents and the seas, the great ranges of mountains, the white frozen tops of the polar regions, etc. etc. (1881: 15)

The imperial gaze is particularly evident in broad surveys such as Spencer's *Descriptive Sociology* and the collective project of *L'Année sociologique*. Perhaps the most striking example was Hobhouse,

Wheeler and Ginsberg's *The Material Culture and Social Institutions of the Simpler Peoples* (1915), a late attempt to overcome the unsystematic use of data in theories of social evolution by providing a statistical base for comparative sociology. Hobhouse and his colleagues surveyed the whole world, collecting information on more than 500 societies. They classified societies by grade of economic development, and tried to establish correlations of development with institutional patterns of law, government, family, war and social hierarchy.

These surveys are virtually forgotten now, but the imperial gaze can also be found in familiar texts such as William Graham Sumner's *Folkways* (1906). The whole world and the whole of history was the field of attention. Few cases delayed the author for more than two sentences. For Sumner the force of the argument did not lie in the depth of his ethnographic understanding. It was provided by the assemblage itself, the synoptic view of human affairs from a great height.

The obvious risk here is incoherence. This problem could be overcome with a variant of the comparative method whose dramatic quality produced some of the best-remembered 'classical' texts. I call this approach grand ethnography, in contrast with the close-focus fieldwork of Franz Boas, W. E. B. Du Bois, or the French specialists on Algeria and Morocco. The usual style of grand ethnography was built on the idea of global difference. It presented holistic accounts of the societies found at the origin and the end of progress, on the understanding that 'In all its leading characteristics—political, legal, religious, economic—archaic society presents a complete contrast to that in which we live.' (Hearn 1878: 4)

The famous contrast of *Gemeinschaft* with *Gesellschaft* is grand ethnography in this sense, identifying polar states of society. Durkheim's *The Division of Labor* was a more rigorous grand ethnography, specifying the basis of the contrast in the division of labour. *L'Année sociologique* took a persistent interest in attempts to distinguish primitive from modern law, in German theories of

Naturvölker and their distinction from *Kulturvölker*, and in attempts to formulate the nature of primitive religion. Grand ethnography was the artistic climax of Comtean sociology, the literary form taken by the theory of progress as the rhetoric of the struggle for existence was bypassed.

Sociology in the political culture of empire

Late nineteenth and early twentieth century metropolitan society had several groups of intellectuals grappling with the analysis of society. The mobilization of European and American workers had produced one intellectual ferment, the mobilization of women produced another. The claim that Harriet Martineau was the 'first woman sociologist' (Hoecker-Drysdale 1992) is anachronistic, but the story of Martineau—novelist, political economist, translator of Comte, travel writer, and reformer—should alert us to the complexity of the milieu in which sociology arose.

Beyond the metropole, there were many intellectuals in these decades who looked at modernity from the standpoint of non-European cultures, and at Europeans from the standpoint of the colonized. Changes in culture and social life were central issues to writers as diverse as al-Afghani in the Islamic middle east, Chatterjee and Tagore in Bengal, and Sun Yat-sen (1927) in China.

From these groups a range of discourses about society emerged, of which sociology was only one. The anarchist Bakunin (1873), criticising Comte on one side and Marx on the other, recognized astonishingly early that a 'science of society' might rationalize the interests of a particular group. Following Bakunin's lead, we should consider the social location in which sociology developed, and the cultural issues to which it was a response.

Sociology developed in a specific social location: among the men of the metropolitan liberal bourgeoisie. Those who wrote sociology were a mixture of engineers and doctors, academics, journalists, clerics, and a few who (like Weber after his breakdown) could live on their family capital.

This is not to say that the sociologists were, generally speaking, either rich or apologists for the rich. Ross (1991) points to the social distance between the academic makers of American sociology and the capitalist entrepreneurs of American industrialization. Weber was a fierce critic of the ruling class of the German Reich, and Durkheim was no friend of the French aristocracy. Nevertheless they were beneficiaries of both class and gender hierarchies. Most lived modest bourgeois lives, supported by the domestic labor of women in patriarchal households. Their social interests were well captured by Comte's slogan 'Order and Progress'.

Men of this sort began to discuss 'the Social Science', as Mill called it, from the 1850s on, in a diffuse movement to apply scientific thinking to society and promote moral improvement. A successful Association for the Promotion of Social Science was set up in London as early as 1857 (Burrow 1966), soon copied in Boston. The same movement produced a heavily moralized 'social science' curriculum in American colleges from the 1860s (Bernard & Bernard 1943). Individual attempts to synthesize the facts of primitive life and social progress, such as Edward Tylor's *Primitive Culture* (1873), counterpointed attempts to establish institutes to formulate a science of man. The latter, in France, gave rise to the first academic chair to be named 'sociology', to which Letourneau was appointed in 1885 (Clark 1973).

In the 1890s social science curricula in American colleges, already fissuring, began to be replaced by more self-consciously scientific courses called 'sociology'. Their claim to scientificity was closely connected with the shift to comparative method and imperial gaze discussed above. Hence the world-spanning content of the first generation of sociology textbooks. Named sociology departments were established, undergraduate courses multiplied, and a market for textbooks rapidly developed (Morgan 1983).

Europe was a little slower to set up departments of sociology, but quicker with associations and journals. By the outbreak of the Great War, sociological societies, journals of sociology, and university courses in sociology, were established institutions in most metropolitan countries. International links were built up, for instance through Worms' *Institut International de Sociologie*, launched in 1893; through visits both ways across the North Atlantic; and through the journals. These provided a practical basis for sociology to develop as an international cultural formation. Historians who emphasise the distinctness of national traditions of sociology (e.g. Levine 1995) under-estimate the extent to which scholars of the period saw themselves as part of an international academic milieu, and conceived of sociology as a universal science.

Overlapping the academic initiatives was a genre of popular sociological writing. A text like Benjamin Kidd's *Social Evolution* could be a considerable best-seller. Within four years of its publication in 1894 this book had gone through 14 printings in England, and had American, German, Swedish, French, Russian and Italian editions.

Sociological thought first circulated as part of the uplifting and informative literature consumed by a new educated reading public who read novelists like Dickens and Eliot, cultural critics like Ruskin and Arnold, and scientists like Darwin and Huxley. Sociology circulated through the same channels as these writers. Thus, Spencer's *The Study of Sociology* (1873) was first published in instalments in magazines, the *Contemporary Review* in Britain and the *Popular Science Monthly* in the United States. It was then issued in book form in a new popular education collection called the 'International Scientific Series'. Spencer's *Principles of Sociology*, an integral part of the vast survey of human knowledge which he called the 'Synthetic Philosophy', was first issued in instalments to subscribers, the first volume coming out in ten parts over three years, while Spencer was writing it.

The relationship between writers and readers was thus far more intimate than professional sociological writing later became.

WHY IS CLASSICAL THEORY CLASSICAL? (1997)

Lepenies (1988) has suggested that European sociology was culturally positioned 'between literature and science', but that exaggerates the contrast. Science too was ethically and politically charged. Darwin, for instance, long hesitated to publish his work on evolution because he knew its religious and political consequences (Desmond & Moore 1992). Sociologists were expected as scientists to provide moral and political teaching. Their teaching especially addressed the dilemma that was inescapable for men of the liberal bourgeoisie: the tension between material privilege and reforming principle.

Nineteenth-century liberalism was itself a complex movement. It was often at odds with radical and democratic movements. But in liberal struggles against the Ancien Régime, commitments were forged which L. T. Hobhouse, recently appointed to the first chair of sociology in England, rousingly declared in his *Liberalism* (1911): civil liberty and the rule of law, fiscal liberty, personal liberty, social liberty, economic liberty, domestic liberty, local, racial and national liberty, international liberty, political liberty and popular sovereignty. These remained culturally powerful beliefs in the public addressed by sociology.

These commitments were challenged by the class and gender inequalities of the metropole (Therborn 1976; Deegan 1988), and even more severely challenged by empire. As Ranajit Guha (1989: 277) observed, the universalising project of bourgeois culture reached its limit in colonialism. Concepts of liberty, rights, and independence were plainly, repeatedly, and brutally violated by what the North Atlantic states were doing all over the world to the colonized.

Sociology, the science of progress that claimed the world as its province and used so extensively the data of empire, was positioned squarely in this contradiction. And it offered a resolution. Sociology displaced imperial power over the colonized into an abstract space of difference. The comparative method and grand ethnography deleted the actual practice of colonialism from the intellectual world built on the gains of empire.

The relation between the imperial powers and the conquered was most directly addressed by the Darwinian wing of Comtean sociology (Spencer, Sumner, Ward, Hobhouse, Kidd, and fringe figures like Crozier). They addressed it by constructing a fiction of 'social evolution' which naturalized global difference. It is no wonder that Spencer became immensely popular in the colonies of settlement, where the idea of the evolutionary superiority of the settlers replaced missionary religion as the main justification of empire.

This was despite the fact that Spencer was personally opposed to imperial conquest. Spencer sharply denounced 'the diabolical cruelties committed by the invading Europeans' in America, the South Seas and elsewhere. Like Gladstone—with whom he discussed the question—Spencer saw forcible conquest as a sign of militarism. But he had no such objection to peaceable settlement and economic competition. In the same passages it is clear he regarded the colonized as 'inferior races', likely to lose out in evolutionary competition (Spencer 1873: 212; Duncan 1908: 224). Even Hobhouse (1911: 43), in full flight expounding the principles of liberalism, blurred them in the case of empire by wondering if the black races were capable of self-rule.

In other writers there was no distance at all between naturalizing progress and justifying empire. The climax of Kidd's *Social Evolution* was a justification for rule of the tropical regions of the world—now languishing under the maladministration of 'the black and coloured races'—by the more progressive peoples of European extraction. Kidd's reconciliation of imperial rule with his belief that natural selection tended towards more religious and ethical conduct, epitomizes the ideological work done by sociology.

The resolution which sociology offered to the dilemmas of liberalism claimed the status of science. Mill and Comte had insisted programmatically that sociology must promulgate 'laws'. This task was accepted by both academic and popular writers in sociology. Legitimacy for laws of progress was provided by the prestige of geology and evolutionary biology. Accordingly, treatises on sociology often expounded organic evolution, and might even start with the evolution of the stars and the solar system (e.g. Ward 1897).

This conception of laws of progress enabled sociology to conflate the problems of empire with the problems of the metropole. The 'social science' of the 1860s and 1870s embraced the social tensions of the metropole as ethical and practical problems. Questions of poverty, class struggle and social amelioration—'the social question' in the terminology of the day—also came on the agenda of the sociological societies and journals in the 1890s and 1900s. In cities such as London, Chicago and Paris there was significant contact and overlap between academic sociologists, Fabian socialists, feminists, progressive liberals, religious and ethical reformers, and social workers (Besnard 1983; Deegan 1988).

What The Social Science contributed to The Social Question was an interpretation of metropolitan problems in the light of an over-arching theory of progress. A characteristic example was the discussion of socialism found in many treatises of sociology. The universal approach of sociologists was to evaluate the goals of the workers' movement in terms of their own model of evolutionary progress—whether the conclusion was endorsement of a mild ethical socialism (as by Hobhouse, Durkheim and Small) or robust rejection (as by Spencer and Sumner).

The crisis and remaking of sociology

[Here followed a section sketching the collapse of evolutionary sociology around the time of World War I, eclipse under fascism and Stalinism, and the remaking of sociology in US universities. It was remade not as a world-spanning meta-discipline but as one among several social sciences, the one that specialised in social difference and problems of order within the global metropole. In this shrunken form, sociology struggled for legitimacy.]

The new concept of sociology and the new origin story

In this conceptual vacuum—as Hinkle (1994: 339) aptly describes the situation after the collapse of evolutionism—the formation of the classical canon began. A condition for this development was a change in sociology's audience. The late Victorian liberal reading public was no more. However the enormous wealth being accumulated in the United States made possible for the first time in history a mass higher education system. Here sociology expanded tremendously in the three decades after World War II (Turner & Turner 1990). A mass audience of students required a teacher training program, which was provided by expanding sociology PhD programs. It was in this milieu, and at this moment, that the pedagogy of classical texts developed.

The crucial step was taken in Talcott Parsons' *The Structure of Social Action* (1937). Parsons was not the first North American theorist to address the intellectual disintegration of sociology (Turner & Turner 1990: 71ff.), but there is no denying the genius of his solution. Parsons purged sociology's history, acknowledging the collapse of the Comtean agenda. He took the empirical problem of post-crisis sociology, difference and disorder in the metropole, and made it the theoretical centre of the discipline (the 'Hobbesian problem of order'). Parsons' later work, establishing the idea of a 'social system', provided a method for thinking the society of the metropole as a self-contained unit. Parsons was no historian and did not claim to be writing the history of sociology. But his reconstruction of the 'emergence' of a social-action model in the theoretical logic of Marshall, Pareto, Weber and Durkheim was understandably read as an origin narrative, and this story created norms for the discipline (Camic 1989).

A canonical view still had to be established against other accounts of sociology. Parsons' vision, however, acquired powerful allies. In his very widely read *The Sociological Imagination*, C. Wright Mills (1959) constructed a composite image of 'the classic social analyst' which he held up as a model of how sociology ought to be done. 'Classical sociology' to Mills was a style of work more than a period—though he conveyed a definite sense that it was more practiced in the past, and included Marx, Weber and Durkheim among his examples. A canonical view was also reinforced by theorists wishing to establish a particular issue as significant. For instance Merton's (1949) account of anomie helped establish Durkheim as classic.

The translation into English of the main European texts incorporated into the canon was accomplished between 1930 and 1950, and a literature of commentary appeared. Levine (1995: 63) aptly remarks of the 1960s and 1970s that 'fresh translations, editions, and secondary analyses of classic authors became one of the faster-growing industries within sociology'. Bendix's very widely read *Max Weber: An Intellectual Portrait* was issued in 1960. Coser's *The Functions of Social Conflict* (1956) was in large part a commentary on Simmel. North American interest even helped to create a Weber revival in German sociology 'after a period of inattention to its classical past', as Lüschen (1994: 11) tactfully put it. German sociologists held a celebration of Weber at their national conference in 1964.

Platt (1995), in a brilliant study of the North American reception of Durkheim, rightly observes the complexity of influences behind the choice of founding fathers: broad historical circumstance, particular academic entrepreneurs or departments, affinity with current trends in the profession. These factors seem to have worked for Weber and Durkheim but against Parsons' other nominee, Pareto. Though Pareto was even more eligible as a systematic theorist, his irony and pessimism were perhaps too obtrusive for his texts to work as foundations for the revived discipline.

The changes are most dramatic in the case of Marx. To Parsons in *The Structure of Social Action* he was part of the background, essentially a minor utilitarian. Some American textbooks of sociology in the 1940s and 1950s got along without any attention to Marx at all. But Marxism remained a force in global culture. It became, for instance, the key intellectual influence in African politics in the decades of decolonization. A progressive American sociologist at this time could find an important resource here. In best canon-making style, Mills issued a collection of Marxist texts, with commentary, in 1962.

However Marx did not become a full-fledged Founding Father in sociology until the discipline's expansion in the 1960s and the radicalization of metropolitan university students. The 'radical sociology' proposed by the US student movement centered on Marx and Marxists (Horowitz 1971), and academic sociology responded. In 1965 the American Sociological Association annual meeting included a plenary session called 'A Re-Evaluation of Karl Marx'. Marx now assumed a more prominent place in accounts of the history of sociological theory (Bottomore & Nisbet 1978), and appeared more often in textbooks for undergraduates. A sociological literature of commentary on Marx multiplied.

The trinity of Marx, Durkheim and Weber was, thus, a late development in the construction of the canon. Durkheim and Weber were the survivors of the canon-making enterprise of Parsons' generation, Marx was grafted on in the next generation, and other candidates fell by the wayside. The trio appears in the role of The Founding Fathers in elementary textbooks in the 1970s (e.g. McGee 1977). In theoretical sociology, a considerable effort of interpretation now tried to make sense of the Marx–Durkheim–Weber grouping as creators of a theory of modernity (e.g. Giddens 1971; Alexander 1982–83).

In most other countries that could afford to have sociology, the discipline was created or re-made in the 1950s and 1960s on the basis of research techniques, research problems and theoretical languages, not to mention textbooks and instructors, from the United States. (For example Japan: Tominaga 1994; Australia: Baldock & Lally 1974; Scandinavia: Allardt 1994.) With the reconstructed discipline came its reconstructed foundation story. Thus world sociology arrived at the situation described in the opening paragraphs of this paper.

WHY IS CLASSICAL THEORY CLASSICAL? (1997)

Reflection

I have argued that the classical canon in sociology was created, mainly in the United States, as part of an effort at reconstruction after the collapse of the first European–American project of sociology; that a new foundation story replaced earlier and very different accounts of the making of sociology; and that this whole course of events can only be understood in the framework of global history, especially the history of imperialism.

In one sense this does not matter; the retrospectively chosen classics actually have little to do with the creative impulses of modern sociology. But the symbolic power of 'classical sociology' remains, and generates distorted pictures of the history of sociology, and of the scope and value of sociology. Nisbet's (1967) list of the 'unit-ideas of sociology' (community, authority, status, the sacred, alienation) was a travesty of history, but had some plausibility as a map of the narrowed territory left after the canon-making was in full swing. Above all, the internalist story directs sociology's attention away from analyses of the social world that come from intellectuals beyond the metropole.

Better connections *have* been made. As Burke (1980) shows, at the very time Durkheim and his colleagues were building the imperial gaze into their sociology, other French social scientists engaged intellectuals of the Islamic world in dialogue about modernity, colonialism and culture. In the same generation, Du Bois moved from a focus on race relations within the United States to a strongly internationalist perspective, with particular attention to Africa. In the first half of the 20th century, black African intellectuals such as Sol Plaatje and Jomo Kenyatta dialogued with the metropole through social science as well as political struggle. The mainstream of metropolitan sociology made little use of such contacts; but this other history is also real, and we need to build on it today.

11

Social science on a world scale (2015)

THE ACCOUNT OF sociology's origin in 'Why is classical theory classical?' was sometimes described as a critique of the 'orientalism' of sociology. There is certainly a parallel with Edward Said's critique of literary and academic visions of the colonised world in his 1978 book *Orientalism*. And like Said's masterpiece, it opened the question of what alternatives can be found. Can we have social science that speaks to major issues without Eurocentric bias, without the concepts, methods or narratives that validate Empire?

I thought it was possible; more, that many examples already existed—though mostly outside of academic discourse. They were the work of intellectuals in colonial and postcolonial societies, in many genres and from all parts of the colonised world. For years I searched for their texts and backgrounds, haunting libraries and second-hand bookshops and pestering colleagues in many countries for advice. At the same time I was trying to understand recent social science from the metropole in terms of its own, unstated, geopolitical context. The two projects simmered together. At a certain point I felt, once again, there was a significant story to tell. It was told in *Southern Theory*, published in 2007.

SOCIAL SCIENCE ON A WORLD SCALE (2015)

This book, too, caught a wave, and one that has kept moving. Other people were working along similar lines, including Farid Alatas, in Singapore, whose excellent *Alternative Discourses in Asian Social Science* was published in 2006. More attention was being paid to the decolonial school of philosophers, to the legacy of Black intellectuals such as WEB Du Bois and CLR James, and to contemporary voices from diasporas in the global North. The work has continued, made more urgent by student movements challenging racism in universities, and by calls to decolonise curricula and workforces.

Higher education was now a global industry and increasingly profit-driven. In 2013 the ham-fisted tactics of corporate-style managers provoked a major strike at the University of Sydney, and I found myself, with the rest of the union, on the picket line. There were alternative ideas about how university work could be done. These became themes of my book *The Good University*, published in 2019.

The struggle pushed me to think more concretely about knowledge work. Postcolonial and decolonial literature discussed ideas, cultures and epistemes. But here also were organisations, workforces, funding streams, divisions of labour, exports and imports, state interventions. These were issues in the research I undertook with Fran Collyer, João Maia and Robert Morrell about the making of new fields of knowledge, published in 2019 as *Knowledge and Global Power*.

In short, we needed an account of the global economy of knowledge, and this chapter is one of my attempts to formulate it. The essay was published in 2015 in *Sociologies in Dialogue*, a new English-language journal established by the Sociedade Brasileira di Sociologia. The journal itself was a contribution to the change we need.

A personal introduction

Around 1968, at the Free University in Sydney, an ambitious research project on class in Australian history was launched by two young scholars, Terry Irving and Raewyn Connell. Free U was an experimental education and research centre set up by activists in the Australian student movement, dedicated to exploring radical questions that the mainstream universities mostly ignored. Free U lasted only a few years, but the research project on class continued. A decade later, its main findings were published in a book *Class Structure in Australian History* (Connell & Irving 1980), which was quite popular for a while. It tried to show, with a wealth of documentary evidence, the distinctive pattern of class formation and class conflict in the settler-colonial society of Australia.

Just a couple of years before we began this project, two radical scholars wrote a book on the distinctive patterns of class formation and class conflict in the postcolonial societies of Latin America. F. H. Cardoso and Enzo Faletto's *Dependencia y desarollo en América Latina*, written in 1966–67 and first published in 1969, was an even more ambitious project, continental in scope. It became a much bigger best-seller, with thirty printings by the time Cardoso ended his term as President of Brasil.

Three things are of interest here. First is the fact that similar intellectual projects could arise at very different points on the global periphery at almost the same time. Both were genuinely innovative, in terms of class analysis in the 1960s—not to mention the conventions of mainstream sociology at the time.

Second is the fact that these projects were entirely unconnected with each other. I doubt that Cardoso and Faletto ever came in contact with Australian social research. At the same time no-one on the Australian left, unless they had personal ties with Latin America, had even heard of CEPAL, the economic think-tank where Cardoso and Faletto worked at the time, celebrated for its critique of dependency and its advocacy of import-replacement industrialization—even though Australia was pursuing a similar strategy at the time. I first heard of their work much later, via English-language translations published in the United States.

Third is the fact that neither project found a connection with the radical class analysis of postcolonial societies being made in the same generation on other continents. Notable work was being done about South African class dynamics during the anti-Apartheid struggles (Wolpe 1972). Notable research was also done in post-independence India. One branch of this became famous, when *Subaltern Studies* was canonized as 'postcolonial studies' in the universities of the global North. Yet Ranajit Guha's (1989) powerful critique of Gramscian models of hegemony as applied to colonial situations, emphasising that colonialism always rested on force, has still not had the impact it should have on class analysis worldwide. The cultural turn in class analysis in the global North has, in fact, moved thinking in the opposite direction—for instance through the influence of Bourdieu's confused concept of 'cultural capital'.

We can lament lost opportunities for connection. But more important, we should analyze *why* the opportunities were lost. Why were the new pages of social science being written around the global South not connected, or only connected via the global North? And what alternatives do we have?

Those questions were addressed in my book *Southern Theory* (Connell 2007), but only in a limited way. I have come to think that a fuller answer requires a new sociology of knowledge, conceived on a world scale. The task of this paper is to outline some elements of this sociology of knowledge, as it affects the making of social science itself.

The global economy of knowledge

A key contribution has been made by the Beninese philosopher Paulin Hountondji (1994), who identifies the problem not as the simple imposition of 'Western' perspectives on the postcolonial world, but as a global division of labour in the production of knowledge, with its roots in imperialism.

The conquest of the world by European (and then North American) power, over the 500 years of modern empire and globalization, not only produced material wealth for the imperial powers. It also produced a rich dividend of knowledge. The colonized world was a fabulous mine of information for European science, across the spectrum from astronomy and geology through biology to the humanities and social sciences. Figures as famous as Charles Darwin and Alexander von Humboldt shared in the collecting, though most was done by humbler colonial officials, missionaries and military forces, and eventually by specialized knowledge workers. As I have shown elsewhere, the assembling of information from colonized societies was a key to the formation of sociology as a discipline (Connell 1997; Steinmetz 2013).

The information was assembled in the museums, libraries, scientific societies, universities, botanic gardens, research institutes, and government agencies of what we now call the global North. This was not just a matter of the imperial centre exercising its greater wealth and power. The process produced a structural division of labour, that is still deeply embedded in modern knowledge systems. The colonized world was, first and foremost, a source of *data*. The metropole, where data from different parts of the colonized world were aggregated, became the site of the *theoretical* moment in knowledge production.

Data were classified, and intellectual structures built and debated, in the knowledge institutions of the metropole. Here two key developments occurred. One was the formalization and routinization of research *methods*, a key dimension of theoretical work. The other was the creation of specialized *workforces* for producing and circulating knowledge, the modern collective intellectual worker (Connell 2019). This process was increasingly centred in universities, with the spread of the German model of a research university, transferred to the United States by the end of the nineteenth century.

In Northern institutions, research was further transformed into applied sciences such as engineering, agronomy and medicine. In this applied form, knowledge was returned to the global periphery. Here it was used by colonial powers, and later by postcolonial states, in the mines, in agriculture, and in government. Applications of global-North science became central to the ideology of 'development' in the second half of the twentieth century.

In our time, the periphery continues to be a rich source of raw materials for the knowledge economy as for the material economy. The global periphery produces data for the new biology, pharmaceuticals, astronomy, social science, linguistics, archaeology, and much more. It is, for instance, a key source of data for modern climate science, as shown in the famous reports of the IPCC, the Intergovernmental Panel on Climate Change. But the metropole continues to be the main recognized site of theoretical processing, now including corporate research institutes and giant databanks.

In this economy of knowledge, intellectual workers in the global periphery are pushed towards a particular cultural and intellectual stance. Hountondji calls this 'extraversion': being oriented to authority external to your own society. In south-east Asia the sociologist Hussein Alatas (1974) called it, less politely, 'academic dependency'.

This stance is familiar to all academics in the periphery. Whatever the discipline, one *must* read the leading journals published in the metropole, and know and cite the leading theorists in the metropole. One must learn and apply the research methods taught in the metropole. Successful career paths include advanced training in the metropole, attending conferences in the metropole, and for the more successful, getting jobs in the metropole. To gain status at home, the most direct method is to gain recognition in the metropole, by publishing in global-North journals. Thus the intellectual frameworks developed in the metropole become embedded in the intellectual work of the periphery—not by imposing direct control, but by the way the whole economy of knowledge is organized.

The problem is not that local content is absent from the research and writing done in the global South. The problem is that local reality is methodically reduced to the status of a 'case' framed by metropolitan concepts. The typical social-science article from the periphery, even when published in a local journal, combines local data or examples with concepts drawn from one or other theorist from the metropole, whether Latour, Foucault, Bourdieu, Butler, Marx, or Habermas. This combination practically defines good practice for social scientists in the periphery.

The pressure to think and write this way has intensified in the neoliberal era. Corporate-style managers in the university sector have introduced an apparatus of performance management, audits, performance indicators and 'league tables'. There is particular pressure to publish in the 'top' journals, which means, necessarily, joining the debates and using the methods recognized in those journals. And surprise! The top journals in the league tables are almost all published in the United States or western Europe. Sociology is no exception: the top 20 journals in the ISI rankings for sociology *all* come from the USA or UK.

Some Northern scholarship about globalization has declared that the distinction of global North from global South is an obsolete binary. Rather there are complex and multidirectional flows and a system without a centre. One recognizes the good intention of such arguments, to acknowledge global complexity and move beyond colonialist stereotypes.

But the facts of gross world economic inequalities, disproportionate military and state power, the transnational corporate economy, and the hierarchical practices of knowledge institutions, remain. (For evidence of continuing hierarchies in knowledge see Collyer 2014; Collyer et al. 2019.) There are large inequalities within the metropole and within the periphery, too. The global economy is a dynamic and often turbulent affair. It does not produce a simple dichotomy. It does produce massive structures of centrality and marginality, whose main axis is the metropole-periphery, North-South relationship.

Recognizing this is crucial to understanding the global politics of theory in social science. Priority for theory produced in the metropole, and marginality for anything of the sort from the periphery, is the *normal functioning* of the global economy of knowledge. Innovations in Latin America, Africa, India or Australia, indeed anywhere outside the metropole, are normally not known to each other until they are adopted and publicized in the global North.

Critiques and alternatives

This situation is no secret, and it is under criticism from different directions. The rise of 'post-colonial studies' in the global North is only one of the currents of critique. Other currents include the 'decolonial' movement, the exploration of alternative traditions in social science and the possibility of postcolonial sociology (Reuter & Villa 2010), indigenous knowledge and the decolonization of methodology, and research on Southern theory, the social analyses produced in colonial and postcolonial societies.

The most clear-cut alternative is provided by the idea of indigenous knowledge. Except where colonization involved absolute genocide, elements of pre-colonization knowledge survived, and in principle offer a standpoint independent of metropolitan hegemony. This has been most vigorously endorsed in Africa (see the discussions in Odora Hoppers 2002), but similar arguments for indigenous knowledge are found in North and South America, in Australia, and elsewhere. The de-colonial school (Mignolo 2007) often comes close to this, proposing a politics of knowledge based on absolute opposition between the colonizing culture and the colonized.

Indigenous knowledge movements present a powerful critique of the imperialist structure of knowledge in mainstream social science, where colonized peoples are still treated as the objects of knowledge. Linda Tuhiwai Smith's influential book *Decolonizing Methodologies* (1999/2012), based on Maori struggles for cultural survival in Aotearoa New Zealand, shows how colonized people can become the subjects of their own knowledge projects and educational practices.

Indigenous knowledge projects generally assume what might be called a mosaic epistemology. In this model, separate knowledge systems sit beside each other like tiles in a mosaic, each based on a specific culture or historical experience, and each having its own claims to validity. Mosaic epistemology offers a clear alternative to Northern hegemony and global inequality, replacing the priority of one knowledge system with respectful relations among many.

However a mosaic approach also faces major difficulties. They were pointed out by Bibi Bakare-Yusuf (2004) in her careful critique of Oyeronke Oyewumi's *The Invention of Women* (1997). Bakare-Yusuf argues that cultures and societies are dynamic, not fixed in one posture. Pre-colonial societies in Africa were not silos, but interacted with each other over long periods of time, absorbed outside influences, and had internal diversity. These arguments are reinforced when we recognize the massive disruption of existing societies by colonialism and postcolonial power. Much contemporary research outside the metropole is done in conditions where 'relative chaos, gross economic disparities, displacement, uncertainty and surprise' are the *norm* not the exception (Bennett 2008: 7).

The indigenous-knowledge retort to the imperialism of Western knowledge has had a political impact, with consequences not always happy. The attempt in South Africa to combat the HIV/AIDS epidemic by using local healing practices in place of antiretroviral drugs, rather than making these approaches mutually supporting, was a devastating mistake that cost many lives (Cullinan & Thom 2009). Hountondji is one who is critical of a silo approach to indigenous knowledge. His concept of 'endogenous knowledge' emphasises active processes of knowledge production that arise in indigenous and colonized societies, and have a capacity to speak beyond them. The emphasis is communication not separation (Hountondji 1994, 2002).

The concept of postcolonial communication, that is, new kinds of connection between knowledge projects in the postcolonial world, is at the centre of other discussions too. For instance it is the key issue in Chilla Bulbeck's (1998) discussion of global feminisms. It is also vital to Gurminder Bhambra's (2014) agenda for 'connected sociologies'.

It is, of course, important to establish that there *are* different sociologies to connect! It matters that we are not all producing local variants of the same product—though that is what defenders of mainstream sociology believe. An important step here is the historical documentation of multiple traditions in social science. They are clearly presented by Sujata Patel in her *The ISA Handbook of Diverse Sociological Traditions* (2010), and by Farid Alatas in his *Alternative Discourses in Asian Social Science* (2006). As João Maia (2011) shows in the case of Brasil, intellectuals of the settler/creole populations also produced social knowledge that had different themes and sensibilities from those of European social science.

This work provides important evidence of the heterogeneity of social knowledge projects around the postcolonial world. It is not just a matter of intensely local knowledge systems embedded in local cultures. Farid Alatas, for instance, shows how the universalism of Islamic thought gave rise to powerful social theories—his key example is the *Muqaddimah* of Ibn Khaldun—which have applications far beyond their place of birth (Alatas 2014).

Yet the framing of the issue in terms of 'diversity' or 'alternatives' still leaves us with a problem: the overwhelming, and indeed *growing*, authority of the global-North 'alternative'. The hegemonic knowledge formation is much more than just another option.

Here the contribution of the decolonial theorists is important. Walter Mignolo (2007) in particular has emphasised that European modernity was formed within imperialism. Aníbal Quijano (2000) developed the important concept of the 'coloniality of power', the institutionalized orientation towards the metropole that persists in colonies even after formal independence. From this idea many have inferred the coloniality of knowledge. Connecting social knowledge from different parts of the world requires a profound *critique* of the Northern-centred global economy of knowledge, and of the processes that produced it and now sustain it.

The exploration of 'Southern theory' starts with this critique *and* the realization that there are alternatives (Connell 2007; Epstein

& Morrell 2012). It can be shown that key categories of Northern social science arise from the experience of the societies of the global metropole and their position in the history of imperialism. These produce characteristic moves in Northern social theory, which I have called the claim of universality, reading from the centre, gestures of exclusion, and the grand erasure of colonialism itself (Connell 2006). Such patterns can be found even in specialised areas of social science. Helen Meekosha (2011), for instance, shows how they have distorted the social-science analysis of disability. Questions about disability look very different when seen on a world scale, prioritising the experience of the colonized.

This critique leads to a view of the history of social science that differs from the familiar tale of European founding fathers and the global diffusion of their ideas. We need to focus, rather, on the *exclusion* of the social knowledge produced in the periphery, that is to say, in colonial societies responding to the consequences of colonization.

Colonized peoples tried to understand what was happening to them. Of course they did! They had their own cultural and intellectual traditions to draw from, as well as the ideas of the colonizers, and the very distinctive experience of *being colonized*. The Southern-theory approach frontally denies the assumption in the mainstream economy of knowledge that powerful theory is only produced in the metropole. From colonized peoples, from settler populations, from postcolonial societies grappling with dependence, violence, and new forms of exploitation, have emerged a wealth of social knowledge. This knowledge contains a strong component of theory, meaning concepts, methodologies, intellectual framings and agendas.

Southern theory is often formulated in different genres from those of Northern academic social science. The resources of Northern universities, especially research universities, were almost never available in the colonial world and not often in the postcolonial world. Yet only a very blinkered view of knowledge would deny the power and originality of thinkers like Heleieth Saffioti, Ashis Nandy, Paulin Hountondji, Samir Amin, Ali Shariati, Celso Furtado, Bina Agarwal,

Achille Mbembe, or collectives such as CEPAL, CODESRIA or the *Subaltern Studies* group, to mention only a few. There is a tremendous resource here to build on.

Workforce and labour process

The discussions just mentioned have been conducted at the level of ideas, texts and discourses. But a sociology of knowledge must be concerned also with the social circumstances in which these ideas are formed and distributed, the social institutions that support (or fail to support) them, the practices of knowledge-making, teaching and learning. These issues too must now be thought through on a global scale.

The first questions concern the intellectual workforce concerned with research-based knowledge. In the university sector, this workforce includes academics, as teachers and researchers, including trainee academics or graduate students (who by some calculations produce about half the knowledge that comes out of universities). But it also involves the non-academic staff, the technical, administrative, maintenance and professional workers whose daily work sustains the teaching and research effort (Connell 2019). Closely related to the university world is a similar workforce in corporate and state research centres, and in hybrid public/private institutions like the Fundação Getulio Vargas in Brasil.

Outside the mainstream economy of knowledge, large institutions are not so dominant. Indigenous knowledge projects are based on decentralized communities that are often very poor. Social movements too may be important producers of ideas and information. Millie Thayer (2010), in a discussion of how ideas and language circulate in feminist activism, has argued that a worldwide 'counter-public', vast and heterogeneous, is constituted by social movement activists, academics, women's organizations, even state and development agency staff. In poorer parts of the developing world, including sub-Saharan Africa, a large part of all social research is produced by

NGOs or by their contract workers, often funded on a small scale by development aid money (Mkandawire 2005).

Several forces have been re-shaping these workforces. The worldwide growth of literacy and the spread of formal education, especially among women, have produced many more actors capable of joining the mainstream knowledge economy. That also means more who are capable of participating in alternative knowledge projects with international reach, such as Islamic feminism.

But other conditions too have changed. The spread of corporate power and the dismantling of developmental states in favour of global market forces has taken resources out of public-sector knowledge projects, and has produced more economic insecurity among knowledge workers. Budget cuts for public universities are a familiar example, and these cuts have not yet reached a limit. The conversion of social movements into NGOs has both formalized alternative knowledge projects and tended to make them less ambitious. In the corporatized world, 'accountability' and 'best practice' in knowledge work usually mean reproducing established Northern-derived research paradigms.

We also need to consider the raw materials of knowledge and how they are used and transformed. In the mainstream economy of knowledge there has been a tendency towards formalizing the data themselves, so the whole analysis is conducted in an abstracted way. In economics, currently the most honoured and influential of the social sciences, statistical analysis and mathematical modelling are central. In sociology, it is noticeable that the *American Sociological Review*, the top journal in global league tables, has a strong preference for statistical analyses of large sets of abstracted data, whatever the topic might be. The style of social science that C. Wright Mills (1959) called 'abstracted empiricism' is not just alive and well, but extremely prestigious.

Yet mathematics as an intellectual tool is not automatically conservative. As Maggie Walter and Chris Andersen show in *Indigenous Statistics* (2016), these methods can be re-purposed for struggles within the settler-colonial state. Indigenous communities can assert data sovereignty and use statistical techniques in defending themselves and claiming resources. This is not indigenous knowledge in traditional form, but it is a strategy of knowledge production relevant to survival and flourishing in the neo-colonial world.

Thomas Piketty in his celebrated *Capital in the Twenty-First Century* (2014) laments the absence of standardized income distribution data sets from much of the world; he excuses the Eurocentrism of his project on this ground. There are nevertheless many attempts at worldwide abstracted data collection, commercial, academic and official. A notable example comes from educational science. What was originally a Scandinavian-based research project on student outcomes has turned into a monster intergovernmental testing and ranking regime, the Program for International Student Assessment (PISA), co-ordinated by the rich countries' neoliberal think tank, the OECD.

The educational *experience* of students in schools is of little interest to the PISA testers, just as the social relations of production are of little interest to Piketty. Knowledge projects coming from severely marginalized groups often emphasise experience. They have the character of 'testimony', as if telling one's life, narrating experience and affirming a reality not found in mainstream sources is itself an important achievement. A striking example is the life stories of transsexual women and men in South Africa, collected by the activist group GenderDynamiX (Morgan, Marais & Wellbeloved 2009).

But testimony alone may not create knowledge with reach and analytic power. Interpretation, structural analysis, and quantitative information are likely to be wanted too. That is, I think, why Southern-theory classics are often notably multi-stranded and might be seen as using hybrid methods. Think of Solomon Tsekisho Plaatje's *Native Life in South Africa* (1916), Bina Agarwal's *A Field of One's Own* (1994), Achille Mbembe's *On the Postcolony* (2001), to take just a handful. They are difficult to fit into any one academic discipline.

Finally, we need to consider the way social-scientific knowledge circulates. As specialized knowledge institutions were created in the global North, a system of communication was created with them. This centred on research reports in journals, of which the Royal Society's *Philosophical Transactions*, dating from 1665, is supposed to be the first; there are now estimated to be 30 000 research journals (not counting all the online pseudo-journals that milk money from the naïve or desperate). Around the journals is a great cloud of textbooks, handbooks, abstracts, bibliographies and reviews—of which a pioneering example was Durkheim's yearly *L'Année sociologique*.

The creation of research journals in the global periphery promised a certain decentralization of the economy of knowledge. But this was undermined from the start by the extraversion of these journals' contents; they rarely offered a robust alternative to journals from Europe or the USA. And then, with the growth of citation counts and league tables, journals from the South have been explicitly relegated to the second or third division. The Internet promised a technological decentralization and democratisation. But this is mostly negated by the commercialization of the Net, and the way rich Northern institutions can use it to establish their agendas as global norms. A notable example is massive open online courses. EdX, the MOOC platform used by MIT, Harvard and other elite US universities, on its website's home page summons readers to 'Start learning from the world's best institutions'. You have to step outside their system to see the arrogance and stupidity of that claim.

There is no simple way to create a genuinely democratic social-science communication system on a world scale. Some international organizations, including the International Sociological Association, are making real attempts to become conduits for multi-centred communication. The ISA's online magazine-format *Global Dialogue* is a notable example, in multiple languages. Attempts at direct South-South linkage are becoming more common (for instance www.southernperspectives.net). They are still on a small scale compared with the mainstream economy of knowledge.

I can see no alternative to a patient process of building connections, organizing translations, funding travel, encouraging joint projects and joint publications, and taking every opportunity to redistribute resources to where they are most needed. This is a long-term approach. That it is not adequate to the need for social knowledge around the postcolonial world, in an era of violence, dictatorship and climate crisis, is all too obvious.

In conclusion

The alternative to a pyramid epistemology, which preserves the dominance of the global North, and a mosaic epistemology, which separates Southern knowledge projects from each other, must be a solidarity-based epistemology (Connell 2015). A solidarity-based approach will look for the connections between knowledge projects as much as the differences between them. At the same time it will be conscious of the history of the global knowledge economy and its gross current inequalities.

A social science that embodies such a view of knowledge must contest the exclusions and hierarchies that grew under colonialism and proliferate in the contemporary world too. Knowledge production is a radically social process. Trying to force it into a mould of competitive individualism, which is at the heart of corporate management strategy, distorts and ultimately trivializes the knowledge project. It is not by chance that universities now employ public-relations workforces, who are closer to top management than the actual research workforce is.

Against the juggernauts of commercialization and global-North dominance, it may seem hopeless to struggle. But many other knowledge projects exist and even flourish. It is by recognizing their presence, their scope and their intellectual power, and building on them, that we can create a social science fit for democratic purposes, on a world scale.

Acknowledgements

Chapter 1

I acknowledge first my co-authors, the late Tim Carrigan and John Lee. We jointly acknowledged the help of Cynthia Hamilton, Helen Easson, Margaret Clarke and other secretarial staff of the School of Behavioural Sciences at Macquarie University, and the staff of the Kuring-gai College of Advanced Education Resources Centre. The work was funded by a grant, 'Theory of Class and Patriarchy', from the Australian Research Grants Scheme.

Carrigan, Tim, Raewyn Connell and John Lee, 1985, 'Toward a new sociology of masculinity', *Theory and Society*, vol. 14, no. 5, pp. 551–604.

Chapter 2

I am deeply grateful to the people with whom I have worked on these ideas, especially Tim Carrigan, John Lee, Norm Radican, Robert Morrell, James Messerschmidt, Taga Futoshi and José Olavarría. Teresa Valdés, Radhika Chopra, Mara Viveros and Kylie Benton-Connell gave key insights and support. An earlier version of this paper was given to the conference 'Les masculinités au prisme de l'hégémonie', École des hautes études en sciences sociales, Paris, 13 June 2013, and published in French as 'Hégémonie, masculinité, colonialité', *Genre, sexualité & société*, no. 13, Spring 2015, article 3429. Part of this research was funded by a Discovery grant from the Australian Research Council.

Connell, Raewyn, 2016, 'Masculinities in global perspective: hegemony, contestation, and changing structures of power', *Theory and Society*, vol. 45, no. 4, pp. 303–18, DOI 10.1007/s11186-016-9275-x.

Chapter 3

Ideas in this paper were developed in joint projects with Sandra Kessler, Dean Ashenden and Gary Dowsett, and with Tim Carrigan and John Lee. I am grateful for the comments of Pam Benton, Lynne Segal and Gary Dowsett, for help given by Helen Easson, and for constructive criticism by participants at the BSA Sociological Theory Group conference in September 1984, where the first version of this paper was given. The research was supported by a grant from the Australian Research Grants Committee, by study leave granted by Macquarie University, and by the hospitality of the Sociology department of the Institute of Education at London University.

Connell, Raewyn, 1985, 'Theorising gender', *Sociology*, vol. 19, no. 2, pp. 260–72.

Chapter 4

My thinking on these issues has been profoundly shaped by Chilla Bulbeck, Teresa Valdés, Radhika Chopra, Mara Viveros, Robert Morrell and Kylie Benton-Connell.

Connell, Raewyn, 2014, 'Rethinking gender from the South', *Feminist Studies*, vol. 40, no. 3, pp. 518–39.

Chapter 5

This work was informed by the large historical project I shared with Terry Irving, later published as *Class Structure in Australian History*, and by many discussions with Ron Witton, my colleague in optimistic times at Flinders University.

Connell, Raewyn, 1975, 'Structure and structural change in the Australian ruling class' in EL Wheelwright and K Buckley (eds), *Essays in the Political Economy of Australian Capitalism*, vol. 1, ANZ Book Co., pp. 227–41.

Chapter 6

'Moloch Mutates' was given as the sixth lecture in the *Overland* series at Trades Hall, Melbourne, on 19 July 2002, which served as the keynote talk for the conference over the following two days. My thanks to the editors of *Overland* for the invitation, and especially to Nathan Hollier, who also edited the book of the conference.

Connell, Raewyn, 2002, 'Moloch mutates: global capitalism and the evolution of the Australian ruling class, 1977–2002', *Overland*, no. 167, pp. 4–14.

Chapter 7

My thinking on these issues was profoundly influenced by my colleagues on the national study of the Disadvantaged Schools Program in Australia, Ken Johnston and Viv White, and by the other contributors to that project. The text is based on the 1992 Paul Masoner International Education Lecture; thanks to the University of Pittsburgh for the invitation to deliver this lecture.

Connell, Raewyn, 1994, 'Poverty and education', *Harvard Educational Review*, vol. 64, no. 2, pp. 125–49.

Chapter 8

I am grateful to colleagues at the Faculty of Education and Social Work, University of Sydney: Patrick Brownlee, Peter Freebody, Lina Markuskaite and Helen Proctor, as organisers of the series of public lectures in which this paper originated; and Nour Dados, for our shared work on neoliberalism.

Connell, Raewyn, 2013, 'The neoliberal cascade and education: an essay on the market agenda and its consequences', *Critical Studies in Education*, vol. 54, no. 2, pp. 99–112.

ACKNOWLEDGEMENTS

Chapter 9

Extract 1: This article is based on research done in the Gender Equity in Public Institutions project. I am grateful to the respondents from five public sector agencies for their gifts of time, information and trust; and to the many colleagues who have worked on this project over its lifetime. Those most involved in this part of the project are co-investigators Toni Schofield and Sue Goodwin, project staff Kathy Edwards, Celia Roberts, Virginia Watson and Julian Wood, industry partners Philippa Hall and Jennifer Perry, and agency representatives who regrettably cannot be named because of confidentiality undertakings. The GEPI project was principally funded by the Australian Research Council, with Industry Partner funding from two New South Wales government agencies, and in-kind contributions by seven New South Wales government agencies and the University of Sydney. The opinions expressed in this article are those of the author alone and do not necessarily reflect the view of any participating agency.

Connell, Raewyn, 2006, 'The experience of gender change in public sector organizations', *Gender Work and Organization*, vol. 13, no. 5, pp. 435–52.

Extract 2: I am grateful to the participants in this study for their generous contributions of time and information. Julian Wood managed the fieldwork and conducted some of the interviews, and Renate Kretschmer conducted others. Research assistance was given by John Fisher and Molly Nicholson. The study was funded by an Australian Research Council large grant, and supported by the University of Sydney.

Connell, Raewyn, 2010, 'Building the neoliberal world: managers as intellectuals in a peripheral economy', *Critical Sociology*, vol. 36, no. 6, pp. 777–92.

Extract 3: I am deeply grateful to the initiator of this interview, known in the report as Robyn; a confidentiality agreement prevents acknowledging her by her actual name.

Connell, Raewyn, 2010, 'Two cans of paint: a transsexual life story, with reflections on gender change and history', *Sexualities*, vol. 13 no. 1, pp. 3–19.

Chapter 10

The project from which this paper came was inspired by my partner, the late Pam Benton. Systematic work began, as explained in the chapter preface, in a course I taught at the University of California, Santa Cruz; I am grateful to all participants and colleagues there, including John Sanbonmatsu, Paul Lubeck, Terry Burke and Behrooz Ghamari-Tabrizi.

Connell, Raewyn, 1997, 'Why is classical theory classical?', *American Journal of Sociology*, vol. 102, no. 6, pp. 1511–57.

Chapter 11

My thanks to the editors of *Sociologies in Dialogue* for the invitation to contribute to their initiative. I'm grateful to the many who contributed to the *Southern Theory* project; and to my colleagues on the 'Arenas of Knowledge' project, Fran Collyer, João Maia, Robert Morrell, Rebecca Pearse, Patrick Brownlee, Nour Dados and Vanessa Watson. That project was supported by a Discovery grant from the Australian Research Council.

Connell, Raewyn, 2015, 'Social science on a world scale: connecting the pages', *Sociologies in Dialogue: Journal of the Brazilian Sociological Society*, vol. 1, no. 1, pp. 1–16.

References

Abdo, Nahla, 2010, 'Imperialism, the State, and NGOs: Middle Eastern Contexts and Contestations', *Comparative Studies of South Abrbsia, Africa and the Middle East*, vol. 30, no. 2, pp. 238–49.
Achebe, Chinua, 1958, *Things Fall Apart*, Heinemann, London.
Ackerly, Brooke A, 2001, 'Women's Human Rights Activists as Cross-Cultural Theorists', *International Feminist Journal of Politics*, vol. 3, no. 3, pp. 311–46.
Agarwal, Bina, 1994, *A Field of One's Own: Gender and Land Rights in South Asia*, Cambridge University Press, Cambridge.
——2003, 'Gender and Land Rights Revisited: Exploring New Prospects via the State, Family, and Market', *Journal of Agrarian Change*, vol. 3, nos 1–2, pp. 184–224.
Al-e Ahmad, Jalal, 1982 [1962], *Weststruckness*, trans. John Green and Ahmad Alizadeh, Mazda Publishers, Lexington, KY.
Alatas, Syed Farid, 2006, *Alternative Discourses in Asian Social Science: Responses to Eurocentrism*, Sage, New Delhi.
——2014, *Applying Ibn Khaldun: The recovery of a lost tradition in sociology*, Routledge, New York.
Alatas, Syed Hussein, 1974, 'The captive mind and creative development', *International Social Science Journal*, vol. 26 no. 4, pp. 691–700.
Alexander, Jeffrey C, 1982–83, *Theoretical Logic in Sociology*, vols 2–3, University of California Press, Berkeley.
Allardt, Erik, 1994, 'Scandinavian sociology and its European roots and elements' in Birgitta Nedelmann and Piotr Sztompka (eds), *Sociology in Europe*, Walter de Gruyter, Berlin, pp. 119–40.
Altman, Dennis, 2001, *Global Sex*, University of Chicago Press, Chicago.
Alvarez, Sonia E, 1999, 'Advocating feminism: the Latin American feminist NGO "boom"', *International Feminist Journal of Politics*, vol. 1, no. 2, pp. 181–209.
Amar, Paul, 2011, 'Middle East masculinity studies: Discourses of "men in crisis", industries of gender in revolution', *Journal of Middle East Women's Studies*, vol. 7, no. 3, pp. 36–70.

REFERENCES

Amin, Samir, 1997, *Capitalism in the Age of Globalization: The Management of Contemporary Society*, Zed Books, London.

Anderson, E, 1991, 'Neighborhood effects on teenage pregnancy', C Jencks and PE Peterson (eds), *The urban underclass*, Brookings Institution, Washington, DC, pp. 375–98.

Angus, L (ed.), 1993, *Education, inequality and social identity*, Falmer Press, London.

Anzaldúa, Gloria, 2007, *Borderlands/La Frontera: The New Mestiza*, 3rd edn, Aunt Lute Books, San Francisco.

Apple, MW, 1982, *Education and power*, Routledge & Kegan Paul, Boston, MA.

——1993, *Official knowledge: Democratic education in a conservative age*, Routledge, New York.

Atwan, R, D McQuade and JW Wright, 1979, *Edsels, Luckies and Frigidaires*, Delta, New York.

Bakare-Yusuf, Bibi, 2003, '"Yorubas don't do gender": a critical review of Oyeronke Oyewumi's *The Invention of Women: Making an African Sense of Western Gender Discourses*', *African Identities*, vol. 1, pp. 119–40.

Bakunin, Mikhail, 1973 [1873], 'Statism and anarchy', *Bakunin on Anarchy*, Sam Dolgoff (ed.), Allen & Unwin, London, pp. 325–50.

Baldock, Cora V and Jim Lally, 1974, 'Sociology in Australia and New Zealand: Theory and Methods', *Contributions in Sociology*, no. 16, Greenwood Press, Westport, CT.

—— and Bettina Cass (eds), 1983, *Women, Social Welfare and the State*, Allen & Unwin, Sydney.

Ball, Stephen J, 2003, *Class Strategies and the Education Market: The Middle Classes and Social Advantage*, RoutledgeFalmer, London.

Barbieri, Teresita de, 1992, 'Sobre la categoría género. Una introducción teórico-metodológica', *Revista Interamericana de Sociología*, vol. 6, nos. 2–3, pp. 147–78.

Barrett, M, 1980, *Women's Oppression Today*, Virago, London.

Bauman, Zygmunt, 1998, *Globalization: The Human Consequences*, Polity Press, Cambridge.

Beauvoir, S de, 1972, [1949], *The Second Sex*, Penguin, Harmondsworth.

Bednarik, K, 1970, *The Male in Crisis*, Knopf, New York.

Bem, Sandra L, 1974, 'The measurement of psychological androgyny', *Journal of Consulting and Clinical Psychology*, vol. 42, pp. 155–62.

Bendix, Reinhard, 1960, *Max Weber, an Intellectual Portrait*, Doubleday, New York.

Bennett, Jane, 2008, 'Editorial: researching for life: paradigms and power', *Feminist Africa*, no. 11, pp. 1–12.

——2010, '"Circles and circles": Notes on African feminist debates around gender and violence in the C21', *Feminist Africa*, vol. 14, pp. 21–47.

Bennoune, Mahfoud, 1988, *The Making of Contemporary Algeria, 1830–1987*, Cambridge University Press, Cambridge.

Bernard, LL and Jessie Bernard, 1965 [1943], *Origins of American Sociology: The Social Science Movement in the United States*, Russell & Russell, New York.

Bernstein, BB, 1974, 'A critique of the concept of "compensatory education"', in D Wedderburn (ed.), *Poverty, inequality and class structure*, Cambridge University Press, Cambridge, pp. 109–22.

REFERENCES

Besnard, Philippe, (ed.), 1983, *The Sociological Domain: The Durkheimians and the Founding of French Sociology*, Cambridge University Press, Cambridge.

Bhambra, Gurminder K, 2014, *Connected Sociologies*, Bloomsbury Academic, London.

Bird, Susan, Ritilio Delgado, Larry Madrigal, John Bayron Ochoa and Walberto Tejeda, 2007, 'Constructing an alternative masculine identity: the experience of the Centro Bartolomé de las Casas and Oxfam America in El Salvador', *Gender & Development*, vol. 15, no. 1, pp. 111–21.

Blagojevic, Marina, 2013, 'Transnationalization and its absence: the Balkan semi-peripheral perspective on masculinities' in Jeff Hearn, Marina Blagojevic and Katherine Harrison (eds), *Rethinking Transnational Men: Beyond, Between and Within Nations*, Routledge, New York, pp. 163–84.

Boehm, EA, 1971, *Twentieth Century Economic Development in Australia*, Longman, Camberwell, Vic.

Bose, Christine E and Minjeong Kim (eds), 2009, *Global Gender Research: Transnational Perspectives*, Routledge, New York.

Bottomore, Tom, 1987, *Sociology: A Guide to Problems and Literature*, 3rd edn, Allen & Unwin, London.

—— and Robert Nisbet (eds), 1978, *A History of Sociological Analysis*, Heinemann, London.

Bourdieu, P, 1977, *Outline of a Theory of Practice*, Cambridge University Press, Cambridge.

Braedley, Susan and Meg Luxton (eds), 2010, *Neoliberalism and Everyday Life*, McGill-Queen's University Press, Montreal and Kingston.

Branford, Victor, 1904, 'The founders of sociology', *American Journal of Sociology*, vol. 10, no. 1, pp. 94–126.

Braverman, Harry, 1974, *Labor and Monopoly Capital*, Monthly Review Press, New York.

Bray, Alan, 1982, *Homosexuality in Renaissance England*, Gay Men's Press, London.

Brennan, DJ, 2002, 'Australia. Child care and state-centred feminism in a liberal welfare regime' in Sonya Michel and Rianne Mahon (eds), *Child Care Policy at the Crossroads: Gender and Welfare State Restructuring*, Routledge, New York.

Brownmiller, Susan, 1975, *Against Our Will*, Simon & Schuster, New York.

Bulbeck, Chilla, 1988, *One World Women's Movement*, Pluto Press, London.

——1998, *Re-orienting Western Feminisms: Women's Diversity in a Postcolonial World*, Cambridge University Press, Cambridge.

Burke, Edmund III, 1980, 'The French tradition of the sociology of Islam' in Malcolm Kerr (ed.), *Islamic Studies*, Undena University Press, Santa Monica, CA, pp. 73–88.

Burrow, JW, 1966, *Evolution and Society: A Study in Victorian Social Theory*, Cambridge University Press, Cambridge.

Business Council of Australia, 2008, *Teaching Talent: The Best Teachers for Australia's Classrooms*, Business Council of Australia, Melbourne.

Butlin, NG, 1964, *Investment in Australian Economic Development*, Cambridge University Press, Cambridge.

Cain, PJ and AG Hopkins, 1993, *British Imperialism: Innovation and Expansion, 1688–1914*, Longman, New York.

Camic, Charles, 1989, '*Structure* after 50 years: the anatomy of a charter', *American Journal of Sociology*, vol. 95, no. 1, pp. 38–107.

Campbell, B, 1984, *Wigan Pier Revisited*, Virago, London.

Campbell, Craig and Geoffrey Sherington, 2006, *The Comprehensive Public High School: Historical Perspectives*, Palgrave Macmillan, New York.

——, Helen Proctor and Geoffrey Sherington, 2009, *School Choice: How Parents Negotiate the New School Market in Australia*, Allen & Unwin, Sydney.

Cardoso, Fernando Henrique and Enzo Faletto, 1979 [1969], *Dependency and Development in Latin America*, University of California Press, Berkeley.

Carneiro, Sueli, 2005, 'Ennegrecer el feminismo', in *Feminismos disidentes en América latina y el Caribe*, Fem-e-libros, México.

Carrigan, Tim, Raewyn Connell and John Lee, 1985, 'Toward a new sociology of masculinity', *Theory and Society*, vol. 14, no. 5, pp. 551–604.

Casanova, U, 1990, 'Rashomon in the classroom: Multiple perspectives of teachers, parents and students' in A Barona and EE Garcia (eds), *Children at risk: Poverty, minority status, and other issues in educational equity*, National Association of School Psychologists, Washington, DC, pp. 135–49.

Centre For Contempory Cultural Studies, Women's Studies Group, 1978, *Women Take Issue*, Hutchinson, London.

Childe, VG, 1954, *What Happened in History*, rev. edn, Penguin, Harmondsworth.

Chisholm, Linda (ed.), 2004, *Changing Class: Education and Social Change in Post-Apartheid South Africa*, Zed Books, London and HSRC Press, Cape Town.

Chodorow, Nancy, 1978, *The Reproduction of Mothering*, University of California Press, Berkeley.

Chopra, Radhika (ed.), 2002, *From Violence to Supportive Practice: Family, Gender and Masculinities in India*, United Nations Development Fund for Women, New Delhi.

——2007, *Reframing Masculinities: Narrating the Supportive Practices of Men*, Orient Longman Private, New Delhi.

Clark, Judith, 2003, 'To Hell in a Handcart: Educational Realities, Teachers' Work and Neoliberal Restructuring in NSW TAFE', PhD thesis, University of Sydney, Faculty of Education, Sydney.

Clark, Terry Nichols, 1973, *Prophets and Patrons: The French University and the Emergence of the Social Sciences*, Harvard University Press, Cambridge, MA.

Cockburn, Cynthia, 1983, *Brothers: Male Dominance and Technological Change*, Pluto Press, London.

——2010, 'Gender Relations as Causal in Militarization and War: A Feminist Standpoint', *International Feminist Journal of Politics*, vol. 12, no. 2, pp. 139–57.

Coleman, JS, 1990, *Equality and achievement in education*, Westview, Boulder, CO.

Collier, Richard, 2010, *Men, Law and Gender: Essays on the 'Man' of Law*, Routledge, Abingdon.

Collyer, Fran, 2014, 'Sociology, sociologists and core-periphery reflections', *Journal of Sociology*, vol. 50, no. 4, pp. 252–68.

——, Raewyn Connell, João Maia and Robert Morrell, 2019, *Knowledge and Global Power: Making New Sciences in the South*, Monash University Publishing, Melbourne; Wits University Press, Johannesburg.

Compton, Mary and Lois Weiner (eds), 2008, *The Global Assault on Teaching, Teachers, and their Unions: Stories for Resistance*, Palgrave Macmillan, New York.

Comte, Auguste, 1875–77, *System of Positive Polity, or, Treatise on Sociology*, 4 vols, Longmans Green, London.

Connell, Raewyn, 1975 [1974], 'Conflict in the Australian ruling class, 1970–72' in M Richards and RA Witton (eds), *The American Connection*, Macmillan, Melbourne.

—— 1977, *Ruling Class, Ruling Culture*, Cambridge University Press, Cambridge.

—— 1982, 'Class, Patriarchy and Sartre's Theory of Practice', *Theory and Society*, vol. 11, pp. 305–20.

—— 1983, *Which Way is Up? Essays on Sex, Class and Culture*, Allen & Unwin, Sydney.

—— 1985, 'Theorising Gender', *Sociology*, vol. 19, no. 2, pp. 260–72.

—— 1991, 'The workforce of reform: Teachers in the disadvantaged schools program', *Australian Journal of Education*, vol. 35, pp. 229–45.

—— 1993, *Schools and social justice*, Temple University Press, Philadelphia, PA.

—— 1997, 'Why is classical theory classical?', *American Journal of Sociology*, vol. 102, no. 6, pp. 1511–57.

—— 2006, 'Northern theory: the political geography of general social theory', *Theory and Society*, vol. 35, pp. 237–64.

—— 2007, *Southern Theory: The Global Dynamics of Knowledge in Social Science*, Allen & Unwin, Sydney; Polity, Cambridge.

—— 2010, 'Understanding neoliberalism' in Susan Braedley and Meg Luxton (eds), *Neoliberalism and Everyday Life*, McGill-Queen's University Press, Montreal and Kingston, pp. 22–36.

—— 2010a, 'Im Innern des gläsernen Turms: Die Konstruktion von Männlichkeiten im Finanzkapital', *Feministische Studien*, vol. 28, no. 1, pp. 8–24.

—— 2010b, 'Building the neoliberal world: managers as intellectuals in a peripheral economy', *Critical Sociology*, vol. 36, no. 6, pp. 777–92.

—— 2011, *Confronting Equality: Gender, Knowledge and Global Change*, Allen & Unwin, Sydney.

—— 2014, 'Margin becoming centre: for a world-centred rethinking of masculinities', *NORMA: International Journal for Masculinity Studies*, vol. 9, no. 4, pp. 217–31.

—— 2015, 'Meeting at the edge of fear: theory on a world scale', *Feminist Theory*, vol. 16, no. 1, pp. 49–66.

—— 2016, '100 million Kalashnikovs: Gendered power on a world scale', *Debate Feminista*, no. 51, pp. 3–17.

—— 2019, *The Good University*, Monash University Publishing, Melbourne; Zed Books, London.

—— and TH Irving, 1973, 'Yes, Virginia, there is a ruling class' in H Mayer and H Nelson (eds), *Australian Politics: A Third Reader*, Cheshire, Melbourne, pp. 31–47.

——, DJ Ashenden, S Kessler and GW Dowsett, 1982, *Making the difference: Schools, families and social division*, Allen & Unwin, Sydney.

——, VM White and KM Johnston, 1991, *'Running twice as hard': The disadvantaged schools program in Australia*, Deakin University, Geelong.

—— and TH Irving, 1992 [1980], *Class Structure in Australian History*, 2nd edn, Longman Cheshire, Melbourne.

——, KM Johnston and VM White, 1992, *Measuring up: Assessment, evaluation and educational disadvantage*, Australian Curriculum Studies Association, Canberra.

—— and James W Messerschmidt, 2005, 'Hegemonic masculinity: rethinking the concept', *Gender and Society*, vol. 19, no. 6, pp. 829–59.

—— and Nour Dados, 2014, 'Where in the world does neoliberalism come from? The market agenda in southern perspective', *Theory and Society*, vol. 43, no. 2, pp. 117–38.

Corrigan, P, 1979, *Schooling the Smash Street kids*, Macmillan, London.

Coser, Lewis A, 1956, *The Functions of Social Conflict*, Free Press, Glencoe, IL.

Crozier, John B, 1911, *Sociology Applied to Practical Politics*, Longmans Green, London.

Cruz Sierra, Salvador (ed.), 2013, *Vida, muerte y resistencia en Ciudad Juárez: Una aproximación desde la violencia, el género y la cultura*, Juan Pablos (ed.), El Colegio de la Frontera Norte, Tijuana; México DF.

CSDH (Commission on Social Determinants of Health), 2008, *Closing the Gap in a Generation*, World Health Organization, Geneva.

Cullinan, Kerry and Anso Thom, 2009, *The Virus, Vitamins and Vegetables: The South African HIV/AIDS Mystery*, Jacana, Cape Town.

Curtis, B, DW Livingstone and H Smaller, 1992, *Stacking the deck: The streaming of working-class kids in Ontario schools*, Our Schools/Our Selves Education Foundation, Toronto.

Dados, Nour and Raewyn Connell, 2014, 'Neoliberalism, intellectuals and southern theory' in Wiebke Keim, Ercüment Çelik, Christian Ersche and Veronika Wöhrer (eds), *Global Knowledge Production in the Social Sciences: Made in Circulation*, Ashgate, Farnham, pp. 195–213.

Daly, M, 1978, *Gyn/Ecology*, Beacon Press, Boston.

Das, Abhijit and Satish K Singh, 2014, 'Changing men: challenging stereotypes. Reflections on working with men on gender issues in India', *IDS Bulletin*, vol. 45, no. 1, pp. 69–79.

Dasgupta, Romit, 2003, 'Creating corporate warriors: the "salaryman" and masculinity in Japan' in Kam Louie and Morris Low (eds), *Asian Masculinities*, RoutledgeCurzon, London, pp. 118–34.

Davis, A, 1948, *Social-class influences upon learning*, Harvard University Press, Cambridge, MA.

Deegan, Mary Jo, 1988, *Jane Addams and the Men of the Chicago School, 1892–1918*, Transaction Books, New Brunswick, NJ.

Delphy, C, 1977, *The Main Enemy*, Women's Research and Resources Centre, London.

Desmond, Adrian and James Moore, 1992, *Darwin*, Penguin, London.

Devine, JA and JD Wright, 1993, *The greatest of evils: Urban poverty and the American underclass*, Aldine de Gruyter, New York.

Dietrich Ortega, Luisa Maria, 2012, 'Looking beyond violent militarized masculinities: guerrilla gender regimes in Latin America', *International Feminist Journal of Politics*, vol. 14, no. 4, pp. 489–507.

Dinnerstein, D, 1976, *The Mermaid and the Minotaur: Sexual Arrangement and Human Malaise*, Harper & Row, New York.
Donaldson, Mike, 1991, *Time of Our Lives: Labour and Love in the Working Class*, Allen & Unwin, Sydney.
Donzelot, J, 1979, *The Policing of Families*, Pantheon, New York.
Dove, Mabel, 2004, *Selected Writings of a Pioneer West African Feminist*, Trent Editions, Nottingham.
Dowsett, Gary W, 2003, 'HIV/AIDS and homophobia: subtle hatreds, severe consequences and the question of origins', *Culture, Health & Sexuality*, vol. 5, no. 2, pp. 121–36.
Doyle, DP and BS Cooper (eds), 1988, *Federal aid to the disadvantaged: What future for Chapter I?*, Falmer Press, London.
Du Bois, WEB, 1978 [1950], 'The problem of the twentieth century is the problem of the color line', *On Sociology and the Black Community*, University of Chicago Press, Chicago, pp. 281–9.
Duncan, David, 1908, *The Life and Letters of Herbert Spencer*, Methuen, London.
Durkheim, Émile, 1964 [1893], *The Division of Labor in Society*, Free Press, New York.
—— 1964 [1895], *The Rules of Sociological Method*, Free Press, Glencoe, IL.
—— (ed.), 1898–1913, *L'Année sociologique*, vols 1–12, Alcan, Paris.
Dworkin, Andrea, 1981, *Pornography: Men Possessing Women*, Perigree, New York; The Women's Press, London.
Edwards, C, 1965, *Bruce of Melbourne*, Heinemann, London.
Ehrenreich, Barbara, 1983, *The Hearts of Men: American Dreams and the Flight from Commitment*, Pluto Press, London.
Eisenstein, Hester, 1984, *Contemporary Feminist Thought*, Allen & Unwin, London.
—— 1996, *Inside Agitators: Australian Femocrats and the State*, Allen & Unwin, Sydney.
Elias, Juanita, 2008, 'Hegemonic masculinities, the multinational corporation, and the developmental state: constructing gender in "progressive" firms', *Men and Masculinities*, vol. 10, no. 4, pp. 405–21.
Embling, J, 1986, *Fragmented lives: A darker side of Australian life*, Penguin, Ringwood.
Encel, S, 1970, *Equality and Authority*, Cheshire, Melbourne.
Epstein, Debbie, Robert Morrell, Relebohile Moletsane and Elaine Unterhalter, 2004, 'Gender and HIV/AIDS in Africa south of the Sahara: interventions, activism, identities', *Transformation*, vol. 54, pp. 1–16.
—— and Robert Morrell, 2012, 'Approaching Southern theory: explorations of gender in South African education', *Gender and Education*, vol. 24, no. 5, pp. 469–82.
Fairbanks, Arthur, 1901 [1896], *Introduction to Sociology*, 7th edn, Scribner, New York.
Fasteau, M, 1974, *The Male Machine*, McGraw-Hill, New York.
Fernbach, D, 1981, *The Spiral Path*, Gay Men's Press, London.
Fine, M, 1991, *Framing dropouts: Notes on the politics of an urban public high school*, State University of New York Press, Albany, NY.
Firestone, S, 1970, *The Dialectic of Sex*, Bantam, New York.
Ford, Michele and Lenore Lyons (eds), 2012, *Men and Masculinities in Southeast Asia*, Routledge, London.
Forsyth, WD, 1935, *Governor Arthur's Convict System*, Longman, London.

Foucault, M, 1979, *The History of Sexuality*, vol. 1, Allen Lane, London.
——1980, 'Introduction', *Herculine Barbin*, Harvester, Brighton, UK.
Franzway, S and J Lowe, 1978, 'Sex role theory: Political cul-de-sac?', *Refractory Girl*, no. 16, pp. 14–16.
Freud, Sigmund, 1918, 'From the History of an Infantile Neurosis', *Standard Edition of the Complete Psychological Works,* vol. 17, Hogarth, London.
——1930, 'Civilization and its Discontents', *Standard Edition of the Complete Psychological Works*, vol. 21, Hogarth, London.
Friedan, Betty, 1976, *It Changed My Life*, Random House, New York.
——1981, *The Second Stage*, Summit, New York.
Game, A and R Pringle, 1983, *Gender at Work*, Allen & Unwin, Sydney.
Ghoussoub, Mai, 2000, 'Chewing gum, insatiable women and foreign enemies: male fears and the Arab media' in Mai Ghoussoub and Emma Sinclair-Webb (eds), *Imagined Masculinities: Male Identity and Culture in the Middle East*, Saqi Books, London, pp. 227–35.
Giddens, Anthony, 1971, *Capitalism and Modern Social Theory*, Cambridge University Press, Cambridge.
——1976, *New Rules of Sociological Method*, Hutchinson, London.
Giddings, Franklin Henry, 1896, *The Principles of Sociology*, Macmillan, New York.
——1906, *Readings in Descriptive and Historical Sociology*, Macmillan, New York.
Ginsburg, MB (ed), 1994, *The Politics of Educators' Work and Lives*, Garland Publishing, New York.
Giroux, HA, 1988, *Teachers as intellectuals: Toward a critical pedagogy of learning*, Bergin & Garvey, Granby, MA.
——1992, *Border crossings: Cultural workers and the politics of education*, Routledge, New York.
Go, Julian, 2013, 'For a postcolonial sociology', *Theory and Society*, vol. 42, pp. 25–55.
Gohar, Saddik M, 2008, 'Toward a Revolutionary Emirati Poetics: Ghabesh's *Beman Ya Buthayn Taluthin?*', *Nebula*, vol. 5, no. 1/2, pp. 74–87.
Goldberg, H, 1976, *The Hazards of Being Male*, Nash, New York.
Goldberg, S, 1973, *The Inevitability of Patriarchy*, William Morrow, New York.
Goodson, IF (ed.), 1985, *Social histories of the secondary curriculum: Subjects for study*, Falmer Press, London.
——1988, *The making of curriculum: Collected essays*, Falmer Press, London.
Gordimer, N, 1979, *Burger's Daughter*, Penguin, Harmondsworth.
Grewal, Inderpal and Caren Kaplan (eds), 1994, *Scattered Hegemonies: Postmodernity and Transnational Feminist Practices*, University of Minnesota Press, Minneapolis, MN.
Grieder, Jerome, 1981, *Intellectuals and the State in Modern China: A Narrative History*, Free Press, New York.
Griffin, C, 1993, *Representations of youth: The study of youth and adolescence in Britain and America*, Polity Press, Cambridge.
Griswold, PA, KJ Cotton and B Hansen, 1986, *Effective compensatory education sourcebook*, US Department of Education, Washington, DC.
Guha, Ranajit, 1989, 'Dominance without hegemony and its historiography', *Subaltern Studies*, vol. 6, pp. 210–309.

Haberman, M, 1991, 'The pedagogy of poverty versus good teaching', *Phi Delta Kappan*, vol. 73, pp. 290–4.
Habermas, J, 1979, *Communication and the Evolution of Society*, Heinemann, London.
Hacker, Helen, 1957, 'The new burdens of masculinity', *Marriage and Family Living*, vol. 19, pp. 227–33.
Hainsworth, DR, 1971, *The Sydney Traders*, Cassell, Melbourne.
Hale, Sondra, 2009, 'Transnational gender studies and the migrating concept of gender in the Middle East and North Africa', *Cultural Dynamics*, vol. 21, no. 2, pp. 133–52.
Hall, AR, 1968, *The Stock Exchange of Melbourne and the Victorian Economy*, ANU Press, Canberra.
Halsey, AH (ed.), 1972, *Educational priority: Vol. I: E.P.A. Problems and policies*, Her Majesty's Stationery Office, London.
Haque, Md Mozammel, 2012, 'Men, masculinities and social change: exploring Khmer masculinities and their implications for domestic violence', PhD thesis, University of Sydney, Sydney.
——2013, 'Hope for gender equality? A pattern of post-conflict transition in masculinity', *Gender, Technology and Development*, vol. 17, no. 1, pp. 55–77.
Harding, Sandra, 2008, *Sciences from Below: Feminisms, Postcolonialities and Modernities*, Duke University Press, Durham, NC.
Haripangest, Adoniati Meyria Widaningtyas, 2009, *Gender Based Advocacy: An Effort to Build Conflict Resolution in Semarang Regency*, Graduate School Gadjah Mada University, Yogyakarta.
Hartmann, H, 1979, 'The unhappy marriage of marxism and feminism', *Capital and Class*, vol. 8, pp. 1–33.
Harvey, David, 2005, *A Brief History of Neoliberalism*, Oxford University Press, Oxford.
Hearn, William Edward, 1878, *The Aryan Household, Its Structure and Its Development*, George Robertson, Melbourne.
Heath, A, 1992, 'The attitudes of the underclass' in DJ Smith (ed.), *Understanding the underclass*, Policy Studies Institute, London, pp. 32–47.
Heath, SB, 1983, *Ways with words: Language, life and work in communities and classrooms*, Cambridge University Press, Cambridge.
Herdt, Gilbert H, 1981, *Guardians of the Flutes*, McGraw-Hill, New York.
Hil, Richard, 2012, *Whackademia: An Insider's Account of the Troubled University*, University of New South Wales Press, Sydney.
Hinkle, Roscoe C, 1994, *Developments in American Sociological Theory, 1915–1950*, State University of New York Press, Albany.
Hoang, Kimberly Kay, 2014, 'Vietnam rising dragon: contesting dominant western masculinities in Ho Chi Minh City's global sex industry', *International Journal of Politics, Culture, and Society*, vol. 27, pp. 259–71.
Hobhouse, LT, 1911, *Liberalism*, Williams & Norgate, London.
——, GC Wheeler and M Ginsberg, 1915, *The Material Culture and Social Institutions of the Simpler Peoples*, Chapman & Hall, London.
Hoecker-Drysdale, Susan, 1992, *Harriet Martineau: First Woman Sociologist*, St Martin's Press, New York.

Hollier, Nathan (ed.), 2004, *Ruling Australia*, Australian Scholarly Publishing, Melbourne.

Horowitz, David (ed.), 1971, *Radical Sociology: An Introduction*, Canfield, San Francisco.

Hountondji, Paulin J, 1976, *Sur la 'philosophie africaine': critique de l'ethnophilosophie*, Maspero, Paris.

—— (ed.), 1997 [1994], 'Introduction: Recentring Africa', *Endogenous Knowledge: Research Trails*, CODESRIA, Dakar, pp. 1–39.

——2002, *The Struggle for Meaning: Reflections on Philosophy, Culture, and Democracy in Africa*, Ohio University Press, Athens, OH.

Howson, Richard, 2006, *Challenging Hegemonic Masculinity*, Routledge, London and New York.

Hoyles, M, 1977, 'Cultural deprivation and compensatory education' in M Hoyles (ed.), *The politics of literacy*, Writers and Readers Publishing Cooperative, London, pp. 172–81.

Huerta Rojas, Fernando, 2006, 'La deportivización del cuerpo: globalización de las identitdades genéricas masculinas' in Gloria Careaga and Salvador Cruz Sierra (eds), *Debates sobre masculinidades: poder, desarrollo, políticas públicas y ciudadanía*, UNAM, México DF, pp. 211–33.

Hunter, Mark, 2004, 'Masculinities, multiple-sexual-partners, and AIDS: The making and unmaking of *Isoka* in KwaZulu-Natal', *Transformation*, no. 54, pp. 123–53.

Indyk, M, 1974, 'Establishment and nouveau capitalists: Power and conflict in big business', *ANZ Journal of Sociology*, vol. 10, no. 2, pp. 128–34.

Interim Committee for the Australian Schools Commission, 1973, *Schools in Australia*, Australian Government Publishing Service, Canberra.

Ito, Kimio, 1993, *Otokorashisa-n-yukue* [Directions for Masculinities: Cultural Sociology of Manliness], Shinyo-sha, Tokyo.

Jewkes, Rachel, Robert Morrell, Jeff Hearn, Emma Lundqvist, David Blackbeard, Graham Lindegger, Michael Quayle, Yandisa Sikweyiya and Lucas Gottzén, 2015, 'Hegemonic masculinity: combining theory and practice in gender interventions', *Culture, Health & Sexuality*, vol. 17, sup. 2, pp. 96–111.

Johnson, Vivien, 1981, *The Last Resort*, Penguin, Ringwood.

Jolly, Margaret, 2008, 'Moving masculinities: Memories and bodies across Oceania', *The Contemporary Pacific*, vol. 20, no. 1, pp. 1–24.

Kemp, CD, 1964, *Big Businessmen*, LPA, Melbourne.

Kessler, SJ and W McKenna, 1978, *Gender: An Ethnomethodological Approach*, Wiley, New York.

Kessler, Sandra, Dean J Ashenden, Raewyn Connell and Gary W Dowsett, 1985, 'Gender Relations in Secondary Schooling', *Sociology of Education*, vol. 58, no. 1, pp. 34–48.

Kidd, Benjamin, 1898 [1894], *Social Evolution*, 3rd edn, Macmillan, London.

Kiddle, Margaret, 1992 [1950], *Caroline Chisholm*, Melbourne University Press, Melbourne.

Kiernan, VG, 1969, *The Lords of Human Kind: Black Man, Yellow Man, and White Man in an Age of Empire*, Little, Brown, Boston.

REFERENCES

Kimmel, Michael, Jeff Hearn and Raewyn Connell (eds), 2005, *Handbook of Studies on Men and Masculinities*, Sage, Thousand Oaks, CA.

Kirmani, Nida, 2011, 'Beyond the Impasse: "Muslim feminism(s)" and the Indian Women's Movement', *Contributions to Indian Sociology*, vol. 45, no. 1, pp. 1–26.

Klein, Naomi, 2000, *No Logo*, Picador, New York.

Kleinhenz, E and L Ingvarson, 2004, 'Teacher accountability in Australia: current policies and practices and their relation to the improvement of teaching and learning', *Research Papers in Education*, vol. 19, no. 1, pp. 31–49.

Knapp, MS, PM Shields and BJ Turnbull, 1992, *Academic challenge for the children of poverty: Summary report*, US Department of Education, Office of Policy and Planning, Washington, DC.

Komarovsky, M, 1946, 'Cultural contradictions and sex roles', *American Journal of Sociology*, vol. 52, no. 3, pp. 184–9.

——1950, 'Functional analysis of sex roles', *American Sociological Review*, vol. 15, pp. 508–51.

——1964, *Blue Collar Marriage*, Vintage, New York.

Korbin, JE, 1992, 'Introduction: Child poverty in the United States', *American Behavioral Scientist*, vol. 35, pp. 213–19.

Kozol, J, 1991, *Savage inequalities: Children in America's schools*, Crown, New York.

Krafft-Ebing, Richard von, 1965 [1886], *Psychopathia Sexualis*, Paperback Library, New York.

Labrecque, Marie France, 2012, *Féminicides et impunité: le cas de Ciudad Juárez*, Éditions Écosociété, Montréal.

Lamas, Marta, 2011, *Feminism: Transmissions and Retransmissions*, Palgrave Macmillan, New York.

Lang, James, Alan Greig and Raewyn Connell, in collaboration with the Division for the Advancement of Women, 2008, *The Role of Men and Boys in Achieving Gender Equality*, 'Women 2000 and Beyond' series, United Nations Division for the Advancement of Women/Department of Economic and Social Affairs, New York.

Lareau, A, 1987, 'Social class differences in family–school relationships: The importance of cultural capital', *Sociology of Education*, vol. 60, no. 2, pp. 73–85.

Laurie, Nina, 2005, 'Establishing development orthodoxy: negotiating masculinities in the water sector', *Development and Change*, vol. 36, no. 3, pp. 527–49.

Lawn, M, 1993, 'The political nature of teaching: Arguments around schoolwork', American Educational Research Association Conference paper, Atlanta, GA, April 1993.

Lazreg, Marnia, 1990, 'Gender and politics in Algeria: unraveling the religious paradigm', *Signs*, vol. 15, no. 4, pp. 755–80.

Lepenies, Wolf, 1988, *Between Literature and Science: The Rise of Sociology*, Cambridge University Press, Cambridge.

Lessing, Doris, 1962, *The Golden Notebook*, Michael Joseph, London.

Letourneau, Charles, 1881, *Sociology, Based upon Ethnography*, Chapman & Hall, London.

Levin, Peter, 2001, 'Gendering the market: temporality, work, and gender on a national futures exchange', *Work and Occupations*, vol. 28, pp. 112–30.

REFERENCES

Levine, Donald N, 1995, *Visions of the Sociological Tradition*, University of Chicago Press, Chicago.

Lewis, Desiree, 2002, 'African Gender Research and Postcoloniality: Legacies and Challenges', paper presented to CODESRIA Gender Institute.

——2007, 'Feminism and the Radical Imagination', *Agenda*, vol. 21, no. 72, pp. 18–31.

Lewis, Glen, 1983, *Real Men Like Violence*, Kangaroo Press, Sydney.

Lewis, Linden, 2004, 'Caribbean masculinity at the *Fin de Siècle*' in Rhoda E Reddock (ed.), *Interrogating Caribbean Masculinities: Theoretical and Empirical Analyses*, University of the West Indies Press, Jamaica, Barbados, Trinidad and Tobago, pp. 244–66.

Lewis, O, 1968, *La Vida: A Puerto Rican family in the culture of poverty, San Juan and New York*, Panther, London.

Lipman-Blumen, J and AR Tickamyer, 1975, 'Sex roles in transition: a ten-year perspective', *Annual Review of Sociology*, vol. 1, pp. 297–337.

Lippert, J, 1977, 'Sexuality as Consumption' in J Snodgrass (ed.), *For Men Against Sexism*, Times Change Press, Albion, CA, pp. 207–13.

Lomas, G, 1960, *The Will to Win*, Heinemann, Melbourne.

Lugones, María, 2007, 'Heterosexualism and the colonial/modern gender system', *Hypatia*, vol. 22, no. 1, pp. 186–209.

——2010, 'Toward a Decolonial Feminism', *Hypatia*, vol. 25, no. 4, pp. 742–59.

Lüschen, Günther, 1994, '25 years of German sociology after World War II: institutionalization and theory', *Soziologie*, no. 3, S11–32.

McCarthy, G, 1973, *The Great Big Australian Takeover Book*, Angus & Robertson, Sydney.

McClintock, Anne, 1995, *Imperial Leather: Race, Gender, and Sexuality in the Colonial Context*, Routledge, New York.

MacDonald, Robert H, 1994, *The Language of Empire: Myths and Metaphors of Popular Imperialism, 1880–1918*, Manchester University Press, Manchester.

McDowell, Linda, 2010, 'Capital Culture revisited: Sex, testosterone and the City', *International Journal of Urban and Regional Research*, vol. 34, no. 3, pp. 652–8.

McGee, Reece (ed.), 1977, *Sociology*, Dryden Press, Hinsdale, IL.

Maciver, DJ and JL Epstein, 1990, *How equal are opportunities for learning in disadvantaged and advantaged middle grade schools?*, Center for Research on Effective Schooling for Disadvantaged Students, Johns Hopkins University, Baltimore, MD.

Maia, João Marcelo Ehlert, 2011, 'Space, social theory and peripheral imagination: Brazilian intellectual history and de-colonial debates', *International Sociology*, vol. 26, no. 3, pp. 392–407.

Mailer, Norman, 1971, *The Prisoner of Sex*, Little, Brown, Boston.

Mama, Amina, 1997, 'Sheroes and villains: Conceptualizing colonial and contemporary violence against women in Africa' in M Jacqui Alexander and Chandra Talpade Mohanty (eds), *Feminist Genealogies, Colonial Legacies, Democratic Futures*, Routledge, New York, pp. 46–62.

——2001, 'Interview with Elaine Salo: Talking about Feminism in Africa', *Agenda*, vol. 50, pp. 58–63.

——2005, 'Gender Studies for African Transformation' in P Thandika Mkandawire (ed.), *African Intellectuals: Rethinking Politics, Language, Gender, and Development*, Zed Books, London; CODESRIA, Dakar.
Marcuse, Herbert, 1955, *Eros and Civilization*, Sphere Books, London.
Marginson, Simon, 1997, *Markets in Education*, Allen & Unwin, Sydney.
——2009, 'National system reform in global context: The case of Australia', paper to international symposium *Reforms and Consequences in Higher Education Systems*, CNUFM, National Center of Sciences, Tokyo, 26 January 2009.
Matos, Marlise and Clarisse Paradis, 2013, 'Los feminismos latinoamericanos y su compleja relación con el Estado: debates actuales', *Íconos: Revista de Ciencias Sociales*, vol. 45, pp. 91–107.
Matthews, JJ, 1984, *Good and Mad Women*, Allen & Unwin, Sydney.
Matthews, T, 1970, 'The All for Australia League', *Labour History*, vol. 17, pp. 136–47.
May, AL, 1968, *Battle for the Banks*, Sydney University Press, Sydney.
Mbeki, Moeletsi, 2009, *Architects of Poverty: Why African Capitalism needs Changing*, Picador Africa, Johannesburg.
Mbembe, Achille, 2001, *On the Postcolony*, University of California Press, Berkeley.
Mead, M, 1950, *Male and Female*, Gollancz, London.
Meekosha, Helen, 2011, 'Decolonizing disability: thinking and acting globally', *Disability and Society*, vol. 26, no. 6, pp. 667–81.
Mernissi, Fatima, 1985 [1975], *Beyond the Veil: Male–Female Dynamics in Modern Muslim Society*, rev. edn, Saqi Books, London.
——1991, *Le Harem Politique: Le Prophète et les Femmes*, Albin Michel, Paris.
Merton, Robert K, 1957 [1949], *Social Theory and Social Structure*, 2nd edn, Free Press, Glencoe, Ill.
Messerschmidt, James W, 2010, *Hegemonic Masculinities and Camouflaged Politics: Unmasking the Bush Dynasty and its War Against Iraq*, Paradigm, Boulder, CO.
Meulenbelt, A, 1980, *The Shame is Over*, Women's Press, London.
Meuser, Michael (ed.), 2010, *Erwägen, Wissen, Ethik*, 2010, vol. 21, issue 3: special issue on hegemonic masculinity.
Meyer, Melissa and Helen Struthers (eds), 2012, *[Un]covering Men: Rewriting Masculinity and Health in South Africa*, Fanele, Auckland Park, South Africa.
Mies, Maria, 1986, *Patriarchy and Accumulation on a World Scale*, Zed, London.
Mignolo, Walter D, 2007, 'Delinking: The rhetoric of modernity, the logic of coloniality and the grammar of de-coloniality', *Cultural Studies*, vol. 21, nos. 2–3, pp. 449–514.
Mill, John Stuart, 1891 [1843], *A System of Logic*, Longmans Green, London.
Millett, Kate, 1970, *Sexual Politics*, Doubleday, New York.
Mills, C Wright, 1959, *The Sociological Imagination*, Oxford University Press, New York.
——1962, *The Marxists*, Dell, New York.
Mitchell, Juliet, 1971, *Woman's Estate*, Penguin, Harmondsworth.
——1975, *Psychoanalysis and Feminism*, Vintage, New York.
Mkandawire, Thandika (ed.), 2005, *African Intellectuals: Rethinking Politics, Language, Gender and Development*, CODESRIA, Dakar; Zed Books, London.

Mohanty, Chandra Talpade, 1991, 'Under Western Eyes: Feminist Scholarhip and Colonial Discourses' in Chandra Talpade Mohanty, Ann Russo and Lourdes Torres (eds), *Third World Women and the Politics of Feminism*, Indiana University Press, Bloomington, IN.

Money, John, 1970, 'Sexual Dimorphism and Homosexual Gender Identity', *Psychological Bulletin*, vol. 74, no. 6, pp. 425–44.

Moodie, T Dunbar, with Vivienne Ndatshe, 1994, *Going for Gold: Men, Mines and Migration*, Witwatersrand University Press, Johannesburg.

Morgan, J Graham, 1983, 'Courses and texts in sociology', *Journal of the History of Sociology*, vol. 5, no. 1, pp. 42–65.

Morgan, Robin (ed.), 1985, *Sisterhood is Global: The International Women's Movement Anthology*, Penguin, Harmondsworth.

Morgan, Ruth, Chris Marais and Joy Rosemary Wellbeloved (eds), 2009, *Trans: Transgender Life Stories from South Africa*, Jacana Media, Auckland Park, South Africa.

Morrell, Robert, 2001, *From Boys to Gentlemen: Settler Masculinity in Colonial Natal 1880–1920*, University of South Africa, Pretoria.

—— and Sandra Swart, 2005, 'Men in the Third World: Postcolonial perspectives on masculinity' in Michael S Kimmel, Jeff Hearn and Raewyn Connell (eds), *Handbook of Studies on Men and Masculinities*, Sage, Thousand Oaks, CA, pp. 90–113.

Mudimbe, VY, 1994, *The Idea of Africa*, Indiana University Press, Bloomington, IN.

Mulholland, Kate, 1996, 'Entrepreneurialism, masculinities and the self-made man' in David L Collinson and Jeff Hearn (eds), *Men as Managers, Managers as Men*, Sage, London, pp. 123–49.

Myrttinen, Henri, 2012, 'Violence, masculinities and patriarchy in post-conflict Timor-Leste' in Michele Ford and Lenore Lyons (eds), *Men and Masculinities in Southeast Asia*, Routledge, London, pp. 103–20.

Nandy, Ashis, 1983, *The Intimate Enemy: Loss and Recovery of Self under Colonialism*, Oxford University Press, New Delhi.

Naples, Nancy and Manisha Desai (eds), 2002, *Women's Activism and Globalization: Linking Local Struggles and Transnational Politics*, Routledge, New York.

National Mutual Life Association, 1969, *A Century of Life*, NML, Melbourne.

Natriello, G, EL McDill and AM Pallas, 1990, *Schooling disadvantaged children: Racing against catastrophe*, Teachers College Press, New York.

Negri, Antonio, 1974, *Crisi dello stato-piano: comunismo e organizzazione rivoluzionaria*, Feltrinelli, Milano.

Neumann, F, 1950, 'Approaches to the study of political power', *Political Science Quarterly*, vol. 65, no. 2, pp. 161–80.

Nichols, J, 1975, *Men's Liberation*, Penguin, New York.

Nisbet, Robert A, 1967, *The Sociological Tradition*, Heinemann, London.

Nnaemeka, Obioma, 2005, 'Mapping African feminisms' in Andrea Cornwall (ed.), *Readings in Gender in Africa*, International African Institute, James Currey and Indiana University Press, London.

Odih, Pamela, 2007, *Gender and Work in Capitalist Economies*, Open University Press, Maidenhead.

Odora Hoppers, Catherine A (ed.), 2002, *Indigenous Knowledge and the Integration of Knowledge Systems: Towards a Philosophy of Articulation*, New Africa Books, Claremont, South Africa.

Ogbu, JU, 1988, 'Cultural diversity and human development' in DT Slaughter (ed.), *Black children and poverty: A developmental perspective*, Jossey-Bass, San Francisco, pp. 11–28.

Olavarría, José (ed.), 2009, *Masculinidades y globalización: Trabajo y vida privada, familias y sexualidades*, Red de Masculinidad/es Chile, Universidad Academia de Humanismo Cristiano and CEDEM, Santiago.

Organisation for Economic Co-Operation and Development, 2005, *Teachers Matter: Attracting, Developing and Retaining Effective Teachers*, OECD Publishing, Paris.

Orland, ME, 1990, 'Demographics of disadvantage: Intensity of childhood poverty and its relationship to educational experience' in JI Goodlad and P Keating (eds), *Access to knowledge: An agenda of our nation's schools*, College Entrance Examination Board, New York, pp. 43–58.

Oyewumi, Oyeronke, 1997, *The Invention of Women: Making an African Sense of Western Gender Discourses*, University of Minnesota Press, Minneapolis.

Paredes, Julieta, 2002, 'Interview with Julieta Paredes of Mujeres Creando', *Green Anarchy*, vol. 9, p. 119, http://www.anarcha.org/sallydarity/julieta.htm.

Park, Robert E and Ernest W Burgess, 1924 [1921], *Introduction to the Science of Sociology*, University of Chicago Press, Chicago.

Parker, RS, 1965, 'Power in Australia', *ANZ Journal of Sociology*, vol. 1, no. 2, pp. 85–96.

Parsons, Talcott, 1937, *The Structure of Social Action: A Study in Social Theory with Special Reference to a Group of Recent European Writers*, McGraw-Hill, New York.

—— and Robert F Bales, 1953, *Family, Socialization and Interaction Process*, Routledge & Kegan Paul, London.

Pascoe, CJ and Tristan Bridges, 2016, 'Introduction: Exploring Masculinities: History, Reproduction, Hegemony, and Dislocation' in CJ Pacoe and Tristan Bridges (eds), *Exploring Masculinities: Identity, Inequality, Continuity, and Change*, Oxford University Press, New York, pp. 1–34.

Patel, Sujata (ed.), 2010, *The ISA Handbook of Diverse Sociological Traditions*, Sage, Los Angeles.

Paxton, Nancy L, 1991, *George Eliot and Herbert Spencer: Feminism, Evolutionism, and the Reconstruction of Gender*, Princeton University Press, Princeton, NJ.

Perkins, Roberta, 1983, *The Drag Queen Scene*, Allen & Unwin, Sydney.

Peteet, Julie, 1994, 'Male gender and rituals of resistance in the Palestinian Intifada: A cultural politics of violence', *American Ethnologist*, vol. 21, no. 1, pp. 31–49.

Peterson, V Spike, 2003, *A Critical Rewriting of Global Political Economy: Integrating Reproductive, Productive and Virtual Economies*, Routledge, London.

Phillips, Jock, 1987, *A Man's Country? The Image of the Pakeha Male: A History*, Penguin, Auckland.

Piketty, Thomas, 2014, *Capital in the Twenty-First Century*, Harvard University Press, Cambridge, MA.

Piven, FF and RA Cloward, 1979, *Poor people's movements: Why they succeed, how they fail*, Vintage, New York.

REFERENCES

Plaatje, Solomon Tshekisho, 1982 [1916], *Native Life in South Africa: Before and since the European war and the Boer rebellion*, new edn, Ravan Press, Braamfontein, South Africa.

Platt, Jennifer, 1995, 'The United States reception of Durkheim's *The Rules of Sociological Method*', *Sociological Perspectives*, vol. 38, pp. 77–105.

Playford, J, 1969, *Neo-capitalism in Australia*, Arena, Melbourne.

——1972, 'Who rules Australia?' in J Playford and D Kirsner (eds), *Australian Capitalism*, Penguin, Ringwood, pp. 108–55.

Pleck, J, 1981, *The Myth of Masculinity*, MIT Press, Cambridge, MA.

Plummer, K (ed.), 1981, *The Making of the Modern Homosexual*, Hutchinson, London.

Poster, Winifred R, 2013, 'Subversions of techno-masculinity: Indian ICT professionals in the global economy' in Jeff Hearn, Marina Blagojevic and Katherine Harrison (eds), *Rethinking Transnational Men: Beyond, Between and Within Nations*, Routledge, New York, pp. 113–33.

Power, M, 1997, *The Audit Society: Rituals of Verification*, Oxford University Press, Oxford.

Prichard, Katharine Susannah, 1990 [1929], *Coonardoo*, Collins/Angus & Robertson, Sydney.

Pusey, Michael, 1991, *Economic Rationalism in Canberra: A Nation-Building State Changes its Mind*, Cambridge University Press, London.

Quijano, Aníbal, 2000, 'Coloniality of power and Eurocentrism in Latin America', *International Sociology*, vol. 15, no. 2, pp. 215–32.

Ratele, Kopano, 2013, 'Masculinities without tradition', *Politikon: South African Journal of Political Studies*, vol. 40, no. 1, pp. 133–56.

——2014, 'Currents against gender transformation of South African men: relocating marginality to the centre of research and theory of masculinities', *NORMA: International Journal for Masculinity Studies*, vol. 9, no. 1, pp. 30–44.

Reay, Diane, 2001, 'Finding or losing yourself? Working-class relationships to education', *Journal of Education Policy*, vol. 16, no. 4, pp. 333–46.

Red Collective, 1978, *The Politics of Sexuality in Capitalism*, Red Collective, London.

Reid, Kirsty, 2007, *Gender, Crime and Empire: Convicts, Settlers and the State in Early Colonial Australia*, Manchester University Press, Manchester.

Reuter, Julia and Paula-Irene Villa (eds), 2010, *Postkoloniale Soziologie: Empirische Befunde, theoretische Anschlüsse, politische Intervention*, Bielefeld, transcript.

Reynaud, E, 1983, *Holy Virility*, Pluto Press, London.

Rich, A, 1980, 'Compulsory heterosexuality and lesbian existence', *Signs*, vol. 5, pp. 631–60.

Roberson, James E and Nobue Suzuki (eds), 2003, *Men and Masculinities in Contemporary Japan: Dislocating the Salaryman Doxa*, RoutledgeCurzon, London.

Robins, D and P Cohen, 1978, *Knuckle sandwich: Growing up in the working-class city*, Penguin, Harmondsworth.

Robinson, Kathryn May, 2009, *Gender, Islam, and Democracy in Indonesia*, Routledge, Abingdon-on-Thames, UK.

Rolfe, H, 1967, *The Controllers*, Cheshire, Melbourne.

Roper, Michael, 1994, *Masculinity and the British Organization Man since 1945*, Oxford University Press, Oxford.

Rosa, Marcelo C, 2014, 'Theories of the South: Limits and perspectives of an emergent movement in social sciences', *Current Sociology*, vol. 62, no. 6, pp. 851–67, DOI: 10.1177/0011392114522171.

Rosaldo, MZ and L Lamphere (eds), 1974, *Woman, Culture and Society*, Stanford University Press, Stanford, CA.

Ross, Dorothy, 1991, *The Origins of American Social Science*, Cambridge University Press, Cambridge.

Rubin, Gayle, 1975, 'The traffic in women: notes on the "political economy" of sex' in R Reiter (ed.), *Toward an Anthropology of Women*, Monthly Review Press, New York, pp. 157–210.

Russell, G, 1983, *The Changing Role of Fathers?*, University of Queensland Press, St Lucia.

Ryan, W, 1971, *Blaming the victim*, Vintage Books, New York.

Saffioti, Heleieth, B, 1978 [1969], *Women in Class Society [A mulher na sociedade de classes]*, Monthly Review Press, New York.

——2004, *Gênero, Patriarcado, Violência*, Fundação Perseu Abramo, São Paulo.

Said, Edward W, 1978, *Orientalism*, Pantheon, New York.

——1993, *Culture and Imperialism*, Vintage, New York.

Sardenberg, Cecilia MB, 2010, 'Women's Empowerment in Brazil: Tensions in Discourse and Practice', *Development*, vol. 53, no. 2, pp. 232–8.

Sartre, Jean-Paul, 1958, *Being and nothingness*, Methuen, London.

——1964, *Saint Genet*, WH Allen, London.

——1976, *Critique of Dialectical Reason*, New Left Books, London.

Savage, DG, 1987, 'Why Chapter I hasn't made much difference', *Phi Delta Kappan*, vol. 68, pp. 581–4.

Schedvin, CB, 1970, *Australia and the Great Depression*, Sydney University Press, Sydney.

Scheerens, J, 1987, *Enhancing educational opportunities for disadvantaged learners: A review of Dutch research on compensatory education and educational development policy*, North-Holland Publishing, Amsterdam.

Seddon, Terri, 1994, 'Teachers' work and political action' in N Postlethwaite and T Husen (eds), *International Encyclopaedia for Educational Research*, Pergamon, Oxford.

Seidman, Steven, 1994, *Contested Knowledge: Social Theory in the Postmodern Era*, Blackwell, Cambridge, MA.

Senate Select Committee On Securities And Exchange, 1974, *Australian Securities Markets and their Regulation*, Australian Government Publishing Service, Canberra.

Shefer, T, K Ratele, A Strebel, N Shabalala and R Buikema (eds), 2007, *From Boys to Men: Social Constructions of Men in Contemporary Society*, UCT Press, Lansdowne, South Africa.

Sideris, Tina, 2005, '"You have to change and you don't know how!": Contesting what it means to be a man in a rural area of South Africa' in Graeme Reid and Liz Walker (eds), *Men Behaving Differently*, Double Storey Books, Cape Town, pp. 111–37.

Silberschmidt, Margrethe, 2004, 'Men, male sexuality and HIV/AIDS: Reflections from studies in rural and urban East Africa', *Transformation*, vol. 54, pp. 42–58.

REFERENCES

Silva, Eduardo, 1996, *The State and Capital in Chile: Business Elites, Technocrats, and Market Economics*, Westview Press, Boulder, CO.

Sinclair-Webb, Emma, 2000, '"Our Bülent is now a commando": military service and manhood in Turkey' in Mai Ghoussoub and Emma Sinclair-Webb (eds), *Imagined Masculinities: Male Identity and Culture in the Middle East*, Saqi Books, London, pp. 65–92.

Sinha, Mrinalini, 1995, *Colonial Masculinity: The 'Manly Englishman' and the 'Effeminate Bengali' in the Late Nineteenth Century*, Manchester University Press, Manchester.

Smith, Linda Tuhiwai, 2012 [1999], *Decolonizing Methodologies: Research and Indigenous Peoples*, 2nd edn, Zed Books, London.

Snow, CE, WS Barnes, J Chandler, IF Goodman and L Hemphill, 1991, *Unfulfilled expectations: Home and school influences on literacy*, Harvard University Press, Cambridge, MA.

Spencer, Herbert, 1954 [1850], *Social Statics*, Robert Schalkenbach Foundation, New York.

——1887 [1873], *The Study of Sociology*, 13th edn, Kegan Paul, Trench, London.

——1893–96 [1874–77], *The Principles of Sociology*, 3 vols, Appleton, New York.

——1904, 'The descriptive sociology' in *An Autobiography*, vol. 2, pp. 305–17, D. Appleton & Company, New York.

Stauffer, Robert H, 2004, *Kahana: How the Land was Lost*, University of Hawai'i Press, Honolulu.

Stearns, PN, 1979, *Be a Man!*, Holmes & Meier, New York.

Steinmetz, George (ed.), 2013, *Sociology & Empire: The Imperial Entanglements of a Discipline*, Duke University Press, Durham and London.

Stevenson, Andrew and Brian Robins, 2012, 'Principals want more power but no strings', *Sydney Morning Herald*, 12 March 2012.

Stiebing, William H, 1993, *Uncovering the Past: A History of Archaeology*, Prometheus Books, Buffalo, NY.

Strober, MH, 1976, 'Toward dimorphics: a summary statement to the conference on occupational segregation', *Signs*, vol. 1, pp. 293–302.

Sumner, William Graham, 1934 [1906], *Folkways: A Study of the Sociological Importance of Usages, Manners, Customs, Mores, and Morals*, Ginn, Boston.

Sun Yat-sen, 1975 [1927], *San Min Chu I: The Three Principles of the People*, trans. Frank W Price, LT Chen (ed.), Da Capo Press, New York.

Suttner, Raymond, 2005, 'Masculinities in the African National Congress-led liberation movement: the underground period', *Kleio*, vol. 37, pp. 71–106.

Swingewood, Alan, 2000, *A Short History of Sociological Thought*, 3rd edn, Palgrave, Basingstoke.

Sydney Morning Herald, 'MySchool: NSW Schools Ranked', special supplement, 27 February 2012.

Taylor, WL and DM Piché, 1991, *A report on shortchanging children: The impact of social inequity on the education of children at risk*, US House of Representatives Committee on Education and Labor, Washington DC.

Teese, Richard and John Polesel, 2003, *Undemocratic Schooling: Equity and Quality in Mass Secondary Education in Australia*, Melbourne University Press, Melbourne.

Thayer, Millie, 2010, 'Translations and Refusals: Resignifying Meanings as Feminist Political Practice', *Feminist Studies*, vol. 36, no. 1, pp. 200–30.
Therborn, Göran, 1976, *Science, Class, and Society*, New Left Books, London.
Thompson, EP, 1968, *The Making of the English Working Class*, 2nd edn, Penguin, Harmondsworth.
Tienari, Janne, Anne-Marie Søderberg, Charlotte Holgersson and Eero Vaara, 2005, 'Gender and national identity constructions in the cross-border merger context', *Gender, Work & Organization*, vol. 12, no. 3, pp. 217–41.
Tiger, L, 1969, *Men in Groups*, Nelson, London.
Tinsman, Heidi, 2000, 'Reviving feminist materialism: gender and neoliberalism in Pinochet's Chile', *Signs*, vol. 26, no. 1, pp. 145–88.
Todd, Arthur James, 1918, *Theories of Social Progress: A Critical Study of the Attempts to Formulate the Conditions of Human Advance*, Macmillan, New York.
Tolson, Andrew, 1977, *The Limits of Masculinity*, Tavistock, London.
Tominaga, Ken'ichi, 1994, 'European sociology and the modernisation of Japan' in Birgitta Nedelmann and Piotr Sztompka (eds), *Sociology in Europe*, Walter de Gruyter, Berlin, pp. 191–212.
Townshend, Charles, 2005, *Easter 1916: The Irish Rebellion*, Allen Lane, London.
Turner, I, 1965, *Industrial Labour and Politics*, ANU Press, Canberra.
Turner, Karen Gottschang with Phan Thanh Hao, 1998, *Even the Women Must Fight: Memories of War from North Vietnam*, Wiley, New York.
Turner, Stephen P and Jonathan H Turner, 1990, *The Impossible Science: An Institutional Analysis of American Sociology*, Sage, Newbury Park, CA.
Tylor, Edward B, 1873, *Primitive Culture: Researches into the Development of Mythology, Philosophy, Religion, Language, Art, and Custom*, 2nd edn, Murray, London.
United Nations, 2013, *Why Do Men Use Violence and How Can We Stop It? Quantitative Findings from the UN Multi-Country Study on Men and Violence*, UNDP, UNFPA, UN Women and UNV, Bangkok.
United Nations Development Programme, 1992, *Human Development Report 1992*, Oxford University Press, New York.
Valdés, Teresa (ed.), 2001, *El índice de compromiso cumplido – ICC: Una estrategia para el control ciudadano de la equidad de género*, FLACSO, Santiago de Chile.
——2007, 'Estudios de Género: Una Mirada Evaluativa desde el Cono Sur' in Luz Gabriela Arango and Yolanda Puyana (eds), *Género, Mujeres y Saberes en América Latina*, Universidad Nacional de Colombia, Bogotá.
—— and José Olavarría (eds), 1998, *Masculinidades y Equidad de Género en América Latina*, FLACSO/UNFPA, Santiago.
——, Ana María Muñoz B and Alina Donoso O (eds), 2003, *1995–2003: ¿Han avanzado las mujeres? Indice de compromiso cumplido latinamericano*, FLACSO and UNIFEM, Santiago and New York.
Vieira de Jesus, Diego Santos, 2011, 'Bravos novos mundos: uma leitura pós-colonialista sobre masculinidades ocidentais', *Estudos Feministas*, vol. 19, no. 1, pp. 125–39.
Viveros Vigoya, Mara, 2001, 'Contemporary Latin American perspectives on masculinity', *Men and Masculinities*, vol. 3, no. 3, pp. 237–60.
——2007, 'De diferencia y diferencias. Algunos debates desde las teorías feministas y de género' in Luz Gabriela Arango and Yolanda Puyana (eds), *Género,*

Mujeres y Saberes en América Latina, Universidad Nacional de Colombia, Bogotá.

Wajcman, Judy, 1999, *Managing like a Man: Women and Men in Corporate Management*, Polity, Cambridge; Allen & Unwin, Sydney.

Walter, Maggie and Chris Andersen, 2013, *Indigenous Statistics: A Quantitative Research Methodology*, Left Coast Press, Walnut Creek, CA.

Walzer, M, 1983, *Spheres of justice: A defense of pluralism and equality*, Basic Books, New York.

Ward, Lester F, 1897, *Dynamic Sociology, or Applied Social Science as Based upon Statical Sociology and the Less Complex Sciences*, 2nd edn, Appleton, New York.

Weber, Max, 1989 [1894], 'Developmental tendencies in the situation of East Elbian rural labourers' in Keith Tribe (ed.), *Reading Weber*, Routledge, London, pp. 158–87.

Weeks, J, 1977, *Coming Out*, Quartet, London.

Wexler, P, 1992, *Becoming somebody: Toward a social psychology of school*, Falmer Press, London.

Wheelwright, EL, 1957, *Ownership and Control of Australian Companies*, Law Book Co., Sydney.

——1974, *Radical Political Economy*, ANZ Book Co., Sydney.

White, Patrick, 1979, *The Twyborn Affair*, Cape, London.

White, V and K Johnston, 1993, 'Inside the Disadvantaged Schools Program: The politics of practical policy-making' in L Angus (ed.), *Education, inequality and social identity*, Falmer Press, London, pp. 104–27.

Whiteford, P, B Bradbury and P Saunders, 1989, 'Inequality and deprivation among families with children: An exploratory study' in D Edgar, D Keane and P McDonald (eds), *Child poverty*, Allen & Unwin, Sydney, pp. 20–49.

Whitty, G, 1985, *Sociology and school knowledge: Curriculum theory, research and politics*, Methuen, London.

—— and M Young (eds), 1976, *Explorations in the politics of school knowledge*, Nafferton Books, Driffield.

Williams, T, 1987, *Participation in education*, Australian Council for Educational Research, Hawthorn.

Williams, Walter L, 1986, *The Spirit and the Flesh: Sexual Diversity in American Indian Culture*, Beacon Press, Boston.

Winter, MF and ER Robert, 1980, 'Male dominance, late capitalism, and the growth of instrumental reason', *Berkeley Journal of Sociology*, no. 24/25, pp. 249–80.

Wolpe, Harold, 1972, 'Capitalism and cheap labour-power in South Africa: From segregation to Apartheid', *Economy and Society*, vol. 1, no. 4, pp. 425–56.

Xaba, Thokozani, 2001, 'Masculinity and its malcontents: The confrontation between "struggle masculinity" and "post-struggle masculinity" (1990–1997)' in Robert Morrell (ed.), *Changing Men in Southern Africa*, University of Natal Press, Pietermaritzburg, pp. 105–24.

Yan, Hairong, 2008, *New Masters, New Servants: Migration, Development and Women Workers in China*, Duke University Press, Durham, NC.

Yates, L, 1993, *The education of girls: Policy, research and the question of gender*, Australian Council for Educational Research, Hawthorn.

REFERENCES

Young, K, C Wolkowitz and R McCullagh, 1981, *Of Marriage and the Market*, CSE Books, London.

Zaretsky, E, 1976, *Capitalism, the Family, and Personal Life*, Pluto, London.

Zhan Junfeng, 2015, *Xing Bie Zhi Lu: Rui Wen Kang Nai Er De Nan Xing Qi Zhi Li Lun Tan Suo [The Road of Gender: An Exploration of Raewyn Connell's Theories of Masculinity]*, Guangxi Normal University Press, Guilin, China.

Zingoni, Eduardo Liendro, 1998, 'Masculinidades y violencia desde un programa de acción en México' in Teresa Valdés and José Olavarría (eds), *Masculinidades y equidad de género en América Latina*, FLACSO/UNFPA, Santiago, pp. 130–6.

Zinn, Maxine Baca, Pierrette Hondagneu-Sotelo and Michael A Messner (eds), 2000, *Gender through the Prism of Difference*, 2nd edn, Allyn & Bacon, Boston, MA.

Index

Africa 86, 87, 203–4, 217, 219, 228; see also global South; South Africa
Agarwal, Bina 78–9
AIDS 4, 46, 47, 228
Association for the Promotion of Social Science 211
Australia 44
  class structure 93–4, 221–2; see also Australian ruling class; Australian working class
  corporations and industries 95–101, 103–6
  economy 112–15
  liberal (conservative) governments 109–11, 118, 121–2, 123, 124, 158
  schools 131–2, 150, 158–9, 170
  see also neoliberalism in Australia
Australian Labor Party (ALP) 3, 102, 109, 124, 125–6, 158–9, 164, 170
Australian working class 39, 125–7, 156, 157

Bakare-Yusuf, Bibi 228
Bakunin, Mikhail 210
Barbieri, Teresita de 80–1
Beauvoir, Simone de 58, 61, 76
Benton, Pam 53–4
biological 'bases' of gender 62, 68–71
biological determinism, critique of 20, 54, 62–5
Bourdieu, Pierre 54, 67, 223

Brasil 79–80, 87, 88
Burgess, Ernest W 200
business and the state 98–101
business leadership 43–4, 101–8, 116–17, 118, 120–2
  managers as business intellectuals 182–8
  new capitalists 103–6
  women managers 117, 179
  see also corporations

capitalism 25, 101–6, 111–13, 127; see also corporations; market ideology; neoliberalism
Cardoso, Fernando 222
Carrigan, Tim 11–12, 30
cathexis 13, 21, 22–3
Childe, Gordon 69
Chile 41, 80, 82, 154–5
China 41, 45
civil servants (state elite) 106–8, 116, 121
class structure 93–4, 221–3; see also ruling class; working class; 'underclass'
Cockburn, Cynthia 15
Coleman Report (1966) 138, 150–1
Collins, Randall 198
Collyer, Fran 221
colonialism 34–40, 84, 213–14, 223, 224–5; see also imperialism
coloniality of gender 73, 83–5
coloniality of knowledge 229
coloniality of power 31, 42–3, 83, 229

262

INDEX

commodification of services 114–15, 154, 155–6, 162–3, 221; *see also* privatisation of public assets and services
Comte, Auguste 199, 205, 206, 207, 208, 210, 211, 214–15, 216
Connell, Raewyn: path toward social science 1–7, 93–4
Connell, Raewyn: works (including co-authored works) 12, 152, 175–6, 182, 188, 198
  Class Structure in Australian History 93, 222
  Gender and Power 54, 70
  The Good University 2–3, 221
  Knowledge and Global Power 221
  Making the Difference 131
  Masculinities 28, 54
  Ruling Class, Ruling Culture 94, 110, 112
  Running Twice as Hard 132
  Schools and Social Justice 132
  Southern Theory 29, 72, 198, 220–1, 223
  Writing for Research 5
corporations
  Australian 95–101, 103–6
  business and the state 98–101
  managers as business intellectuals 182–8
  power-oriented gender practices in 25, 39, 43–6, 48, 85
  share ownership 115–16
  see also business leadership
cultural deficit (concept in education policy and practice) 135–7, 141–2

Darwin, Charles 199, 213
data analyses 232–3; *see also* knowledge production
data source, global South as 76, 78, 224–6
de Valera, Eamon 38
Dinnerstein, Dorothy 57
disadvantage, measurement of 134–5; *see also* education and poverty
Disadvantaged Schools Program (Australia) 131–2, 150
The Division of Labor in Society (Durkheim) 203, 204, 206, 209
division of labour 15, 19, 36, 61–2, 176–8; *see also* hegemonic masculinity; 'sex roles' concept

Donzelot, Jacques 66
Du Bois, WEB 207, 219
Durkheim, Émile 197, 198, 199, 200, 201, 203–4, 206–7, 208, 209, 211, 215, 216–17, 218
Dynamic Sociology (Ward) 199–200

economic development 39–42; *see also* corporations; neoliberalism
education
  commodification 114, 162–3, 221
  competition in 114, 119, 143, 157, 163, 164–5, 170
  concept of 159–62
  curricular justice 148–9
  curriculum 144–6, 147, 165
  educational reform strategies 137–8, 148–51
  expansion of 107–8
  knowledge base 166–70
  neoliberalism and 114, 119, 120, 152, 153–71
  policymaking 168, 170–1
  pseudo-knowledge 161, 168–9
  technical and further education 157–8, 164
  testing and performance ranking 138, 163, 165–8, 170, 233
  see also knowledge production; schools; teachers; universities
education and poverty 131–51
  curricula 144–9
  false assumptions 134–9
  rethinking the issues 139–48
  school as institution 142–4
  schools' exercise of power 140–2
  strategy of change 148–51
Eisenstein, Hester 64, 68
employment policy, neoliberal 40–1, 114, 119, 164
Encel, Sol 95, 96, 98, 106, 108
epistemologies 77–8, 227–8
ethnography 137, 206, 207, 209–10, 213
Eurocentrism 33, 76, 77, 83, 88; *see also* global North; metropole

Faletto, Enzo 222
families
  demography of poverty 136

income and expenditure differences
    141–2
  relationships inside 14, 17–18, 41, 81
  sexuality and family 66
femininity, historicity of 68; *see also*
    women
feminism 25–6, 55, 58–9
  categoricalism 61–5, 71
  circulation of ideas and language 232
  coloniality of gender 73, 83–5
  future sites of knowledge production
    85–90
  in global North 33, 72, 73, 74, 75–6
  global scholarship 73–8, 228
  in global South 74, 76, 78–86
  see also gender, social theory of;
    gender equality/inequality; women's
    movement
'femocrats' (feminist policymakers and
    administrators) 85–6
Fernbach, David 68
fiction 35, 66, 84–5
fieldwork examples
  gender in organisational life 175–82
  gender transition 188–93
  managers as business intellectuals
    182–8
Foucault, Michel 66, 76
Free University, Sydney 221–2
Freud, Sigmund 21, 55
Friedan, Betty 58

gay liberation movement 25, 26, 53–4,
    61, 71
gender, social theory of 54–71
  analysis of social structure 65–8
  biological 'bases' 62, 68–71
  coloniality of gender 73, 83–5
  issue in early sociology 206–8
  power analysis and categoricalism 61–5,
    71
  scope 56–8
  'sex roles' concept 19, 54, 55, 57–61, 69
gender equality/inequality 29, 46, 59
  changes and gender justice 46–8
  gender discrimination 179–82
  gender order 84
  'league tables' and indicators 76–7
  in organisational life 175–82

power-oriented gender practices in states
    and companies 43–9
  see also feminism; 'sex roles' concept;
    women, subordination of
gender relations 13–15, 56–8
  disruption by and among colonisers
    35–7
  and economic development 39–40
  gender in resistance movements 37–8
  male sexist behaviour 179–82
  postcolonial societies 38–40
  psychodynamics 20–2, 23
  sex/gender system 13, 20, 33, 67
  violence in 24, 33, 35, 48, 61, 85
  see also gender, social theory of;
    masculinity/masculinities
gender research 32–4, 74–87; *see also*
    feminism; knowledge production
gender transition 23, 188–93
Giddens, Anthony 54, 67
Giddings, Franklin 199, 200, 201, 208
Ginsberg, M 209
'global difference' idea in sociology 74,
    201–9
global economy of knowledge 31, 223–31,
    234
global North
  empires 203–8
  feminism in 33, 72, 73, 74, 75–6
  knowledge institutions 224–5, 233–4
  neoliberalism 153–4, 155
  North-centred global economy of
    knowledge 31, 223–31, 234; *see also*
    knowledge production
global South 72–3
  as data source 76, 78, 224–6
  feminism in 74, 76, 78–83, 85–6, 88–9
  gender studies 87–8
  indigenous knowledge 227–33
  knowledge production 75–90, 229–31
  neoliberalism 154–5
  research and scholarship 222–3, 225–7
  Southern perspectives 31–4, 48–9,
    229–31, 233
globalisation
  Australian economy 112–15
  idea of 29, 75, 185–7
  metropole-apparatus 42–6, 185
  neoliberal development 41–2, 153–5

grand ethnography 209–10
Grupo Iniciativa Mujeres, Chile 82
Guha, Ranajit 32, 223

hegemonic masculinity 14, 15, 16–20, 24–30, 39–40
  decolonising the discussion 31–4, 227–8
  definition and concepts 29, 30, 32–4, 48–9
  postcolonial understanding 32–4, 42–8
hegemony and empire 32, 34–43, 48–9
  disruption of gender order 35–7
  hegemonic projects in and after resistance 37–9
HIV/AIDS 4, 46, 47, 228
Hobhouse, LT 206, 208–9, 213, 214, 215
Hollier, Nathan 110
homosexual people 19, 56, 57, 63, 68; *see also* gay liberation movement
homosexuality (male) 14, 15–16, 18, 19, 21–2, 56, 68
Hountondji, Paulin 223, 225, 228
Howard government (Australia) 109–11, 121–2, 123, 124

ICC (*Indice de compromiso cumplido* [index of achieved commitments]) 82–3
imperialism 203–8, 213–15, 223–4, 229–30; *see also* colonialism
India 32, 41, 45, 46–7, 87, 88, 223
indigenous knowledge 227–33
Indonesia 87, 88
information and communication technology (ICT) and management 182–5
intellectual workers 182–8, 224–5, 231–5
Introduction to the Science of Sociology (Park and Burgess) 200
Ireland 38
Irving, TH 93, 221–2

Japan 39–40
journals 75, 226, 232, 233–4

Kennett government (Victoria, Australia) 118, 123, 124, 158
Kidd, Benjamin 212, 214

knowledge production 5–6, 31, 48–9, 221, 232
  coloniality of knowledge 229
  communication of knowledge 5, 226, 232, 233–5
  education knowledge base 166–70
  epistemologies 76–8, 227–8, 235
  future sites of 85–90
  global economy of knowledge 31, 223–31, 234
  in global South 76, 78–83, 86–90, 229–31
  indigenous knowledge 227–31
  intellectual workforce 182–8, 224–5, 231–5
  NGOs 86–7
  postcolonial communication 228–31
  see also education; research
Komarovsky, Mirra 57, 60

Labor Party *see* Australian Labor Party (ALP)
labour *see* work
language shifts in feminist writing 64
L'Année sociologique (journal from Durkheim's group) 198, 201–2, 208, 209–10, 234
Latin America 38, 40–1, 79–83, 86, 87, 88, 154–5, 222; *see also* global South
Lee, John 11–12, 30
Letourneau, Charles 200, 205–6, 207, 208, 211
Lugones, María 83–4

Maia, João 221
male supremacy *see* hegemonic masculinity; women, subordination of
managers *see* business leadership
market ideology 114–28, 185–7, 232; *see also* capitalism; neoliberalism
Martineau, Harriet 210
Marx, Karl 76, 197, 199, 200, 210, 217–18
Marxism 79–80, 93, 217–18
masculinity/masculinities
  boys' conflict in schools 142
  decolonising the discussion 31–4, 227–8
  forms of 15–21, 25–7
  in global perspective 28–49

hegemony and empire 30–42
managerial 43–6, 48
in neoliberal development 40–2, 48
postcolonial understanding 32–4, 42–8
psychodynamics 20–2, 23, 24
social analysis of 11–27
transformations 22–7
see also gender relations; hegemonic masculinity
mass media 19, 43, 119, 186
The Material Culture and Social Institutions of the Simpler Peoples (Hobhouse, Wheeler and Ginsberg) 209
Matthews, Jill 54, 68
Mead, Margaret 57, 58, 61, 76
men
  CEOs *see* business leadership
  gender transition 23, 188–93
  male homosexuality 14, 15–16, 18, 19, 21–2, 56, 68
  sexist behaviour among 179–82
  see also gender equality/inequality; masculinity/masculinities
men's movements 16–17, 24, 25–6, 59
Messerschmidt, James 29, 30
Metropole (imperial centre) 31, 155–6, 185, 216
  and creation of sociology 204–5, 210–11, 215, 219
  empires 213–15
  hegemonic projects 45–6
  knowledge institutions 224–30, 233–4
  and masculinity 42–4, 48
  see also Eurocentrism; global North; globalisation
metropole-apparatus 42–3, 45–6
México 34, 42, 48–9, 85, 86, 87
Mill, John Stuart 205, 207, 211, 214
Millie Thayer 89, 231
Mills, C. Wright 216–17, 218
Mitchell, Juliet 54, 67, 76
Morrell, Robert 36–7, 221

National Organization for Women (US) 58
Negri, Antonio 110, 113–14
neoliberalism 34, 48
  contested 86

definition and dynamics of 153–6
impact on education 114, 119, 120, 156–71
impact on welfare state 112, 118–22, 127
masculinities 40–2
metropole-apparatus 42–6
support and opposition 122–6
neoliberalism in Australia 111–28, 156–7
  commodification of services 114–15, 154, 155–6, 162–3, 221
  cultural barrenness 119
  cultural change 117–20
  impact on education 152, 156–71
  political leadership 120–2
  privatisation of public assets 113–20, 123, 154, 185–6
  support and opposition 122–8
  vulnerability 124–5
NGOs 47, 48, 82, 86–7, 232
the North *see* global North

Pareto, Vilfredo 200, 216, 217
Park, Robert E 200
Parsons, Talcott 57, 58, 61, 216, 217
patriarchy 13, 58, 61, 62, 80, 81; *see also* hegemonic masculinity
Perkins, Roberta 23
Playford, John 95, 98, 103, 106
political leadership 102–3, 107, 120–4
power *see* gender relations; hegemonic masculinity; imperialism; women, subordination of
The Principles of Sociology (Giddings) 199, 200
The Principles of Sociology (Spencer) 202, 206, 207, 212
privatisation of public assets and services 113–20, 123, 154, 155, 185–6; *see also* commodification of services
progress, concept of 205–15; *see also* sociology as a discipline
public sector
  civil servants (state elite) 106–8, 116, 121
  commodification *see* commodification of services; privatisation of public assets and services
  culture change 117–20, 175–7

gender in workplaces 175–82
  managers as business intellectuals 182–8
  neoliberalism impact on 112–22
Pusey, Michael 110, 121, 156

Quijano, Aníbal 31, 83, 229

race as issue in early sociology 206–8
Readings in Descriptive and Historical Sociology (Giddings) 201
research 1–6
  biomedical research 166–7
  education research 131–2, 137–9, 168
  gender research 32–4, 86–7
  see also education; knowledge production
research journals 75, 226, 232, 233–4
resistance movements 37–8
Rich, Adrienne 68
Robert, ER 25
Rubin, Gayle 13, 54, 67–8, 70, 81
Ruling Australia (Hollier) 110
ruling class
  American 25, 26, 117
  Australian 93–108
    business and the state 98–101
    corporations, 95–101, 103–6
    leadership of 101–3, 116–17, 120–2
    state elite 106–8, 116, 121

Saffioti, Heleieth 79–80, 81
Sartre, Jean-Paul 21, 54, 70, 139
schools
  Disadvantaged Schools Program 131–2, 150
  funding differences in USA 144
  power in 140–3
  school system in Australia 131–2, 158–9, 170
  testing and performance ranking 138, 163, 165–8, 170, 233
  violence in 142
  see also education; teachers
'sex roles' concept 54, 55, 57–61, 69; *see also* division of labour; gender, social theory of
sex/gender system *see* gender relations
sexism *see* gender equality/inequality
sexual politics 13, 23–7, 56–8

gender categoricalism 61–5, 71
  nuances of language 64
  see also feminism; gay liberation movement; gender, social theory of; women's movement
sexuality 18, 20–3
  as issue in early sociology 206–8
  male homosexuality 14, 15–16, 18, 19, 21–2, 56, 68
  writings on sexuality and family 66
A Short History of Sociological Thought (Swingewood) 199
Simmel, Georg 199, 200, 217
Social Evolution (Kidd) 212, 214
social movements 88–90, 231; *see also* gay liberation movement; 'men's movement'; women's movement
social relations *see* gender, social theory of; gender relations
social reproduction 33–4, 160
social science
  critiques and alternatives 227–31
  decolonising the discussion 31–4, 227–8
  global economy of knowledge 31, 223–7, 234
  multiple traditions 229
  workforce and labour process 231–5
  see also sociology as a discipline
social structure in social theory 54, 55, 58, 60, 65–7, 70, 81; *see also* gender, social theory of
sociology as a discipline 197–8, 234
  classical theory origin stories 198–200, 219
  content and method 205–10
  curricula, teaching, texts, commentary 211–13, 216–18, 234
  first academic chairs 199, 200, 211, 213
  global difference and empire 201–9
  journal rankings 226, 232
  new concept and new origin story 216–19
  in political culture of empire 210–15
  popular works 212
  Southern-theory approach 229–31, 233; *see also* global South
sociology of knowledge *see* knowledge production

sociology of masculinity *see* masculinity/masculinities
the South *see* global South
South Africa 37, 39, 41, 46, 87, 88, 228, 233
South America *see* Brasil; Chile; Latin America
Spencer, Herbert 199, 202, 205–7, 212, 214, 215
the state
  business and 98–101
  in feminist thinking and gender studies 85–6
  school as embodiment of state power 140–3
  see also 'femocrats', public sector
subordination of women *see* women, subordination of
Sumner, William Graham 207, 209, 214, 215
Swingewood, Alan 199

teachers 150–1, 164–8, 170–1; *see also* schools
teachers' work 138, 145, 146–8, 149, 150–1, 159–61; *see also* education
technical and further education sector 157–8, 164
Thayer, Millie 89, 231
Thompson, Edward 54, 55, 67
Todd, Arthur 205
Tönnies, Ferdinand 199, 200, 207
transition, gender *see* gender transition
transsexual women and men 23, 188–93
truth and pseudo-knowledge in education 161, 168–9
Turkey 39, 40

UN Commission on the Status of Women 29
UN World Conferences on Women 73, 82
'underclass' concept 133, 136–7, 142
universities 2–3, 137–8, 169
  corporate-style management 152, 157, 221, 226, 235
  funding cuts 112, 157, 232
  gender studies in global South 87–8
  patentable knowledge 167

workforce 87, 157, 164, 224, 231
see also education; knowledge production

Valdés, Teresa 82
violence
  of colonialism 34–7
  in gender relations 24, 33, 35, 48, 61, 85
  reduction programs 47–8
  in schools 142

Ward, Lester F 199–200, 206, 207, 214
Weber, Max 197, 199, 200, 204, 211, 216–17, 218
welfare state and neoliberalism 112, 118–22, 127
Wheeler, GC 209
Wheelwright, Ted 95–7, 98
Winter, MF 25
women
  'femocrats' 85–6
  gender division of labour 15, 19, 61–2, 176–8
  historicity of femininity 68
  as managers 117, 179
  in neoliberal regimes 40, 41, 42
  in resistance movements 38
  see also gender, social theory of
women, subordination of 13–14, 15, 17, 56, 65, 67, 83–4
  gender discrimination experienced 179–82
  sexual domination of 21–2, 35, 61–2
  see also gender equality/inequality
women's movement 53–4, 71, 73, 88–90
  Women's Liberation 11, 24–5
  see also feminism
work
  division of labour 15, 19, 36, 61–2, 176–8
  gender in workplaces 175–82
  teachers' work 138, 145, 146–8, 149, 150–1, 159–61
workforce casualisation 40–1, 87, 164
working class 17–18
  in Australia 39, 125–7, 156, 157
  and educational institutions 136, 140–2, 150, 159, 165–6